MAILMAN

U.S.A.

MAILMAN

U.S.A.

BY WILLIAM C. DOHERTY

PRESIDENT, NATIONAL ASSOCIATION
OF LETTER CARRIERS

DAVID McKAY COMPANY, INC.

New York

Dedicated

CONTENTS

MAILMAN

U.S.A.

RANDOM THOUGHTS ON BEGINNING A BOOK

I WANT to say at the very outset of this book that I am very prejudiced in favor of the 125,000 letter carriers who deliver the mail to the homes and business offices of America.

However, I am not alone in this. Most of the people in this country share my prejudice. Ask the average American what he thinks of when someone mentions the United States postal service, and in nine cases out of ten the answer will be: "The mailman."

More than the postmaster, the postal clerk, or even the Postmaster General himself, the man who marches the streets of urban America in uniform of gray, delivering the nation's mail, stands as the living symbol and personification of the greatest system of communications ever devised by the human mind.

This is due to many causes. One of these is the fact that the letter carrier is easily identifiable by reason of his uniform and is seen by almost every city-dweller in the nation at least once a day, six days a week.

Another is the aura of tradition that surrounds the letter carrier. This tradition dates at least as far back to the Bible. The couriers, who are the spiritual forefathers of today's letter carriers, are mentioned in II Chronicles, I Samuel, I Kings, and in the Books of Job and Esther. In the eighth century before the Christian Era, Hezekiah, a great and good king in Israel, used the existent posts to invite all the citizens of Judea and Israel to attend the restoration of the true Passover after years of pagan desecration. Couriers carried the Epistles of Paul, Peter, Timothy, and James to their distant destinations and thereby helped hold the fledgling Christian world together. And, of course, the fleet messengers of Darius the Persian were immortalized by Herodotus in the fifth century before Christ by those words which, in loose translation, are engraved above the entrance of the General Post Office in New York City and which have become the official slogan of the letter carriers of America: "Neither snow nor rain nor heat nor gloom of night stays these couriers from the swift completion of their appointed rounds."

But to me there is an even more compelling reason why the letter carrier has been taken to the public heart as a personification of the entire postal service.

I refer to the over-all *character* of the individuals who carry on their backs those messages which not only maintain the communicational ties that make our huge commercial and industrial complex possible, but which also convey the most intimate and personal messages between our humblest citizens through their predestined straits.

After all, why does a man become a letter carrier?

No one in his right mind joins the postal service in the expectation of becoming rich.[1] The commercial world offers many jobs

[1] And, thanks to the rigid Civil Service requirements, no one *can* join the postal field service unless he is in his right mind. This does not necessarily apply, however, to the higher echelons of the Post Office Department since the only requirement for those appointments is Presidential nomination plus Senate confirmation—a far less exacting test than the Civil Service examinations.

that pay higher salaries, offer swifter advancement, equal security, and far less arduous labor. Anyone joining the field service of the Postal Establishment must know he is signing up for a career of hard work at comparatively low wages and with benefits and promotions dropping as slowly and as grudgingly as the tears of charity.

So why do they do it?

I feel certain that each man who joins up must have deep within himself, even though he might be unconscious of it, a driving urge to be of service to his fellow man, and there are few professions or occupations on earth which can satisfy this compulsion so directly and to the same extent as does the business of moving and delivering the mails.

Still, granting that this inner compulsion exists, why do men choose to be letter carriers rather than postal clerks? After all, the job of postal clerk, while requiring the same amount of intelligence and skill as that required by the job of letter carrier, still enables the person occupying such a job to work indoors, secure from the vagaries of wind and weather, and even to sit down during most of the time he is performing his chores.

In my opinion there is one advantage built into the job of letter carrier that is paramount in the mind of anyone who likes and enjoys people and which easily outweighs all the disadvantages: the letter carrier has the daily opportunity of meeting the public on its own terms and in its own natural habitat. He has the privilege of observing at close quarters the human drama and of being an active participant in the ever-changing activities of Vanity Fair.

I know whereof I speak. I carried the mail for many years in my native city of Cincinnati. I know the people who make up the body of letter carriers in the United States both as individuals and as an outstanding group of citizens. I know their emotions and their reactions because they are almost exactly the same as my own. And I can remember no satisfaction as great as that which I enjoyed when, even as a substitute carrier before I became a regular, I was privileged to deliver into the homes along my route the eagerly awaited messages from loved ones in distant places; or even, on those occasions when the call of common humanity demanded it, to assist in assuaging the grief of those who had received tragic news.

I am quite aware that every general statement is at least partially untrue, but nevertheless I think it is safe to say that on the average the typical letter carrier is an extrovert and the average postal clerk is an introvert.

Of course, there is no special virtue in being either an extrovert or an introvert. All the members of the human family are the way God made them, and any society would be unbearable if it consisted entirely of one type or the other. But it is true and natural that an extroverted personality should seek and obtain work that keeps him in constant contact with people, while an introverted personality will normally gravitate to the more technical or the purely clerical type of work.

To the average extrovert letter carrier there is nothing quite so exhilarating as the sight of someone on a doorstep along his route eagerly awaiting his arrival with the mail. To such a person the feeling of being *liked* or *wanted* in the performance of his duties is in itself a *raison d'être*.

The life of a letter carrier is endowed with infinite variety. To anyone who genuinely likes mankind there is nothing dull about the job. Not only are the human contacts satisfactorily diversified, but since human nature is gloriously unpredictable, the letter carrier in the course of his duties is regularly exposed to generous helpings of the drama of life.

Hundreds of letter carriers have been impromptu midwives, and just as many have eased and comforted the dying in their final moments.

The files of the Post Office Department contain innumerable cases of heroism on the part of the nation's mailmen. Just at random I can think of Johnny Johnson of San Francisco, who recently discovered a four-year-old girl with her clothing on fire. He saved her from a flaming death by beating out the fire with his bare hands and tearing the smoldering garments off her body.[2] In the little town of Spur, Texas, Carrier Ray Gilcrease noticed that an eleven-year-old boy in a house along his route had been knocked unconscious and all but fatally electrocuted by a faulty wire connection. He broke into the house and applied artificial respiration with such skill that the youngster's life was saved. Also in recent times Ed Osterland, of Indianapolis, risked his own life to beat out flames engulfing the clothing of a three-year-old boy, and in Louisville, Kentucky, Carrier Boyd Montgomery, by using his head and his heart saved an eighteen-month-old girl from drowning.

The recent records of the Boston Post Office disclose stories of letter carriers who have averted tragedy by detecting escaping gas in patrons' houses and directing the evacuation of the premises. They also show several cases of letter carriers who have discarded their packs and have dived into the icy waters of the Charles to rescue drowning persons. There are also in the contemporary records accounts of letter carriers who have plunged into burning buildings to rescue the trapped occupants and of others who have saved lives by employing first-aid techniques in treating those who have been gravely injured and were bleeding to death.

I happen to be familiar with the Boston story because the *Boston Globe* recently ran a feature story on the saga of heroism among letter carriers in that city. However, the same courage and devotion to the human family exist among letter carriers every-

---

[2] For this act of heroism Johnson received a hundred-dollar achievement award from the Post Office Department, from which, ironically, eighteen dollars had been deducted for income taxes. Surely a country as rich as the United States could afford to make awards of this sort tax deductible! Certainly heroes are as deserving of tax leniency as are oil producers with their 27½-per-cent tax deductible allowance!

where in the nation, and every city has a tradition as inspiring as that of Boston in this regard.

Scores of carriers have given up their lives in performing, on behalf of their fellow men, acts of courage and daring far beyond and above the call of duty. Many more have narrowly escaped death or serious injury in such humane endeavors. There is also an impressive roster of carriers who have made unbelievable sacrifices in order to "complete their appointed rounds."

I need point only to Reinhold Dreahn, of South Dakota, who froze to death while attempting to deliver mail on his route during a blizzard; also the brothers Hitchcock of Ohio, who attempted a joint effort of delivering mail in spectacularly foul weather and were rescued, finally, when they were wedged neck-high in twin ice cakes. Their clothing was hacked off them like pieces of medieval armor and, miraculously, they lived to tell the tale.

And when postal tragedies are recounted the case of substitute Carrier Bill Osborne of Bowling Green, Kentucky, springs immediately to the mind. Bill was a twenty-nine-year-old veteran of World War II when, at 7:50 A.M. on January 26, 1949, the bright and promising world that lay before him literally blew apart.

In the course of casing the mail he would be delivering along his route that day, he came upon a small package, mailed from Newark, New Jersey, and addressed to a nonexistent house address. He turned to point out the misaddressing to his supervisor when the time bomb in the package went off with a sickening roar. The explosion ripped both his arms off at the elbow and blew out both his eyes.

During his Gethsemane Bill never lost a moment's consciousness and his incredible guts made it possible for him not only to survive the tragedy, but eventually to rise above it.

Because of the inadequacy of federal compensation laws covering cases such as this, the National Association of Letter Carriers started an Osborne Fund. Not only did they show great generosity themselves, but they carried the appeal to federal employees in every field and eventually raised almost $80,000. Part of this money paid for the enormous surgical bills and part has been invested wisely so as to provide a future for Bill and his family. He and his wife have had two children since that time, and their intelligence and courage have enabled them to create a happy and useful life together.

The Postal Inspection Service has never been able to apprehend the fiend responsible for this vile and senseless act.

But it is probably unfair to mention only these few cases of gallantry and danger when there are so many others of at least equal significance. However, almost everyone who reads this book will have his own catalogue of heroic acts performed by the warmhearted and wonderful people who carry the country's mail.

All this has given to the letter carrier a position of dominance in the public mind unchallenged by any other element in the postal service, despite the fact that the total number of letter carriers represents less than one-quarter of the half million men and women who make up the work force of the United States Postal Establishment.

It is unfortunate but true that most people take their mail service pretty much for granted. In my opinion it is as unwise as it is ungrateful for anyone to take any of the blessings of liberty for granted, and there is none among these blessings more important or more vital to survival than freedom of communications as epitomized by the postal service.

After all, it is impossible for tyranny and free communications to exist in nature together. By an extension of Gresham's Law, one inevitably throws out the other. Despotism requires that each man be made an island, separated by a wall of fear from other human beings, prohibited by law and force of arms from exchanging ideas and hopes with his neighbors. Since a despotism is by its very nature the rule of a minority, it is essential to its success that the enslaved subjects be kept divided and disorganized, unaware of their potential combined power. A free and uncensored mail service would be fatal to such a plan. Because of this, freedom of communications has always been tyranny's first target and freedom's first creation.

To realize more fully the importance of what we have, we should think for a moment of what the benighted and beleaguered slaves behind the iron curtain would do for just a *touch* of the freedom which we all are inclined to accept like the air we breathe. In those bleak latitudes of fear, an indiscreet word of criticism against the slave masters could well lead to a living death in a dark dungeon, or to being led blindfolded between twelve gleaming rifles and a wall. Whole generations of human beings have grown up in those muted meridians without knowing what it is to write their opinions freely in a letter or even to hear with pleasure the cheerful sound of mail being thrust through the slot in their own front doors. In Soviet Russia and her satellites the approach of the postman, to the ordinary human being, is at best a matter of deep suspicion and, at worst, a matter of overpowering dread. The mail service is the only entirely secret and private communication that we have.

Actually, the concept of the sanctity and privacy of a personal or business letter is entirely an American one. When the Founding Fathers wrote this principle into law they were breaking virgin ground. Under the Hanoverian kings of England, postmasters in the colonies were not only permitted but *instructed* to open whatever personal letters they pleased in order to detect incipient subversion at its source. This practice had so inhibited and enraged the revolutionaries that, once they had won the war, they considered the hitherto unheard-of principle of the sanctity of the mails as a *sine qua non* of the liberty they had fought so hard to achieve.

When this new concept worked in the newly fledged republic without fomenting internal strife, it was tried elsewhere, until at last it became the symbol of freedom in every land where men could walk upright without fear and call no man master and worship God as they saw fit.

Our system of communications as embodied in the mail service is the golden thread that holds the tapestry of freedom together. Everyone who works in this great enterprise, from the Postmaster General down to the lowest-paid worker contributes significantly, each in his own way, to that ever-growing tapestry. But it is the rewarding role of the letter carrier to be the recognizable beginning and end, the alpha and the omega, of the noble and essential business of maintaining communication among free human beings through the postal service. Although the letter carrier has a multitude of other duties inside and outside of the Post Office, the fact remains that he is best known as the man who picks up your letter from the mailbox in which you deposit it and starts it on its way, and as the man who eventually delivers that letter to the front door of the person to whom you have written it.

This is a proud role and a gratifying role. It is a source of pride to me to know that the overwhelming majority of letter carriers in the United States understands fully the responsibilities and implications inherent in their role.

CHAPTER 2

THE LETTER CARRIER
AND THE POSTAL SERVICE

IT IS A pity that too few Americans know the facts about their
postal system. Here is a tremendous system of communications, the only government function that directly touches every
person in the country every day of every week in the year, and
yet public knowledge of its size and operation is so slight that it
borders on the ridiculous.

This condition of ignorance illustrates a kind of national
apathy toward our federal government. Government has grown
so big in recent times that the people of this country have all but
given up hope of ever comprehending its workings. No longer
do people consider government something they own and control;
they consider government something that *happens* to them. They
grumble about the things in government that they don't like, but
by and large they seem to be content to leave the running of the
country to the politicians, and to hope that things will turn out
for the best somehow, someday.

We have no divine assurance that things *will* turn out for the best. We enjoy no special exemption from the lessons of the past. Since the beginning of recorded history it has never been true that liberty has been won or lost in a single day. The progression upward or downward has always been gradual, almost imperceptible. Apathy is the element most erosive to the fabric of freedom. If allowed to spread unchecked, it invariably eats away at the fabric until it is irretrievably ruined.

In the case of the Post Office public ignorance has produced a kind of apathy that has been expensive and extremely deleterious to the service. The American people, generally, cannot be bothered to learn about their post office. This is so true that I find myself amazed whenever I do happen to come across a lay person who knows anything at all about the postal service.

By and large, the only civilians who do bother to learn the facts of postal life are those whose livelihood depends upon the service and whose incomes are dependent on low postage rates. I do not blame these individuals. It is their business to know certain phases of the Post Office inside and out, and it is their undisputed right to protect their interests in the Congress. But, of course, it is only natural that their approach to postal problems is somewhat one-sided.

This apathy and lack of knowledge on the part of the public has led to a corresponding apathy and lack of knowledge on the part of the majority of the members of the Congress. As a result, the Post Office Committees in both Houses are very low on the Congressional prestige totem pole, despite the fact that many able and courageous men and women have sat on them.

Few Americans even know the size of their postal system. It is not only the most important business in the world, but it is also among the biggest. It employs more than 525,000 men and women in approximately 36,000 post offices.[1] It has a cash turn-

---

[1] In 1900 there were almost 77,000 post offices. However, as the automobile developed and roads improved, the number of rural post offices has been whittled down each year as they were replaced by rural letter-carrier service.

over of about twenty-three billion dollars a year. As a mere side-line it operates, as the postal savings system, one of the largest savings banks in the world.

At a conservative estimate, the average letter carrier walks about twelve miles every day delivering the mail to patrons along his route. (Of course, the distance varies according to the size and kind of route involved.) This means that the 125,000 letter carriers in the United States march about one and a half million miles a day, or the equivalent of three round trips to the moon.

During the past year your postal system handled more than sixty billion pieces of mail, or almost three hundred and fifty pieces for every man, woman, and child in the country.[2] This is more than the mail volume of all the other countries of the free world put together; it is more than two-thirds of the mail volume of the entire world. The annual increase in volume of one year over another is often larger than the total mail volume of many European countries.

And the annual "deficit" of the Post Office Department is now around six hundred million dollars.

It is important to remember that the Post Office Establishment does not have the use of the revenues it takes in. These go straight into the United States Treasury. The Post Office Department operates under appropriations voted to it by the Congress. It first makes a budget request which is usually whittled down by the Bureau of the Budget, which feels it has to justify its governmental existence by reducing expenditures. When the request goes before the Appropriations Committees of the Congress it is usually cut down much further, since some members of these committees feel they can only justify their political existence by telling their constituents what tremendous sums of money they have saved them. When an appropriations request is larded with excess fat this system works satisfactorily. When it is an honest

[2] Figures taken from the Postmaster General's Annual Report, 1959.

budget with no fat in it, the subsequent cuts are plainly unrealistic and, if allowed to stand, can result only in impaired services and inadequate working conditions.

Although I have publicly and violently disagreed with Postmaster General Arthur E. Summerfield over many of his policies, I have always respected his courage and his real, if sporadic, desire to effect improvements in the postal service. Parsimonious appropriations have frustrated him in many of his efforts. His own insistence on balancing the postal budget has made many other efforts abortive.

One of the most important of these has been the program of providing new postal facilities all over the nation. In the twenty-year period between 1938 and 1958 Congress failed to appropriate as much as a single dime for the construction of new postal facilities. In that period the postal volume doubled. The average post office was about fifty years old and it was bursting at the seams. In several large cities (notably Denver and Seattle) postal employees were sorting the mail out on the street, even in freezing weather, because there wasn't any room in the buildings. Postal employees were trying to give the American people twentieth-century service out of nineteenth-century post offices—an obvious impossibility.

This tendency on the part of the Congress toward inattention to the physical needs of the postal service was and is extremely short-sighted, since obsolescence feeds upon itself and, when left unchecked, becomes dynamic.

To his credit, General Summerfield has tried to modernize postal facilities, and he has made good use of existing means of leasing postal facilities that have been built by private capital. This program has prevented absolute chaos from enveloping the postal system.

But, despite manifold and manifest improvements, Summerfield's efforts have been only a fleabite compared to the over-all problem. And I am convinced that if the average American knew the conditions under which the mail must be handled in the average post office he would swear off complaining about the inadequacy of the postal service and would start giving thanks for the dedication and loyalty of the army of postal employees who overcome such obstacles in making the service as good as it is.[3]

Postal employees on the payroll of the richest and most powerful country in the history of the world are still forced, in many communities, to work under conditions that would be embarrassing in even the most impoverished areas of the earth.

With the mail volume increasing enormously, not only as far as total pieces are concerned but also in terms of per capita use, the postal service will collapse under its own weight within the next twenty years unless national administrations stop being mesmerized by balanced budgets, and unless the Congress stops treating the Post Office like some unwanted and embarrassing love child. This is a problem that will not walk away if we pretend it isn't there. It has to be faced squarely, and the more we procrastinate and try to ignore it, the worse it becomes.

The lack of knowledge on the part of the average person concerning his postal service has led to a general misunderstanding as to what a letter carrier actually does to earn his pay. This has given an opportunity for postal administrators to attempt to disguise and distort the real duties of a letter carrier whenever pay legislation is discussed, in order to make these duties seem insignificant and unimportant. Less than five years ago the Civil Service Commission, whether through ignorance or malice I know not, went so far as to compare the duties of a letter carrier with those of a Western Union messenger. This insult rankles even now in the mind of every person of even minimal honesty who knows the facts of the postal service.

[3] I refer to conditions particularly in Detroit; Philadelphia; Harrisburg, Pennsylvania; Portland, Oregon; Houston; Boston; Mobile; and Oakland, California. There are many others.

So, what does a letter carrier do? Let's follow an average carrier through an average day.

He gets up usually before 5 A.M.[4] It is usually necessary for him to get to the post office by 6 A.M. and, since low postal salaries generally do not allow him and his family to live in quarters close to the downtown area where the post office or the postal station is located, early rising and commuting to and from work represent a way of life with a carrier.

A letter carrier begins his day by sorting, street by street and number by number, the mail that has been distributed to him by the postal clerks. He must also pick up and sign for collect-on-delivery packages and for registered, certified, and custom duty mail destined for his route. He must also pick up the keys to the various boxes along his route.

The carrier is held financially responsible for the loss of all such mail, if a loss does occur.

There are other financial risks involved in a carrier's life. For instance, when he delivers a registered letter, regulations state that he must give it to the person to whom it is addressed or to his "authorized agent." Regulations, however, fail to define explicitly what an authorized agent is, nor do they explain how a letter carrier can distinguish such an authorized agent from an impostor. The carrier is therefore caught on the horns of a dilemma.

If he is overly cautious and refuses to give the registered letter to someone claiming to be an authorized agent the patron might become indignant.

If, on the other hand, he takes a chance and does hand over a registered letter to someone in the addressee's home, he had better be right! He is taking his financial life in his hands. If he's wrong, it's Katy bar the door! The financial loss that is claimed will come out of his pocket.

---

[4] I am outlining the duties of a typical letter carrier. Naturally there are variations in the routine.

In addition to all this, the carrier, before he begins his rounds, must cull out of his mail all "nixies," i.e., all letters wrongly addressed, all letters inaccurately handled by post office clerks, mail addressed to people who have moved to other locations, mail for people who have gone on extended vacations and have left a forwarding address, and so on. He has all the relative information marked down in his route book, and he must check his mail against the book and turn in all the "nixies."

He must work against a rigid time schedule to "box" his mail. Then he must set up his relays. That is, he must arrange his mail so it can be distributed by truck to the eight or ten collection and storage boxes along his route. Postal laws and regulations hold that a letter carrier can carry only thirty-five pounds of mail on his back at a time.[5] A letter carrier's load for an entire route can average five hundred pounds, and on days on which the big slick magazines are due for delivery, the total load can be much greater. Therefore, arranging the relays in advance requires intelligent planning on the part of the carrier as well as an intimate knowledge of his route.

All this represents a sizable bit of work, and as a general rule, it is accomplished before the carrier starts his daily march along the sidewalks of America.

Once he begins his march he must keep up a rigid and exacting schedule. Regulations stipulate that he must complete eight hours within ten hours of the day, and he gets no overtime unless permission has been granted by his supervisor in advance. If the carrier falls behind in his schedule he will immediately fall under suspicion of loitering. Carriers are under constant surveillance by the Inspection Service, and very little quarter is given when they are suspected of even minor violations of postal laws and regulations.

In addition to his regular job, the letter carrier is often asked

[5] However, there are no scales in the relay boxes and many carriers, in their zeal, are inclined to ignore this limitation.

to perform duties quite extraneous to the postal service but extremely helpful as far as the government and the average citizen are concerned.

Since the mailman knows a great deal about the people along his route he is continually called upon to assist in such enterprises as the taking of the census, the registration of enemy aliens in time of war, the distribution of adjusted service certificates, the recording of all working people under the Social Security Act, and so on. Both the Postal Inspection Service and the Federal Bureau of Investigation often depend upon the letter carrier to supply information concerning suspected criminals who might be living on his route.

There is one further thing, an intangible but vital aspect of the letter carrier's service, which is generally overlooked. He is a most important public relations man for Uncle Sam. He is the most intimate and the most human contact the average citizen has with his government. In many cases a citizen's entire attitude toward his government is based upon his relationship with his letter carrier.

When the need arises, and it arises often, letter carriers voluntarily and on their own time walk their routes to collect money for charitable causes such as the muscular dystrophy campaign and the March of Dimes. They develop a close and unique association with those families whom they serve. It is not unusual for this association to extend over three generations. The letter carrier delivers the birth announcements throughout the neighborhood. He delivers the annual birthday greetings, the invitations to parties, the graduation cards and the wedding invitations. He delivers the anniversary cards each year, and finally, the death announcements and cards of condolence. More often than not, he attends the wakes and the funerals of people he has known and served throughout their lives.

Whenever a movement develops in the Congress to increase postal salaries the high echelon of the Post Office Department, who are usually exemplary gentlemen in their way but almost always mesmerized by the desire for balanced budgets and for making the postal service into a public utility rather than a public service, bolster their opposition to raising our salaries by implying that the letter carrier is a mere pack horse and, as such, is probably overpaid as it is.

This is a stratagem that invariably makes me see red, since I know that those who propound it know better. I think, from this sparse account of what a letter carrier actually does to earn his meager pay, the average reader will agree that my resentment against this vile tactic is justifiable.

CHAPTER 3

BEGINNINGS
OF UNIONIZATION

THE National Association of Letter Carriers is the biggest and most successful of all the postal unions.

Since letter carriers are in the federal service, they are denied the right to strike, to bargain collectively, or to demand a union shop or a check-off. Yet, the association today has 125,000 members, more than the total number of active carriers in the postal service. (This is because several thousand letter carriers who have retired, or who have been promoted to supervisory positions, loyally continue to hold cards in the NALC.)

All improvements in wages and working conditions must come from the federal government. This has meant that, purely as a matter of survival, the National Association of Letter Carriers has had to develop to a very fine point the gentle art of lobbying. Success in this field plus the natural affection which most congressmen feel toward the letter carriers of the nation have combined to give to the association a position of dominance and respect unequaled by any other voluntary labor organization in or out of government.

However, the road to success has all been uphill. Ever since free city delivery was instituted by the Post Office Department in Cleveland, Ohio, in 1863, there have been local mutual benefit organizations among the letter carriers. Since in those days letter carriers were selected by the postmasters more for their ability to carry their political precincts than for their ability to carry the mail, the effect of the postal employees on Congress was more on a personal influence basis than on an organizational basis.

Actually, during the second half of the nineteenth century, the flagrant submission by all parties to the spoils system made effective organization impossible. Men were hired and fired on a purely political basis, regardless of merit, and every change of administration meant an inevitable shake-up of every major post office in the land.

The postmaster was almost always one of the leading politicians in the town, and all his employees were at his personal mercy. He set working conditions and pay scales. There was no job security. If a politician was hurt at the polls, his friends in the post office would inevitably be hurt also. Whereas a letter carrier today can be fired for partisan political *activity,* in those days the best way to be fired was to display partisan political *inactivity.*

Although some political favorites were given sinecures in the post office, most of the tours of duty were rugged and long, averaging from ten to twelve hours a day. Postal inspectors could, theoretically, set a man's tour of duty for alternating hours throughout the entire day and there was nothing the employee could do about it except quit.

For the first ten years after the inauguration of city delivery service, salaries for letter carriers varied between $200 and

$1,000 a year with an average of $460.[1] Since all carriers did just about the same kind and the same amount of work, the inequality between rates of pay was obvious. However, it gave the politician postmaster a handy lever by which he could reward political faithfulness and punish political deviation.

Postmaster General Marshall Jewell tried in 1875 to adjust the inequities by raising the minimum salaries and reducing the maximum salaries. However, congressional tight-fistedness in regard to appropriations for city delivery forced the Department to make serious cuts in the carriers' salaries and the emphasis was a great deal more on reduction than it was on increasing.

Even though the letter carriers were not organized nationally they were able to call the attention of a sympathetic public to their plight by explaining their case to their patrons as they delivered the mail.

At this juncture one of the first and certainly one of the most loyal friends of the letter carriers ever to sit in the Congress came to the fore. He was Representative Samuel Sullivan "Sunset" Cox of New York,[2] a man who, along with Representative John J. O'Neill of St. Louis will always be revered by postal workers in this country.

Congressman Cox introduced a bill in 1877 calling for a fixed

[1] Cf. Sterling Denhard Spero, *Labor Movement in a Government Industry* (New York: George H. Doran Company, 1924), p. 59. Carriers could, however, supplement their income by collecting certain fees from their patrons.

[2] Samuel Sullivan Cox (1824–89) was one of the most remarkable and versatile public figures of his time. He was a Congressman from Ohio during the early part of his political career and later represented Manhattan's East Side in Congress. An irrepressible Democrat with a flashing wit, he was a consistent and selfless champion of the nonprivileged groups within our borders. The letter carriers of Brooklyn, New York, still make an annual pilgrimage to his grave in Greenwood Cemetery. He was the first real political hero of postal employees, and he performed his heroics when the going was roughest. After Cox's death the letter carriers raised $10,000 to erect a statue in his memory. It stood for many years in Astor Place, in lower Manhattan, a few blocks from the Cox home. In 1924 the eight-foot sculpture was relocated in Tompkins Square Park, Avenue A and Seventh Street, within the boundaries of Cox's old Congressional District.

rate of pay for all letter carriers. In 1879 the legislation was passed which set carriers' salaries at $800 and $1,000 per annum with the pay of carriers in smaller cities being set at $850. A third grade, called "auxiliaries," was created with a salary of $400 per annum.

The law, when passed, encountered considerable opposition and even subversion in the field. Postmasters resented having their wings clipped, and often refused to pay letter carriers their just salaries. The Department dilly-dallied interminably in classifying its employees and placing the law into action. Promotion from auxiliary to regular was in many communities next to impossible. Postmasters saw no reason why they should pay a letter carrier one thousand dollars per year when they could get an auxiliary to do the same work for him at less than half that sum.

However, because of the insistence of the Congress that its wishes be obeyed and its intent respected, the fixed pay rate became the rule in the service and conditions were greatly altered for the better.

Although the conditions described above literally cried out for unionism and an aggressive program of labor organization, the political climate within the post offices made such action almost impossible.

The big change came in 1883. Congress passed the Pendleton Civil Service Act.[3] Judged by the standards of today, this act is a poor thing indeed, and insofar as the employee was concerned, it resembled a sieve more than it did a bulwark. But compared with the primitive conditions that existed prior to its enactment, the Pendleton Act was a giant step forward, since it drastically reduced the role of the politician in the lower echelons of the postal service.

[3] Senator George H. Pendleton, of Ohio, was the "Father of Civil Service." He was a resident of my home town, Cincinnati. His crusade to eliminate the "spoils system" from government defeated him in his bid for re-election. Postal and federal employees showed no gratitude. A sad commentary indeed!

But as the Congress lost its power of patronage over the rank-and-file employees it also lost interest in their welfare. As the friendliness of the politicians dramatically diminished, the letter carriers (and other postal groups) saw immediately that they had to unify nationally or Congressional indifference would eventually reduce them to peonage.

Postal administrations and the postal worker live constantly in an uneasy state of balance upon the horns of a dilemma. Because of a strange concatenation of causes, the postal employee is trained in highly specialized skills, very few of which are applicable in the outside civilian world. If he leaves the postal service he must learn a new trade for which his postal experience has given him a minimal amount of experience. Contrariwise, the skills of the postal worker are so specialized and are achieved after so much experience and hard work that if a walk-out of any proportion by postal workers ever did take place, the entire postal service of the nation would be fouled up for months and even years. The skills of a letter carrier, a clerk, or a supervisor are not cheaply bought, nor are they easily attained. As the postal service has become more complex, as the volume and the *per capita* use of the mails have risen so stratospherically, it is no longer possible to insert inexperienced, green men into career jobs and expect the mails to move accurately and swiftly.

Postmasters, though they perform an essential function in management, are not quite as indispensable nor are they as difficult to train or replace. If every first- and second-class postmaster in the country were to leave the service tomorrow, the mail would somehow get delivered. But if every letter carrier, every postal clerk, or every supervisor were to leave the service, there would be no conceivable chance of getting the mail to the homes of America. By this I mean no insult to postmasters. There are thousands of very fine postmasters in the country and they do a very commendable, professional job. Many of them I count among my close personal friends. Indeed, a great many of them have been graduated from the ranks of the National Association of Letter Carriers.[4]

Career postal employees and the top management of the postal establishment live in a state of dual dependence upon each other. Neither could exist profitably without the other. Sometimes the relationship is uneasy but it is permanent. At such times this relationship reminds me of the married couple who continuously held each other's hand because if they ever let go they would tear each other apart. At other times the hand-holding is genuine and affectionate. After all, postal administrators are transient and can and do differ violently in their attitude toward labor, but the aims and objectives of labor are consistent and do not vacillate according to the vagaries of political winds.

With the decline of Congressional interest in postal employees, however, the delicate balance of power between management and the rank-and-file was thrown out of kilter and the only way to restore that balance was for the rank-and-file to organize and replace personal political influence with unified nationwide power which could be reflected significantly at the polls.

The only weapon left to the letter carriers was (and still is) the fact that individually and as a group they are liked and admired by the American public at large and that they visit each home in America every day, six days a week. Since people talk

[4] I have had, over the years, many happy experiences with such postmasters and former postmasters as Raymond A. Thomas and Joseph Gallagher, of Philadelphia; Patrick Connelly, of Boston; Charles J. Backlet and Hobart A. Wehking, of Cincinnati; Raymond Holmquist, of Pasadena, California; John Coan, of Indianapolis; Joseph Glennon, of East Orange, New Jersey; Louis Reilly, of Newark, New Jersey; Albert Goldman, Robert Bragalini, and Robert ("Ray") Shaffer, of New York City; Sam Valliere, of Miami; Joseph Franz, of Cleveland; Roy Williams, of Lexington, Kentucky and William E. Kelly, of Brooklyn. There are many others, of course. It is inevitable that postmasters and letter carriers should have occasional differences but, by and large, these differences have been ironed out without rancor. Despite widely differing objectives at times, the National Association of Letter Carriers has got along well with the National Association of Postmasters and there have been occasions when the two associations have been mutually helpful to each other.

to their letter carriers as old friends, and vice versa, this is a formidable bargaining point with the Congress.

The passage of the civil service law also gave the letter carrier and other postal employees a greater stake in the career service. When they were hired for political reasons only, the fact that their tenure would almost certainly be short lived inclined them to accept, even though grumblingly, inadequate working conditions and wages. The job was a stopgap, not a career. But the Pendleton Act was intended to create a career service (although the intention was imperfectly worked out) and the job suddenly became far more secure, far more attractive. Since the politicos, once they had bowed to the public will and had reluctantly voted for a patronage free career service, were now starting to chisel away at the law and destroy what they had, for temporary political advantage, created, the need for organization among postal employees became urgent.

Up until this time lobbying in the Congress had been performed by letter carriers on an individualistic, catch-as-catch-can basis. A local group would appoint someone to represent its membership in Washington, and that representative would operate in behalf of his local brothers (who were paying his way) rather than for letter carriers as a whole. Because of the political prominence of some of these representatives, this system, though haphazard, was not entirely without beneficial effect. But this individualistic system was swiftly becoming inadequate for bearing the burden of increasingly complex governmental relations.

The seeds of effective organization grew out of the vacation situation. Vacations for letter carriers in these early days were entirely within the gift and the discretion of the local postmaster. Except in New York City, however, vacations were taboo. In New York City the postmaster was in the habit of granting ten days' leave a year to his letter carriers, provided that the carriers not on leave would combine their forces, on the basis of three men doing the work of four, so as to cover the routes of their vacationing brothers.

However, departmental employees in Washington were habitually granted thirty days' annual leave. This was because they were political appointees and often from homes far distant from the nation's capital. With the relatively primitive transportation facilities existing, an extended leave was necessary if they were to be able to reach their homes, remain to fraternize and politick effectively, and then to return to their desks.

The letter carriers of the New York area, in an action of unprecedented boldness, petitioned the Department for the same leave privileges as those enjoyed by the departmental employees in Washington. The solicitor, or law officer, for the Department tore up the petition and declared that there was no law existing under which the local postmaster could legally grant any annual leave whatsoever. The Postmaster of New York City was ordered to discontinue the granting of vacation time.

The New York City and Brooklyn letter carriers were indignant, and they interested Congressman "Sunset" Cox in their righteous crusade. The Congressman was finally able, after one disappointment, to effect a compromise by which letter carriers throughout the country would be granted fifteen days of annual leave with pay per annum. Letter carriers all over the country began to realize their own potential strength, since this crusade, although organized and manned in metropolitan New York, had nationally beneficial results.

National unionization was on its way.

CHAPTER 4

THE HARD
ROAD UPWARD

MEANWHILE, the Ancient and Holy Order of the Knights of Labor was emerging from its cocoon of fraternal existence and was beginning to show some muscle in the nation's economic and industrial life. Those who were not engaged in crafts which were generally considered "skilled" looked to this organization as the potential savior of their future well-being. During the 1880's its membership approached the three-quarter million mark and its locals numbered almost six thousand.

For more than two decades the eight-hour day was standard for "laborers, workmen and mechanics." When the letter carriers asked the Department for the same consideration that private industry granted its employees they were coldly turned down on the grounds that they were not eligible because they were neither laborers, workmen, nor mechanics. The carriers' groups in New York City, Brooklyn, Chicago, Omaha, and Buffalo, among other communities, secretly joined the Knights, often without notifying any other group and without being notified of any other group's affiliation.

When the Knights of Labor introduced an eight-hour bill for letter carriers in 1886, the reaction of the Post Office Department was frenetic. No effort was spared in the attempt to blow the fledgling movement out of the water before it was securely afloat.

The leading antagonist in the field was the postmaster of New York City, H. G. Pearson, a violent enemy of labor. He attempted to fire, out-of-hand, one hundred and fifty carriers who had joined the Knights. Fortunately, the Knights had become a potent political factor and 1886 was an election year, so the Department reluctantly ordered Pearson to go easy and to reinstate his intended victims.

However, the internecine war continued in the dark alleys of bureaucracy. Organization men were given assignments as far as possible from their homes. Now that vacations were allowable, letter carriers were peremptorily ordered to take annual leave with as little advance notice as possible. One favorite and despicable gambit was to make independent-minded carriers take their vacations over the Christmas holiday season, thus not only reducing their actual number of days of leave, but also preventing them from benefiting from the generosity of their patrons during the Yuletide holidays. Many carriers, because of the low wages, depended upon these gifts to maintain their families. If a letter carrier were known to be a member of the Knights it was common practice all over the country to stick him on spectacularly undesirable routes. Spies were set upon suspected carriers. When the Knights of Labor held a great mass meeting in support of the eight-hour day at Cooper Union, New York City, in 1888, Postmaster Pearson infiltrated the meeting with his espionage agents. However, the inevitable informational leakage occurred and affiliated letter carriers took cover in time to escape detection.

In league with the Knights, the letter carriers participated effectively but legally (within the limits of a very loosely written law) in the Congressional elections of 1886, and the fact that a surprising number of advocates of an eight-hour bill were elected or re-elected to the Congress, and an equally surprising number of enemies of such a bill were defeated, created greater respect in legislative circles for the letter carriers and for the labor movement generally. It is apparent that a significant number of uncommitted Congressmen got the message, because a viable eight-hour law passed the Congress and was signed by President Grover Cleveland in 1888.

While this struggle was going on, most letter carriers learned the need for concerted, organized action and the weakness inherent in having separate locals operating independently and often at cross purposes. As early as 1887 an organization calling itself the Letter Carriers' National Association was petitioning the Congress for an eight-hour law.[1] However, the word "national" was a euphemism, since there is no indication of the group having any membership outside Pennsylvania and, perhaps, Ohio, and it did not survive to acquire any wide acceptance.

The real birth of the National Association of Letter Carriers occurred in August 1889, when the carriers of Milwaukee, Wisconsin, sent out a call for all other carriers to meet in their city during the annual encampment of the Grand Army of the Republic scheduled for that year. Since the local organizations were suspicious of official traps and apprehensive of detection by departmental spies there was no overt affirmative response to this call. However, since a large number of letter carriers had served with the Union forces in the War Between the States (which had concluded only twenty years previously) persuasion and proselyting went on well during the encampment. The handful of heroic organizers announced formation of a national association, drew up a bill of grievances consisting of twenty articles, and sent

---

[1] Spero, p. 68.

out a call to all carriers for a national convention to be held the next year in Boston.

Because these veterans of the war were not officially representing any group, their action was viewed at first with some suspicion among letter carriers, and with alarm among postal officials. The small group of instigators was offering charters in a practically nonexistent association at fifty dollars apiece, and there was a natural caution lest there might be some hanky-panky afoot. There was, in fact, general resistance until the New York Letter Carriers' Association (which by this time dominated Gotham's Knights of Labor group) saw the potential in the idea and called representatives of all the important elements of local carrier groups into conference to iron out the existing differences and allay existing suspicions. As a result of this conference a bonafide convention was held in Boston and a real and living association was formed.

The first president of the Association was William H. Wood, of Detroit, a veteran of the Civil War, who was elected at Milwaukee at that informal 1889 convention. At the Boston convention in 1890, John J. Goodwin, of Providence, Rhode Island, became president.

However, the most significant result of the 1890 convention was the election of John F. Victory, of New York, as national secretary. Mr. Victory, an extremely able man and a writer of great verve and talent, was not only a letter carrier but also owned a major interest in a paper devoted to the interests of postal employees entitled *The Postal Record*. This paper, on December 1, 1893, became the official organ of the National Association of Letter Carriers and ever since has been indispensable to the growth and development of the organization on a national as well as a local level.

CHAPTER 5

THE SEEDS
OF OPPRESSION

NOTHING historically has aided the growth of trade unionism
both in and out of government more than has the consistent imbecility of management in dealing with rank and file
employees.

Certainly this is true of the growth and development of the
National Association of Letter Carriers. The stern and stupid
measures of certain postal administrations did more to unify the
letter carriers of the nation than anything the most dedicated and
adroit labor organizers could possibly have done.

It is the blessing of God Almighty that the human spirit is
indestructible. It resists persecution and even flourishes under
despotism. Therefore, the more that postal administrations
sought to suppress the NALC and to subjugate its membership,
the more the Association grew in numbers and solidarity.

Ironically, a little more intelligence and insight on the part of
postal management could have made the young NALC relatively

ineffective from the very outset. Dissidence and jealousies among the membership threatened to tear the Association apart before it could get really started. If postal management had emulated Machiavelli rather than adopting the tactics of a Nero, the subsequent history of the organization could have been quite different. However, instead of taking the Biblical advice of being "wise as serpents and harmless as doves," the leaders of the Department were consistently harmless as serpents and wise as doves. And doves are stupid. Don't let anyone tell you differently.

As a result of the initial successful NALC convention in 1890, fifty-three cities asked for, and received, charters in the new national organization. However, some of the most populous cities, notably New York, Chicago, and Brooklyn insisted on maintaining their affiliation with the Knights of Labor, and in those communities leadership in the local assemblies of the Knights meant automatic leadership in the local branches of the NALC.

This somewhat unhealthy situation was aggravated when the devotees of the Knights of Labor tried to bring the entire NALC under the domination and control of the Knights.

Secretary Victory, by far the most effective and influential officer in the NALC at that time, threw his own considerable influence, as well as the influence of *The Postal Record,* against this attempt to force affiliation upon the Association. He felt strongly (and subsequent events proved him correct in this belief) that the Knights of Labor were on their way out as an effective labor organization. He saw no reason for the struggling NALC to board a sinking ship. He also felt that the NALC was not yet sufficiently strong to affiliate with a large national labor group. Affiliation, in his opinion, could only mean an eventual loss of identity and a loss of control by the Association over its own affairs.

The bitterest controversy between the two factions was in New York City itself, and two delegations from that city, one representing the Empire City Branch of the NALC, and the other the Knights of Labor, demanded to be seated at the 1892 national convention in Indianapolis. After presentation of arguments on both sides, the non-Knights of Labor group was seated in the convention, and the Knights were rejected.

This led to a dangerous split in the texture of the NALC. The Knights of Labor letter carriers broke off relations with the rest of the NALC membership. They published a rival paper and they made their own separate appeals to the Congress on behalf of their letter carriers. Congress became so confused by the controversy that it tacitly refused to consider any legislation involving letter carriers until the feuding was ended.[1]

Then, at this perilous juncture in the history of the NALC, the Post Office Department unwittingly came to the rescue!

With exquisite timing, someone in the Department whose brains had been, to say the least, informally assembled, decided to interpret the eight-hour law of 1888 in such a way as to cause universal outrage. Soon after this came the inauguration of the nefarious "spotter" system. And, finally, there came the "gag rule." By the time all this had been done the National Association of Letter Carriers was a solid, militant, loyal, effective, and growing organization. The dove-like stupidity and the snake-like animosity of departmental officials put the NALC in business for all time.

Trouble with the eight-hour law started with the historically recurrent obsession on the Department's part with balanced budgets rather than with improved service.

Population growth was necessitating an extension of free delivery, but appropriations were not sufficient to provide for the necessary expansion of the carrier force. So the Department decided to circumvent the law in order to make ends meet.

The law stated that a letter carrier, if he is "employed a greater

---

[1] This situation exists today among the postmasters, who have two rival groups, and among the postal clerks, who have four or five organizations among which their strength is dissipated.

number of hours a day than eight . . . shall be paid extra for the same in proportion to the salary now fixed by law." [2]

This language was perfectly clear to anyone except a government lawyer. When the Department started working letter carriers more than eight hours a day without extra compensation, the Association complained.

But some legal "genius" decided to make of the law a Procrustean bed to meet the immediate demands of the administration. The Department decreed that an eight-hour day *really* meant a fifty-six hour work week and that, therefore, a carrier who worked six nine-hour days *actually owed the government two hours of work at the end of the week!*

Congressman "Sunset" Cox, one of the principal writers of the law, indignantly rejected this outlandish interpretation, but the Department was adamant.

The National Association of Letter Carriers fought a test case all the way up to the United States Supreme Court [3] and won smashing victories all the way.

When the fighting had ended and the dust had cleared, the Congress had to appropriate $3,500,000 to settle the thousands of claims for overtime which had been caused by departmental obstinacy.

This was an historic case and a significant victory. The David-like NALC had annihilated the Goliath-like Department and labor and management all over the United States sat up and took notice. The prestige of the NALC grew enormously almost overnight.

Secretary Victory used this growth in NALC prestige to make peace with the Knights of Labor and the subsequent love feast was so successful that the national head [4] of the Knights of Labor,

[2] 25 Stat. 157.
[3] 148 U.S. 124 (1893) Post *vs.* U.S.
[4] His real title was General Master Workman of the Ancient and Holy Order of the Knights of Labor.

John N. Parsons, who also was a letter carrier, was elected to the presidency of the National Association of Letter Carriers. He served well and honorably in this capacity for five successive terms.

With their historical, and sometimes hysterical, pig-headedness the departmental officials unwittingly continued to do everything possible to consolidate the gains the NALC had achieved. They persecuted prominent members of the Association and sought to bribe others by holding out the promise of advancement if they would cooperate by guiding Association policies in directions most acceptable to the Department. This infiltration by departmental "stooges" could have created a fatal fifth column within the Association in those early and formative days, and perhaps could have succeeded in making the NALC a mere company union. But the Department once again snatched defeat out of the jaws of victory. It instituted the "spotter system."

It seems the civil service laws were inhibiting the administration from bestowing as much patronage on the faithful as they would like, so the Post Office created new jobs for party hacks by making them "spotters" or, in plain language, spies.

The spotters were chosen from the outside. They had no postal experience and their job was to stealthily watch the letter carriers on their rounds and report every semblance of an infraction of rules.

The Department, of course, said that this ignoble system was designed to create greater efficiency and economy. It was just a coincidence that it also created jobs for the hungry hordes of political supporters which quadrennially plague every national administration. The beauty of the plan, from the Administration's point of view, was that it enabled the postmasters to fire letter carriers for alleged or actual infractions of rules, and thereby create openings on the civil service lists which could be filled by the reasonably qualified among the politically faithful.

The spotters, naturally enough, attempted to justify their existence by overzealousness in the performance of their duties. In many large metropolitan areas (particularly in Cleveland and Philadelphia) as many as one-third of the entire carrier force were up on charges at one time and were battling ineffectually for retention in the service.

The most insidious part of this attack upon the civil service was the manner in which charges were preferred. In almost all cases letter carriers were hauled before the postmaster approximately six months after the alleged offense was supposed to have taken place, and were interrogated about their precise movements on a day they had long since forgotten.

The Association, quite rightly, saw in this system an attempt to undermine its power and influence, since (by another odd coincidence) prominent members of the fledgling NALC were most often the targets for the spotters' persecutions.

At the NALC national convention in Cleveland in 1894 there were several sycophantic letter carriers who sought to curry favor with Postmaster General Bissell by attempting to defend the spotter system. This proved to be too much for an eloquent and righteously indignant brother from Philadelphia, who departed from the customarily cautious oratory which characterized NALC conventions at that time by delivering a passionate attack upon the Cleveland administration generally, and the Postmaster General and his spotters in particular. His fiery words had hardly stopped echoing through the hall when he received word from the Post Office Department that he had been fired.

It is perhaps symptomatic of the labor-management relationship of that time that the name of this hero is lost to us. The postal administration had the labor organizations so cowed that in the official transcript of the convention proceedings there is no mention of this delegate's speech or of the reaction it had on the rest of the convention!

It is easy to look back from the vantage point of today and blandly criticize the leaders of the late nineteenth and early twentieth century for lack of aggressiveness against intolerant management. There is no comparison between the sociological and political climate of those days and now. Labor had comparatively little support in the Congress and very little among those powers who controlled both major political parties and, through ownership of the press, public opinion. Especially in government, management held all the aces when it dealt with labor. Opposition to management's demands was bound to be both futile and unpopular.

And yet one cannot help but wish that the leaders of the postal organizations had shown more courage at this crucial juncture in the history of labor-management relations in government, for, if they had, the dismal record of the next quarter of a century might have been very different.

"If the trumpet give an uncertain sound," asks St. Paul, "who shall prepare himself for the battle?" The employee organizations became confused and overcautious in the face of concentrated management aggression, and management skillfully exploited the situation until it had labor pretty well on the run.

This premeditated campaign of oppression reached its climax in the adoption of the notorious "gag rule" of 1902.

CHAPTER 6

THE GAG RULE

THEODORE ROOSEVELT, by the standards of his day and by many standards even of our day, was a trail-blazing liberal. It is ironic, therefore, that he should have been responsible for the initiation of the "gag rule," the most flagrant violation of the constitutional right of free speech in the history of governmental labor-management relations.

It all started in 1901. The postal service at that time was in miserable shape. The average salary of a letter carrier was only $903, and the average salary of a post office clerk was an even more pitiable $818 a year. In addition, clerks were still being refused protection under the eight-hour-day law and promotions were being awarded on an out-and-out political basis.[1]

All this added up to serious trouble. Recruitment was almost impossible and experienced employees were quitting in droves.

[1] There was also a syndicate in the Department and in post offices which was selling promotions.

Those employees who stayed in were being brutally overworked and the deterioration of the service was steady and swift.

There were bills before the Congress to raise postal salaries, to create a system of classification, and to provide for automatic promotions. All these pieces of legislation would have improved service by improving working conditions. Nothing could be done about them, however, because the chairman of the House Post Office Committee, Congressman Eugene F. Loud, of San Francisco, was a labor-baiter of the most primitive kind and he insisted on keeping all curative postal legislation bottled up in his committee.[2]

This was a frustrating situation, and the letter carriers, assisted by the postal clerks, bombarded the Congress and the White House with petitions, prayers, and appeals.

Because of their desperate plight, the employees may have seemed overly aggressive to government and business leaders of the time. In any case, their activities were sufficiently disturbing to the *status quo* to lead to President Roosevelt's issuance, on January 31, 1902, of the first "gag rule," which forbade all federal employees of every description "either directly or indirectly, individually or through associations, to solicit an increase of pay or to influence or attempt to influence in their own interest any other legislation whatever, either before Congress or its Committees, or in any way save through the heads of the Departments in or under which they serve, on penalty of dismissal from the Government service."

It was James C. Keller, president of the National Association of Letter Carriers, who first saw completely the disastrous impli-

---

[2] Congressman Loud once said that men became letter carriers only because their lives had been failures. (His son-in-law was a post office inspector.) Loud, however, was far from typical of the kind of men San Francisco has sent to Congress. One contemporary congressman, Rep. Jack Shelley, is a former high official of the California Federation of Labor and has always been a courageous and intelligent friend of labor. Congressmen Richard Welch and Franck Havenner, also of San Francisco, had excellent labor records in the Congress.

cations of this order. He prepared a memorandum which he presented in person to President Roosevelt, pointing out that the letter carriers had not yielded up their citizenship when they joined Uncle Sam's payroll. If the Post Office Department continued to refuse to present the postal employees' case to the Congress Keller told the President that the NALC would continue to exercise the right, guaranteed by the Constitution of the United States, of direct petition.

Typically, Roosevelt was at first delighted with this show of spunk on the part of Keller and the NALC. He wrote a note on the memorandum calling it "an admirable document" and giving it his unqualified approval. He then forwarded the document, plus his endorsement, to Postmaster General Henry C. Payne.

The Postmaster General's reaction was, roughly, "I heard you the first time." Since there had been no formal rescission of the order he said he would continue to enforce it. Roosevelt forgot about his original enthusiasm. He never did anything to soften the "gag rule."

Of course, the order was essentially unenforceable. There is no way to stop a letter carrier, or anyone else, from talking to his Congressman. But it did give the Deparment's patronage dispensers a dandy weapon. The principal practical danger of the gag rule was that it could be used as a punitive measure at any time at the will and pleasure of the Postmaster General. From a moral point of view, the rule was indefensible.

There was no hope of economic relief for postal employees as long as Representative Loud was chairman of the Post Office Committee. He was adamant and vociferous in stating his opinion that letter carriers were being overpaid as it was. He wanted to reduce even the average $903 pittance they were receiving as an annual wage.

The postal employees secured for themselves a strange ally at this time. They called on William Randolph Hearst in New York City. Mr. Hearst had started his newspaper career by inheriting from his father the *San Francisco Examiner,* and the *Examiner* had a large circulation and considerable influence in that city. Hearst was sympathetic and helpful. He turned over the power of the *Examiner* to William Wynn, Loud's Democratic opponent in the 1902 congressional elections and this support, backed by the vigorous but undercover campaigning of postal employees, defeated the labor-hating congressman.

This was the first time in history that postal employees, and particularly letter carriers, made their political potential pay off at the polls. Unfortunately the subsequent pusillanimous policies of postal union organizations caused this victory to backfire.

The politicos were scandalized and scared at this revolutionary turn of events. The Civil Service Commission, under official prodding, conducted a full-scale investigation but, although the evidence of political activity among postal employees was incontrovertible, it was impossible to pin the blame on any individual or any group of individuals. No dismissals were ordered and only a vague warning was issued.[3]

This did not satisfy the Department one little bit. After all, this was a Republican administration and Loud was not only a prominent Republican but he was also the darling of the Postmaster General. Punitive measures were in order. The knives were unsheathed and whetted.

In 1903 the jurisdiction over city delivery service was transferred in the Department to the Fourth Assistant Postmaster General, Joseph Bristow. Bristow was also in control of the Department's Inspection Service.

Bristow was aided by the hue and cry developing around the news, which had just begun to leak out, of the widespread illegal trafficking in jobs and promotions being carried on in post offices throughout the country. Since he was given a free hand to inves-

[3] The Post Office Department placed Loud's postal inspector son-in-law in charge of the investigation. Attempts were made to penalize letter carriers who admitted they had even *voted* against Congressman Loud.

tigate this scandal, he became the actual dominant force in the Department, wielding even more power than the Postmaster General himself.

Bristow was one of the must rugged antilabor individuals ever to hold government office. He refused to recognize any organization of postal employees. He denied that they had any right to petition. He tried every gambit at his disposal to crush or outlaw all employee organizations. He went so far as to tell the letter carriers that he "did not need, did not want and would not have" their cooperation. [4]

Of course, President Keller was target number one. He had shown more courage than wisdom by actually going out in person to San Francisco to help direct the anti-Loud campaign. He then traveled up and down the West Coast, telling the world what he had done. The Department told the postmaster at Cleveland that Keller, a letter carrier in that city, was to receive no leave whatsoever in the future unless consent was specifically given by the Department in advance.

Keller happened to be in Washington in 1904 when he was summoned to General Bristow's office and ordered to appear for duty in the Cleveland Post Office at 6:30 A.M. the next morning. Keller pointed out to Bristow that there was no train which could possibly get him to Cleveland on time. Bristow smilingly allowed that this was just too bad, and sent an order for his dismissal to the Cleveland postmaster on the spot, even before Keller was given a formal letter of charges.

Unfortunately, the National Association of Letter Carriers did not react to this situation with the courage and solidarity which have characterized its organizational behavior ever since. It may be that Bristow's savagery was too much for them. Also, President Keller's lack of discretion, plus his somewhat flamboyant personality, might have caused a reaction to set in among letter

[4] Cf. Spero, p. 101.

carriers. Whatever the reason, the NALC more or less turned its back on Keller and concentrated its efforts on trying to conciliate the Department. Keller was defeated for the national presidency of the Association at the national convention in Portland, Oregon, in 1905. He was succeeded by J. D. Holland of Boston, Massachusetts, who served one two-year term and then yielded to William E. Kelly of Brooklyn, who served as president from 1907 until 1915.

The Department reacted to this show of weakness on the part of the NALC in the same way that a tiger reacts to fear in a human being. It took all semblance of initiative away from the employee organizations and embarked on a reign of terror which reads like something out of the most lurid *doctrinaire* novels of the period.

The Post Office Department's attitude toward trade-unionism was much like that of the mother in the old nursery rhyme who admonished her daughter to "hang your clothes on a hickory limb, but don't go near the water." As Postmaster General Cortelyou told the National League of Postmasters in 1905, organizations within the Department "must have for their objective improvements in the service, or be of a fraternal or beneficial character. With any other purpose in view they are detrimental to the service, their members, and the public. . . ." [5]

The president of the American Federation of Labor, the revered Samuel Gompers, tried his best to have President Roosevelt rescind the gag order which, by its very implications, was making postal organizations impotent and their members, serfs. He even introduced it as an issue in the Congressional campaigns of 1906, but the public tide was running the other way and all efforts proved unavailing. The public and the Congress could not care less. As a matter of fact Roosevelt responded to pressure by gutting the civil service laws through a personal amendment

[5] Report of the Postmaster General, 1905, p. 12.

which permitted department heads to remove employees without notice and without "reasons in writing" or the usual "proper answer" which had been the necessary prelude to any terminating action on the part of the government toward an employee.

It is not necessary to recount the history of these bitter times in detail. Suffice it to say that the "gag rule" was used as a bludgeon to silence the complaints of every organization leader and every postal employee who felt himself abused in any way whatsoever.

For instance, the railway postal clerks at that time were forced to work under conditions so appalling that they were unable to obtain life or accident insurance except at rates so exorbitant that they could never afford it. They worked in wooden cars which, squeezed as they were between the engine and the steel cars of a train, were often reduced to matchwood in even minor railroad mishaps. In the year 1909 alone there were 742 casualties, including twenty-seven fatalities, among railway mail employees. Mail cars were so old and so dilapidated that rain and cinders poured through the seams. Roofs were mere sieves. Clerks were forced to sort mail by oil lamps which were both lethally dangerous in old wooden rolling stock, and were also inadequate in the illumination they afforded. Toilets in mail cars were not enclosed and had neither flushing nor disinfecting devices. Drinking-water coolers were rarely cleaned and the ice in these coolers was never separated from the water as the regulations required. (Since most of the ice was cut raw from lakes and ponds, the filth that had been frozen into the ice during the winter merely melted into the drinking water.)

However, the complaints of the railway clerks were ignored by the Department and when they reached other ears they led to summary dismissals. When a postal transportation clerk in Houston, Texas, happened in some horror to show a newspaperman a long-dead rat which he had fished out of the drinking cooler of his mail car, he was summarily dismissed from the postal service because he had violated the "gag rule."

In Chicago, Charles D. Duffy, the local leader of the letter carriers, and Oscar F. Nelson, head of the postal clerks' local, smuggled members of the Illinois State Commission on Occupational Diseases into the post office one night. These public officials reported to postal authorities that there was not a single business concern in the entire state which tolerated filthy conditions such as were prevalent in the Chicago Post Office. There was no ventilation, no method of dusting or disinfecting. The same drinking cup was common to hundreds of employees. Toilet conditions were beyond description. The incidence of consumption and typhoid among postal employees was therefore astronomical.

When the story broke, the authorities did not move to correct conditions. Instead, they fired Nelson out-of-hand for having violated the "gag rule." The National Federation of Post Office Clerks turned right around and elected Nelson their national president at their next convention. Duffy was fortunate in that he escaped dismissal. His part in this episode was not known until the heat had died down.

W. S. Shallenberger, Assistant Postmaster General (Transportation), in 1906 even extended the "gag rule" so that all postal employees working on trains were forbidden to discuss publicly the conditions under which they worked, or even to criticize the policies of the railway companies in regard to postal personnel. In other words, it was not only forbidden to criticize the Administration, it was also forbidden to criticize private corporations doing business on a contract basis with the government, even when those corporations were violating the terms of their contracts and endangering the lives of postal personnel.

The Administration piously claimed that it would listen with fatherly attention to any and all justifiable complaints from its employees. They said they always had the employees' welfare at

heart. But when a clerk in Texas wrote to his district superintendent to complain that his buddy had been killed in the wreck
of a railroad car that had many times been reported unsafe, the
Department coldly replied that it had no control over the construction of post-office cars and "all men who did not care to
assume the necessary risks had no place in the Railway Mail
Service." [6]

Spero, in his fine book *Labor Movement in a Government
Industry,* cites cases of postal inspectors and railway authorities
conspiring to "frame" postal mail clerks who made themselves
troublesome by reporting inadequate equipment or dangerous
conditions to the authorities. Clerks who reported unsanitary
conditions were ordered to change their reports, stipulating that
conditions were sanitary after all. Non-compliance meant dismissal.

As far as the Department's kindly avuncular ear extending to
hear employee complaints was concerned, the payoff came in
the following bulletin dated November 5, 1910, and issued by
C. E. Dennison, chief clerk of the Tenth Division of the Railway
Mail Service, located in Aberdeen, South Dakota:

> Instructions have been received from the superintendent to
> inform all clerks in this jurisdiction who are continually making
> exaggerated and unfounded reports regarding the physical con-
> ditions of their cars, that *unless the practice is stopped their re-
> ports will be referred to the Department with recommendations
> not to their liking.*[7]

Because Roosevelt had been considered a liberal, postal employees had hoped for sympathetic treatment at his hands. They
were sorely disappointed. Since William Howard Taft looked like
a kind of beardless Santa Claus, they thought he would infuse

[6] Hearings: House Committee on Post Offices and Post Roads, January 1912,
p. 554.
[7] Need I say that the italics are mine?

the service with warmth and humanity. They were equally disappointed in this hope.

Taft's Postmaster General was Frank H. Hitchcock, of Massachusetts, who had been an obstinately anti-employee First Assistant PMG under George Cortelyou. Once he was in the saddle, Hitchcock exhibited an almost maniacal determination to ride herd on the entire postal employee force. He was determined to "take up the slack" in a postal service that was already starved, overworked, underpaid, and thoroughly browbeaten.

Whenever any employee so much as let out a peep against Hitchcock's slave-driving policies he was thrown out into the streets for violation of the "gag rule." However, postal jobs were becoming so burdensome that they were hardly worth holding any more, so Hitchcock's brutal methods merely caused dissension to spread and increase. Men grow boldest when they have least to lose. Dissension increased to such an extent that, during Hitchcock's regime, the postal service saw its first threat of something approximating a strike. In certain areas employees, particularly in the transportation service, signed resignations en masse and threatened to submit them en masse unless specific conditions were alleviated. It was obvious, in each case, that the men meant business, and mass resignations would disrupt the service almost beyond repair. The Department in each case was forced to make concessions. But these were merely local affairs and oppression on a national level continued unabated.

Needless to say, the postal service, as a result of moronic administrative policies, was fast becoming the favorite target of the cartoonist's pen, the butt of the low comedian's jokes. The once great service, which had been the pride of the American public, a symbol of our democracy, had degenerated into a national laughing stock.

The turnover among the employee force became so great that it was impossible to find people to fill the key jobs requiring skill and judgment. The average of resignations among the clerk and carrier forces rose to more than 20 per cent a year. In Chicago, during the first six months of 1906, there were five hundred and fifty resignations among the clerks alone.

Those who remained on the job were unhappy, uncertain, dispirited, scared, and gagged.

However, "gag rule" or no "gag rule," the plight of the employees became more and more the concern of the publisher, the public, and the politician. The sympathy of the people of the country—largely because the nation's letter carriers were talking to their patrons on every street in every city and town of America —was turning steadily and rapidly in favor of the postal employees and against the postal Administration.

The Administration controlled the nation's press, but the letter carriers had access to the national ear and the national heart. This made the difference. Relief was on the way.

CHAPTER 7

THE LLOYD-
LAFOLLETTE ACT

IT would be pleasant indeed to record at this point that *The Postal Record,* the official organ of the National Association of Letter Carriers had been militantly opposing the despotism of the Department during these troubled years. Unfortunately, this was not the case. The official attitude of the NALC was "wait and see." Every effort was made to propitiate the powers that be. The pages of the *Record* are almost entirely innocent of controversy and, except for a few instances, there is nothing in their columns during these years to indicate that everything in the relationship between the Administration and the letter carriers wasn't for the best in the best of all possible worlds.

The real honors for militant journalism in the fight against the "gag rule" must go to a truly remarkable little periodical called *The Harpoon.*

Editor and driving force of *The Harpoon* was a railway postal clerk named Urban A. Walter, who had contracted tuberculosis in the service and had retired to Phoenix, Arizona, to regain his health.

Since Walter was already out of the service he could afford to sail into the Administration with both fists flying and without fear of reprisal. This he did, using methods that were sometimes flamboyant but almost always effective. His prose carries a bite even after half a century.

The Harpoon caught on immediately. By its third month of publication it received more than a thousand favorable newspaper notices.[1] Its circulation jumped to a not inconsiderable 12,000, and before the anti-gag rule fight was over Walter had even doubled that figure.

Although *The Harpoon* was primarily a paper for railway clerks, it aimed at the abuses being inflicted on all postal employees and especially at the violation of their civil rights embodied in the "gag rule." *The Harpoon* became the rallying point for all post office workers, a source of strength and inspiration.

The Postmaster General reacted to the growing influence of *The Harpoon* in typical fashion. That is, he behaved stupidly. When the magazine started running horrifying and revealing pictures of wrecked and splintered railway cars, the Administration let it be known all the way down the line that the paper was very much in its disfavor and that it would not be healthy for any clerk to be observed reading it.

In 1911, when Walter sent out an appeal bulletin asking every man in the postal service to join *The Harpoon's* campaign against the "gag rule," his mailing was held up in the Denver post office and he was arrested by postal inspectors for alleged violation of the postal laws. He was finally released on $1,000 bail and the subsequent publicity, naturally, earned his campaign a far greater degree of sympathetic attention than it would otherwise have

[1] Cf. Spero, p. 125.

received. The March 1911 issue of *The Harpoon* sold more than 200,000 copies.

Meanwhile, needled by continuing failure in its attempts to suppress trade unionism in the Postal Establishment, the Administration became hysterical. Supervisors were told to inform all new employees that membership in labor organizations would mean trouble for them throughout their careers. They were also told to communicate this warning orally, not put it in writing.[2] Men were fired right and left simply because they refused to give up their union membership. Inspectors were accused of spending more time checking up on the unions than they spent in preventing or detecting mail depredations.

Part of the hysteria was caused by the stupidly naive reports of the Inspection Service, particularly in regard to the American Federation of Labor, to which postal groups were more and more turning their eyes. The fact that the inspectors didn't know what they were talking about did not in the least deter them from making positive and derogatory statements.

The chief inspector, for instance, presented Postmaster General Hitchcock with a confidential memorandum on the activities of the AFL which reads like an undercover analysis of the Mafia.[3] "It appears that this organization before granting admission . . . requires a secret oath," the memorandum read. "The central organization does not seem to be incorporated; it is responsible to no laws and to no government; in spite of the tremendous industrial, economical and social influence which it asserts it manages its affairs without public accountability; its oligarchies raise and spend vast sums of money in ways of which the public has no knowledge; its operations are veiled in mystery and reach out to every corner of the country."

[2] House Hearings: Lloyd Bill, p. 10. See testimony of AFL president, Samuel Gompers.
[3] Senate Doc. 866 (Sixty-second Congress, Second Session), p. 241.

Postmaster General Hitchcock made himself ridiculous by swallowing this obvious asininity hook, line, and sinker. In fear and trembling for the future of the country and the postal service, he considered it his holy duty to crusade even more energetically against any and all "secret organizations" within the postal service.

Meanwhile the Congress was beginning to wake up to the deteriorating conditions within the postal service. The mounting unpopularity of President Taft had removed from the Department its immunity from Congressional scrutiny and disapproval. Senator "Fighting Bob" LaFollette of Wisconsin sent out thousands of questionnaires to postal employees seeking information on the "gag rule," the Department's suppression of unions, and other abuses. He received a tremendous number of replies and picked up vast quantities of priceless information from the field.

It can be imagined what effect this questionnaire had on the Department! Senator LaFollette complained that his mail "was subjected to an espionage almost Russian in character." He charged that postal inspectors were opening and reading his mail in direct violation of the law.[4] Naturally, efforts in the field were made to discourage employees from answering the questionnaire.

However, once the ball started rolling in the Congress there was no stopping it. President Taft, on May 14, 1911, tried to stem the rising tide of anti-gag feeling by stating, in a speech at Harrisburg, Pennsylvania, that "government employees are a privileged class . . . upon whose entry into government service it is entirely reasonable to impose conditions that should not be and ought not be imposed upon those who serve private employers." He did not say in what way the government employees

---

[4] Congressional Record (Sixty-second Congress, Second Session), p. 10729. Times have changed. If the Inspection Service ever tried to do this to a senator today, heads would be rolling all over the place.

were privileged under his Administration. "Trapped" would perhaps have been a better and more honest word.

But despite everything the Administration could do, the pressure in the Congress for anti-gag legislation became overwhelming. In some desperation the President began to make concessions insofar as the "gag rule" was concerned, but they were too late and too little. On April 18, 1912, the House wiped out the infamous rule by passing the Lloyd Bill as an amendment to the Post Office Appropriation Bill for fiscal 1913. It passed with only one dissenting vote, that of the leader of the Republican minority.

Victory was not quite so easy in the Senate, where Bob LaFollette was leading the fight for justice. There was a need for assurances in the bill that affiliation with the AFL would not lead to a series of strikes within the government service. When these assurances were forthcoming in an amendment written by Senator Reed, the legislation passed handily and was signed into law on August 24, 1912.

The Lloyd-LaFollette Act is the most significant piece of legislation ever to be passed insofar as federal workers are concerned. It was the Emancipation Proclamation and the Magna Carta rolled into one.

Most of all, it gave the employees freedom of expression. During the ten years of the gag rule's existence employee leaders were kept under the Department's thumb. They had to move cautiously at all times, and they felt they had to be especially careful not to annoy the Administration.[5]

During this period of comparative liberalism employee groups discarded their previous subservience and moved in to achieve sig-

---

[5] President William E. Kelly, of the National Association of Letter Carriers, for instance, refused to testify in favor of anti-gag legislation until he was issued a subpoena by the Senate Committee. Unsolicited testimony could easily have led to his dismissal from the service.

nificant gains in the Congress. One of the most significant of these was a workable eight-hour law.

Letter carriers and clerks for years had a justifiable complaint in that, while their actual tours might be eight hours, those tours could be spun out over a much longer period during which they had constantly to be on call. There were many cases in which a carrier's day lasted fourteen hours, although he actually worked only eight of those hours, and it was not uncommon to find instances where the work day lasted as long as sixteen or eighteen hours.

The Reilly Act,[6] which passed August 4, 1912, gave the necessary relief in that it stipulated that carriers and clerks in first- and second-class offices "shall be required to work not more than eight hours a day, provided that the eight hours of service shall not extend over a longer period than ten consecutive hours." The law also provided for *pro rata* overtime pay, compensatory time, and the closing of post offices on Sundays.

Naturally the Department fought the bill, as it had always fought any progressive legislation to assist postal employees. But, by this time, the Department had had it. The Congress was Democratic and the Administration, Republican, so there was no love lost between the executive and legislative branches. The hearings on the Lloyd-LaFollette Bill had brought a number of nasty facts into the light of the noonday sun and the Congress was in no mood to listen to the Postmaster General's whining [7] to the effect that liberal legislation would wreck the service and destroy the national economy.

Postal employee leaders, unfettered for the first time in ten years, testified in favor of the law and against the stand of the

[6] Rep. John L. Reilly of Connecticut, father of the bill, was another congressman who has earned the undying gratitude of postal employees.

[7] Considering Postmaster General Hitchcock's frustration at this point, I think it is allowable to say that "this whine came from sour grapes."

Department without fear of punitive action or reprisal. For the first time in a decade, in other words, they were permitted to act like American citizens.

It looked like the beginning of a bright new day for postal employees.

CHAPTER 8

BURLESON

I WAS born a Democrat. I proudly live as a Democrat. I shall
die a Democrat. Therefore, the story that will be told on the
following pages is painful to me. Nonetheless it is a story that
must be told.

During the years 1902–1912, postal employees, and particularly letter carriers, suffered under Republican oppression like
the children of Israel under the Pharaohs. There was always the
hope that the Democratic party, the traditional friend of the
working man, would throw the minions of entrenched capitalism
out of their lofty places in government and that the laboring
man would then come into his own.

In the 1912 elections the miracle happened at last. The Bull
Moose party wrecked the regular Republican organization, and
Woodrow Wilson was swept into the presidency.

Letter carriers generally rejoiced. The years of bondage were over. No longer would the children of Israel be called upon to make bricks without straw. Hallelujah!

It did not turn out that way. Not quite.

For reasons known only to himself President Wilson chose for his Postmaster General a preposterous Texan by the name of Albert S. Burleson whose attitude toward postal employees made even Postmasters General Hitchcock and Cortelyou look like flaming liberals.

Mr. Burleson served as Postmaster General for eight years. They are the darkest eight years of postal history as far as the employees are concerned. He brought to office a nicely balanced combination of stupidity and sadism which has made his name infamous among postal employees for all time.

Burleson took office on March 4, 1913, the very day on which the Lloyd-LaFollette Act and similar remedial legislation became effective. Almost as soon as he lowered his right arm after taking the oath of office he called for reinstatement of the "gag rule" and announced that it was his intention to make the postal service yield a surplus no matter what the cost in human endeavor and human suffering.

To the dismay of the postal employees, he declared open warfare on their organizations and refused to deal with his workers except as individuals.

In his eagerness to create a surplus he fought every and all increases in wages even when soaring living costs were drastically devaluating the purchasing power of the dollar.

When he felt he could get away with it, he ignored all the protective legislation that had been passed in favor of postal employees, or he perverted the laws to his own brutal ends.

His annual report for fiscal 1914 is a remarkable document both for audacity and for flint-heartedness. He announced a "surplus" of $3,600,000. He also requested that the Reilly eight-in-ten hour law be repealed and that the Department be permitted to return to a forty-eight-hour week, with carriers being "allowed" to work twelve hours a day. He requested that grade promotions be made once every two years instead of once a year. He requested that substitute carriers and clerks be reduced in salary by as much as ten cents an hour. He even urged that the rural service should be turned over to private industry.

Even with an overwhelming Democratic majority in the Congress he had no chance whatsoever of passing legislation of this sort, particularly since the newly emancipated carriers and postal clerks, once they recovered from their initial shock, went roaring up to Capitol Hill to oppose Burleson's antediluvian policies. The effective work of the postal organizations in this skirmish embittered Burleson permanently against trade unionism in government. His original cold hostility was transformed into white-hot fury.

Failing to get what he wanted from the Congress, he began to exercise his executive prerogatives with wild abandon, to an extent far beyond his rights.

First of all, he sent out a notice, dated February 4, 1915, to all postmasters, saying: "Work of carriers *collecting* mail is less exacting than that performed by carriers in *effecting deliveries* of mail. It is therefore desired that, in the future, the maximum salary of letter carriers assigned to the *collection* of the mail be fixed at $1,000 per annum." The maximum salary for letter carriers generally, at this time, was $1,200.

Burleson had no right to do this. There was no distinction in the law between carriers and collectors, and the National Association of Letter Carriers had consistently, from the very beginning, refused to recognize such a distinction; and the Congress, just as consistently, had agreed.

Forms were issued to postmasters for carriers in the collection service to sign, which were, to all intents and purposes, a waiver of their rights. The carriers in the collection service were given the choice of "voluntarily" accepting a two hundred dollar a year reduction in salary or of being dismissed from the service for insubordination.

The NALC petitioned the Congress directly on this issue and the Congress not only reinstated the collection-carriers to their original salary levels but forbade Burleson to make any more such arbitrary artificial distinctions.

Burleson, who had served with minimal distinction in the Congress himself, still refused to take the dictates of the legislative branch very seriously. He instituted "efficiency rating systems" which were a transparent ruse by which he could hold postal salaries at an abnormally low level. Wholesale salary reductions resulted.[1]

An all-out attack was made upon what Burleson called "superannuated" employees (i.e., those who were getting the top salaries by virtue of seniority).

For an exercise in human charity I recommend reading the speech of First Assistant Postmaster General Daniel C. Roper of South Carolina to the annual convention of the National Association of Postmasters in 1914. He was furious at postmasters for being human beings. "Some postmasters refrain, from humanitarian reasons, from recommending demotions and removals in accordance with declining efficiency of employees," he said. "The only proper course for the Department and for the postmasters is to put on notice all employees that they will be continued in office only so long as they are capable to earning the salaries paid them and that salaries will be scaled down and readjusted from time to time to meet the declining efficiency and earning power of clerks and carriers."

---

[1] Cf. *Congressional Record* (Sixty-fifth Congress, Second Session), p. 5905. Between 1915–17, seven hundred and twenty-nine letter carriers were reduced from regular to substitute. In the six previous years only fifty-nine had been thus reduced.

This was aimed at those members of the employee force who had devoted the greater part of their extremely useful lives to the movement of the United States mails. The salaries which had to be scaled down were, at a maximum, $1,200 a year, which was a scandalously low figure in the expanding economy of 1914. Substitutes, who worked just about as hard and as long as regulars, were lucky to average thirty-five dollars a month.[2]

Supervisors were forced to exact the most stringent economies if they expected to keep their jobs, let alone achieve promotions. This led not only to almost universal violation of the work-hour laws, but also to widespread falsification of the records by supervisors with the complete but tacit approval of the Department.

Naturally enough, Burleson's contempt of the laws protecting employees led to defensive action by the newly emancipated postal organizations. And, as can be expected in a person of General Burleson's mentality and caliber, each attempt on the part of the postal organizations to by-pass the Department and petition the Congress directly was interpreted as an act of subversion.

The Railway Postal Clerks, long the center of the anti-union storm where postal management was concerned, continued to receive the brunt of the Administration's attacks. Burleson's general superintendent of railway mails, A. H. Stephens, declared as his policy, almost immediately upon taking office, that: "We have no use for labor unionism within the government service and certainly labor unionism will not be permitted in the railway mail service." [3]

---

[2] Substitute carriers were required to appear for work every day along with the regulars and remain in the post office awaiting a possible call for work. They were being paid at a rate of between thirty-five and forty cents an hour. Burleson wanted to reduce this rate to thirty cents. Up until 1907, incidentally, substitute carriers were paid by the regular carriers for whom they had substituted. They had to grab their men as they left the pay window.

[3] *Harpoon*, April 27, 1915, No. 66.

When Senator Borah, of Idaho, introduced legislation to prevent the Department from instituting inhuman speed-up methods and unrealistic efficiency tests, railway postal clerks signed petitions asking the other members of the U.S. Senate to support his bill. Stephens counterattacked with a speech to the railway postal clerks at Indianapolis in which he said that whenever a clerk signed that petition he would be "up before the general superintendent of this service for removal," and he added, "I have the power, the authority and the inclination and the decision to remove him from the service." Superintendent Stephens may have been weak in syntax but he made it quite clear that he just did not believe in the Lloyd-LaFollette law.

Next, Burleson took after the rural letter carriers' organization. He had a passionate desire to eliminate the rural service and sell the franchise to private industry, because, as he said, the rural service was costing money.[4] He therefore did everything within, and even far beyond, his power to destroy the rural letter carriers' organization and to undermine its influence with the Congress.

Burleson was surrounded, as could be expected, by men who shared his archaic views. Fourth Assistant Postmaster General (Facilities) James I. Blakelee, of Pennsylvania, in the *Report of the Postmaster General for Fiscal 1916,* pulled out all the stops. He referred to postal organizations as "pernicious postal parasites" and charged that their existence depends upon their ability to arouse discord and dissension between administrative officials and their employees. (Since postal organizations were at this

---

[4] Burleson's cost accounting may have been inaccurate in this case. While the rural service is responsible for the *delivery* of eight times the number of letters it *collects for delivery,* still it must be remembered that the mail generating in urban communities and delivered on rural routes would never be generated if rural routes didn't exist. By using this yardstick some accountants have held that the rural mail service actually makes money and always has. Cf. *Financial Policy for the Post Office Department,* p. 161.

time fighting for their very survival, this charge could hardly have been meant to be taken seriously.)

He also added:

> They report to the associations that maintain them in luxury in this city, from whence they circulate reports concerning their numerous activities, and the many benefits they demand and receive, whereas in fact they do not perform one substantial service, except to limit the earning capacity of that type of postal employee who is entitled to far greater consideration for expert service rendered, while at the same time promoting the interest of that employee who is negligent, inefficient and whose duty could be performed by a school boy.
>
> They attempt to interfere in the administration of discipline and in the promotion and demotion of employees solely because of their affiliation with different organizations in the service and without regard to the merits involved.
>
> The public must be freed from these insidious influences for the reason that they are demoralizing the spirit of honesty and loyalty that constitutes sincerity in the service of the people.

Meanwhile, the First Assistant Postmaster General (Operations), Roper, sent to various postal conventions a paper, which he did not care (or dare) to read before those gatherings in person, attacking the Lloyd-LaFollette law. His paper, which, when read to the convention of the NALC, was entitled, "The Recognition of the Human Element in the Postal Service" [5] stated: "Organizations of postal employees have no official status which may be recognized by the Department. They are not *per se* a part of the postal service nor are they essential to its conduct or

---

[5] It is sad that men with the most wicked intentions usually clothe them with pious titles which indicate the absolute opposite of their intentions. Communist-front groups often name themselves after Thomas Jefferson or Abraham Lincoln. Fascist groups or pro-Fascist groups prior to World War II assumed superpatriotic titles. The process still goes on, as evidenced by the numerous "Right to Work" bills which intend exactly the opposite of what the name implies.

its welfare." (This was even more blunt and more uncompromising than anti-union sentiments expressed in previous administrations.) Roper added that direct petition to the Congress, if allowed to continue unchecked and unguarded, would "imperil either the position of the employees or the integrity of the service." He did not say how.

Burleson began to flex his muscles. He showed he meant business by firing out-of-hand President E. J. Ryan, of the Railway Mail Association, and Fred L. White, president of the National Association of Rural Letter Carriers, on the very same day. Both were dismissed for daring to criticize Burleson's policies.

World War I gave Burleson an excellent opportunity to vent his distaste for labor unions. He constantly compared letter carriers' salaries with those of soldiers at the front and asked that postal salaries be cut. He issued, on April 6, 1917, an order forbidding any further absences from work except to employees actually on the current payroll.[6] (Employees in the armed services, of course, were excepted.) Although the Postmaster General explained the order as a patriotic war measure, its real intent was to wound the employee organizations. The Department had traditionally granted leave without pay to the top officers of the employee organizations so they could take care of the affairs of their unions. This practice was now stopped.

The first national officer to suffer from the order was President Edward J. Gainor of the National Association of Letter Carriers. Upon issuance of the Postmaster General's order Gainor returned to his home in Muncie, Indiana, and resumed his work of carrying the mail. Despite the obvious impossibility of conducting the affairs of the NALC while actually working a full day in the post office, Gainor was unable to get any leave without pay. When Burleson even denied him leave to attend the national

[6] P.O.D. Order 210.

convention of the American Federation of Labor, Gainor had to make a choice. He resigned his job as a letter carrier.[7]

Burleson also fired the top leadership of the National Federation of Postal Clerks on trumped-up or trivial charges. In most cases the postal unions continued their leaders in office and gave them permanent salaries despite their dismissals from the service. Burleson pointed to this as evidence of union subversion and made it a practice to disparage the petitions and objections of employee groups by saying they came from "disgruntled former employees." [8] The Department made it a rule to listen to employee groups only if they were composed entirely of men actually on the payroll at the time of discussion.

Not surprisingly, the service fell to a new low during Burleson's regime. Despite the difficulty of applying their special skills to "civilian" work, postal employees left the service in ever-increasing numbers in order to enter the war industries and replacements became more and more difficult to find. Bi-weekly civil service examinations were held in many localities in a desperate attempt to recruit help. In many other localities civil service requirements were quietly thrown out the window. Instead of seeking intelligent workers capable of learning specialized skills, the Department was reduced to hiring anyone it could find.[9]

The Post Office also was forced to keep a standing order with the U.S. Employment Service in some communities for any kind of available labor. Whenever the Employment Service was forced to send someone to the Post Office in these localities, however, it was understood that the postal job was only a stopgap until

[7] E. J. Gainor, who is revered by letter carriers as the father of the shorter work week, served as president of the NALC from 1915 to 1941. He was my immediate predecessor in that position and a man for whom I always had a great affection.

[8] Burleson at this point would have been hard put to find an employee in or out of the service who was "gruntled."

[9] Cf. Hearings, House Committee on Post Office Expenditures, August 26, 1919, pp. 4, 5, 6.

the person could find a decent position somewhere else. As far as employment was concerned, the Post Office was the absolute bottom of the barrel.

Meanwhile, Burleson was becoming the subject of sharp attacks in the Republican press, particularly in the *Chicago Tribune,* which gave him a savage going over. The populace was growing angry over the impaired service. The Congress, realizing that Burleson was a political liability and would be an issue in the 1920 presidential campaign, made an intensive investigation of management-labor relations, which disclosed enough horror stories to shock the most case-hardened politician. Over the vociferous objections of the Postmaster General and his staff, the Congress finally passed the Classification Act of 1920, which raised letter carriers' and clerks' salaries to $1,440 a year on entrance and to a maximum of $1,800 a year. Although this salary level was far below what it should have been in relation to rising costs, it gave some relief to those who needed it badly.

When Warren G. Harding was elected President in 1920, Burleson left office, an embittered and discredited old man.

A self-made man who boasted unabashedly of his millions, Burleson was chronically unable to understand the needs and aspirations of his employees. He became a notorious victim of the monomania of economy above all else and subjugated everything, including every human instinct, to the chimerical ideal of creating a financial "profit" in the Post Office Department.

Even in this he was less than a success. His administration showed a "profit" in three of the five *peacetime* years in which he served and a "deficit" in two. Fiscal years 1917, 1918, and 1919 are classified as *"war"* years and during such years the Post Office always shows a "profit" since most of the transportation costs of the Department are borne by the military. This means it is not a real "profit" but a mere bookkeeping transaction. In his final fiscal year Burleson left behind him a "deficit" of

$17,750,000, which, up to that time, was the second highest in the entire history of the Department.

Burleson differed from his predecessors mainly because of the sociological climate in which he operated. In the years 1902–1912 the tide was running strongly with the capitalists. Organized labor was comparatively weak and was widely feared by the ignorant. (Of course, management played expertly and heartlessly at times upon this fear, creating a false and frightening image of labor unions generally.)

Although Hitchcock, Cortelyou, and other postmasters general of that period were reprehensible in their treatment of their employees, they were in their way reflecting the general attitudes and the behavior of management in private industry. But during the years 1912–20 the world moved. World War I altered labor's position considerably, and for the better. Organized labor became the necessary partner of management both in the preservation of the economy of the nation and of the nation's security. Burleson, therefore, was swimming against the tide and broke himself by attempting to impose upon the labor force of the Postal Establishment labor-management concepts that were hopelessly outmoded.

Burleson refused to accept the movement of the world and when the world moved anyway, without his permission, he became infuriated and spiteful. This was his tragedy and the major cause of his failure. He simply refused to accept the twentieth century as a fact, and he was convinced that if he continued to ignore it the century would one day disappear like a bad dream. Instead, it was Burleson who disappeared.

His successor was Will H. Hays, of Indiana, who later became the czar of the motion-picture industry. Hays operated on the theory that whatever Burleson had done was wrong, and he conscientiously attempted to overturn all that had occurred during the past eight years. As a result, he became a topflight Postmaster General and his was the first truly modern administration in the history of the Postal Establishment. There have been few modern administrations since.[10]

[10] Postmaster General Hays had honest reservations regarding the wisdom of and the need for affiliation with the AFL. He didn't accept the fact that his successors might be less fair and less honorable than himself. Nonetheless, he was a good friend of the letter carriers. When the NALC offered him a lifetime honorary membership he insisted that the word "honorary" be stricken out. He asked that he be allowed to pay annual dues like every other carrier. He continued to pay his dues faithfully during all his years as czar of the movie industry and up until the time of his death in March, 1954.

CHAPTER 9

AFFILIATION
WITH THE AFL

BURLESON has been called the father of the postal unions. His toughness and vindictiveness caused the unions to stiffen in their resistance to autocratic power and eventually drove them headlong into the American Federation of Labor.

The AFL had shown an interest in organizing postal workers ever since 1897, when the struggle for the eight-hour day was in full force.

There was very little pro-affiliation sentiment among the carriers and clerks in those early days, however, except in the largest post offices. The Chicago Post Office Clerks joined the AFL in 1900, but at the biennial convention of the clerks in 1902 they were denied seats. It was generally felt that affiliation with the AFL would interfere with the civil service oath. However, the relationship between postal unions and the AFL was friendly and warm. In 1906 the National Federation of Postal Clerks, consisting of seven locals (Chicago, San Francisco, Milwaukee, Louisville, Salt Lake City, Nashville, and Muskogee) joined the AFL as a national union with one thousand members.

The Department's reaction was predictable and violent, and constant attempts were made to punish those who favored affiliation. Postmasters General Hitchcock and Cortelyou were egged on in their efforts to suppress unionism by the wild reports of the Inspection Service which pictured the AFL as some kind of dangerous anti-American secret society similar to the Ku Klux Klan.

The National Association of Letter Carriers was cautious in its approach to affiliation with the AFL. As early as 1900 President Samuel Gompers of the AFL made overtures to the NALC and even addressed the national convention of the carriers in that year. In 1902 President Keller of the NALC and Gompers held some exhaustive discussions on the pros and cons of affiliation.

The NALC leadership, however, felt it was in the final stages of organizing the association into an effective postal body and therefore affiliation should be postponed. Committees were formed to investigate the matter but as the Administration's attitude toward affiliation toughened it was decided that it would be "highly inexpedient, if not to the last degree dangerous" if the NALC were to become involved in any "entangling alliances with any other organization." [1]

Although there was a very real concern among the leaders of the NALC that their organization would lose its identity and its autonomy if it were to join the AFL, it must be admitted that fear of the big stick the Postmaster General was carrying also had a decisive effect upon their deliberations. It is true that, in view of the sociological climate of the times, affiliation could have done more harm than good. Retribution from management would undoubtedly have been swift, savage, and wholesale.

[1] Postal Record, October 1905, p. 227.

Despite the efforts of the more zealous affiliationists, the issue was dead in the NALC until 1910, when the accumulated injustices perpetrated by postal management brought it very much to life again.

The affiliated National Federation of Postal Clerks started the ball rolling by requesting permission from the AFL to do some wholesale pirating of members from the NALC. The NALC, naturally, resisted this effort and, after consultation with the AFL leadership, it was agreed that letter carriers would not be admitted to the AFL unless the carriers' association were to join as a body.

In 1913 the NALC national convention was held in San Francisco, and a referendum was ordered on the question of affiliation. Burleson was comparatively new in office at that time, and the full extent of his vicious anti-labor program was not yet recognized. The referendum which took place early in 1914 was a fiasco as far as the affiliationists were concerned. The vote was 18,769 to 3,968 against affiliation.

However, Postmaster General Burleson almost immediately extended and fortified his tyranny and thus gave tremendous ammunition to the advocates of affiliation. In 1917 the Postal Clerks and the Brotherhood of Railway Clerks merged under the title of the National Federation of Postal Employees and started to move toward formation of a single, powerful postal union under the aegis of the AFL. When small groups of letter carriers started deserting the NALC and clamoring for admittance to this superunion, the leadership of the NALC complained to the AFL. This time the AFL washed its hands of the controversy. They refused to protect the NALC from proselyting unless the letter carriers agreed at last to affiliate.

This was the situation when the NALC held its national convention in Dallas, Texas, in 1917. Discontent among employees of the postal service was at a rolling boil, and the NALC was threatened with eventual disintegration if it did not affiliate.[2]

President E. J. Gainor was conservative by nature, but above all he was intellectually honest. He fundamentally distrusted entangling alliances with nonpostal organizations, and he honestly feared for the future identity of the NALC in the event of affiliation with the AFL. When the issue was brought up unexpectedly on the floor of the convention, Gainor suggested another national referendum. This created a furore among the delegates. Gainor momentarily lost control of the convention, as member after member testified that his constituents were almost unanimously in favor of immediate affiliation. There was no doubt whatsoever that the sentiment of the convention was overpoweringly in favor of affiliation and against any unnecessary delay in achieving this end. The rules were suspended, and by a voice vote the national secretary was instructed to take steps immediately to effect affiliation as soon as possible. This was done and, at the same time, an agreement was worked out with the National Federation of Postal Employees by which they surrendered jurisdiction over letter carriers, and those letter carriers who had defected to the NFPE were welcomed back without prejudice.

A subsequent referendum to test the action of the convention showed a vote of 23,551 in favor of affiliation and only 1,971 against.

In other words, the tactics of "Bully" Burleson had completely reversed the sentiment of the NALC in less than four years. In 1914 affiliation was defeated by 14,801 votes. In 1918 it passed by 21,580 votes.

In 1914, 83 per cent of the letter carriers of the country voted against affiliation with the AFL. In 1918, 92 per cent voted in favor of affiliation. It seems hard to believe that practically the same group of people was voting in both referendums.

[2] Cf. Postal Record, October 1917, pp. 270-275, 327-328.

What happened, of course, was that the letter carriers came to realize from bitter experience that if Postmaster General Burleson was against affiliation, then affiliation must be precisely what the letter carriers needed most.

Actually, the move was long overdue.

Since the NALC joined the AFL it has never looked back. It has grown steadily in strength, in prestige, and in effectiveness. Ever since the decision to affiliate was made the National Association has never had cause for anything but satisfaction and gratification.

I have written earlier about the unique position which postal employees, because of their very specialized skills, hold in the government service. While it is true that any strike or movement of mass resignation among postal employees would result in a chaotic disruption of the postal service, it is also true that postal employees leaving the service would be at a loss to employ their skills remuneratively in any other line of business. During the years 1902–1917 the Department exploited this latter advantage mercilessly. Postal employees were told that if they didn't like their jobs they could quit any time they wanted. Because employee organizations were relatively weak, the balance was all in favor of postal management.

Affiliation with the AFL changed all that. Since the only arena in which postal employees could make progress was and is the political arena, affiliation gave them a broader political base upon which to operate. It increased the power of their voice many times over. They no longer represented, when they called upon the Congress, a mere handful of postal employees; they represented the millions upon millions of their laboring brethren throughout the nation. This served to correct the balance.

The predictions of the Cassandras have been proved false. These prophets of gloom and doom predicted the ruin of the mail service as soon as affiliation was effected. No such ruin occurred. There never has been a threat of a strike since the letter carriers joined the AFL. There never has been a question of divided loyalties. But, on the other hand, there never has been any danger of a return by postal management to the applied and continuing bullying of postal employees which characterized those dark and bitter years prior to affiliation. As a matter of fact, the only threats to the integrity of the postal service since that time have come from postal *management,* which tends to subjugate considerations of service to considerations of false economy.

On the day the National Association of Letter Carriers joined the American Federation of Labor it joined the Big Leagues, and it has remained firmly established in the Big Leagues ever since.

It should be added that President Gainor of the NALC, despite his early misgivings, became an able member of the Executive Council and served as a national vice-president of the AFL. In 1924 he was chosen to go to England as an official AFL delegate to the British Trades Union Congress. This is the kind of recognition that has been bestowed many times since that time on the president of the National Association of Letter Carriers. For instance, I myself have the honor of serving as a national vice-president of the AFL–CIO and have been sent overseas at least a dozen times as a fraternal representative at foreign labor gatherings. I take pride in the fact that I was sent to London as a "founding father" of the International Congress of Free Trade Unions and that I am the only American ever to have been sent twice to represent the parent union as a fraternal delegate to the British Trade Union Congress. And, I want to make it clear that the pride I take in this distinction is not personal; it is because of the recognition of the National Association of Letter Carriers implicit in such an important assignment.

CHAPTER 10

MY OWN ROAD
TO THE POST OFFICE

ALTHOUGH I come honestly and through inheritance by my
labor union affiliations, the road that led to my association
with the postal service was a long and devious one.

I was born on February 23, 1902, in Cincinnati, Ohio, into
a family devoted to both the labor union movement and the
Roman Catholic Church. My parents were both born in this
country, but all four of my grandparents were born in Ireland.
(To those who might have suspected that I have just a *touch* of
the Gael in me, I would like to add that there is not a drop of
non-Celtic blood in my rather ample body.)

My father, Lawrence Michael Doherty, was a railroad man
and an ardent unionist until his death in 1952. My mother,
Katherine Ryan, is still very much alive and a constant joy to
all who know her.

There were six children in our family, and although things
were never easy at home insofar as money was concerned, my

father and mother managed to make ends meet through a combination of courage, self-sacrifice, and intelligent planning.

However, when I was still a student at Blessed Sacrament parochial school in Cincinnati, a series of tragedies hit the Doherty family and played havoc with the family budget. This made it necessary for me to quit school, get a job, and help win bread for the family.

Through the artful and completely excusable connivance of my mother, who in her anxiety may perhaps have exaggerated my age just a little, I began to work for the Postal Telegraph Company as a messenger.

From the very first I became fascinated with the telegrapher's key and resonator and determined that this was where my future lay. I spent my spare time studying and attending the Cincinnati School of Telegraphy. I was graduated at the ripe old age of sixteen (Mother's understandable and necessary little white lie about my age was still having far-reaching effects) and was almost immediately appointed manager of the Postal Telegraph office at Springrove and Harrison Avenue in Cincinnati, where I had begun as a messenger.

There were two permanent benefits I derived from this experience for which I shall always be grateful. One is the skill of the telegrapher, which I still retain. The other, which is immeasurably more important, was of a romantic nature.

As a result of my skill as a telegrapher I made the first blind date of my life—or, for that matter, the first date of any kind.

It is the custom of telegraphers during slack hours to chat back and forth in Morse Code. One of my first correspondents was a telegrapher at the main office who signed "his" messages "GD." This gave rise to some ribald comment on my part as to the significance of the initials. I received an immediate and sharp rebuff and was informed that this "he" was a "she" and that "GD" stood for Gertrude Dacey, and no nonsense about it.

I was fascinated. As dearly as I love the Spangenbergers,

Rauckhorsts, Wehkings, and Gropengeisers of this world, I am still partial to the Irish, and Dacey is one of the fine old Irish names dating back to Norman times. As soon as I finished my profuse apologies I summoned enough courage to ask for a blind date. Eventually I succeeded and it was a case of instantaneous puppy love on both our parts.

That first date led to marriage some years later, to nine wonderful children and to (thus far) thirty unbeatable grandchildren.[1]

Our romance was interrupted at this point, however, by unforeseen circumstances. In 1919 the Commercial Telegraphers Union of America went out on strike.

The strike was doomed to failure from the start because the Western Union operators refused to walk out, but nonetheless, as a loyal union man of seventeen, I had no moral choice except to join the picket lines with my union brothers.

This meant my returning to the status of a burden to my parents rather than being an additional wage-earner. My father was very proud that I had stuck to the union principles and he vowed he would take care of me as long as it was necessary, but good feeling does not, of itself, put meat and potatoes on the table. So in June 1919 I enlisted in the U.S. Army. (Once again, I was technically underage, but Mother's innocent fabrication was still paying dividends for me.)

[1] This figure has been revised upward twice during the writing of this book. I know it's considered bad form to boast about one's family, but this is my book so I'm going to do it anyway. Bill Junior is a graduate of Catholic University and is Inter-American representative of the PTTI; John Timothy is now director of the International Labor Center at St. John's College, Annapolis; James Francis, a graduate of Georgetown, is a prominent labor lawyer in Philadelphia; Thomas Aloysius, recently out of the Air Force, is a jet mechanic; and, as this is being written, Joseph Patrick is an Air Force lieutenant on Okinawa. Our four fine daughters, Mary Seton, Catherine Ellen, Gertrude Patricia, and Margaret Frances, have all been an equal source of pride and inspiration to me. And, of course, if I were to begin to write down what I owe to the former telegrapher who signed her initials "GD" I would have to write an entirely new book.

Eventually, I was directed to join Company D, 53rd Telegraph Battalion, Signal Corps,[2] at the Presidio in San Francisco and to proceed with them to Siberia, where the weirdest chapter in our entire military history was being written.

Soon after arriving at Vladivostok I was to learn that World War I was not yet over. Several components of the 31st Infantry were virtually annihilated through a surprise attack in the still of the night by a horde of Russian Cossacks.

These Cossacks were the original Russian gangsters. They were professional cavalry fighters who at the war's end and the collapse of the old regime had, like Othello, found their occupation gone. So, rather than become unemployed nomads, they sold out to the Bolsheviks and fought not for principle but for plunder and for the sheer sadistic love of slaughter.

As an army telegrapher I worked on the Chinese Eastern Trans-Siberian railroad, which originated its run in Harbin in Manchuria, an experience that gave me more anxious moments than did the guns of the Bolsheviks. (The old expression, "That's a hell of a way to run a railroad," is, in my opinion, a translation from the Chinese and came from observing this famous and strategic line in frenzied operation.)

The Siberian military adventure was an odd one altogether but people were killed in it just as tragically and just as hideously as in our more orthodox wars.

The United States had decided to support the weak and short-lived Kerensky government against the Bolsheviks, a diplomatic blunder which plagues us to this day. The Bolsheviks merely overwhelmed the opposition, finally massacring the forces of Admiral Kolchak at Golden Horn Bay, and seizing Vladivostok almost overnight.

From where I was stationed I could hear the cannonading

---

[2] If the assignment of a professional telegrapher to a telegraphic battalion sounds like an improvement over most army classification, don't be misled. I was first assigned to the Medics!

close by and, despite the fact that I received from a grateful government a Victory Medal with a Battle Clasp, I must in all honesty admit that this was the closest I ever got to actual combat.[3]

However, since the Bolsheviks had reduced the railroad station to rubble and cut all the telegraph lines, there was nothing for a telegrapher to do for a while except act the tourist. In this capacity I learned for the first time the technique of Communist recruitment.

Before the capture of Vladivostok there was no pro-Communist talk to be heard and no Communist red ribbons to be seen anywhere in the city. When the Bolsheviks took over, they massacred the citizenry at will, piled up the bodies in the gutters, stole their pants and shoes, and left them there. (There was no danger of putrefaction setting in for a while since the weather averaged more than thirty degrees below zero.)

The citizenry took a good look at what happened to people who didn't wear red ribbons and they got the message. The next day it was impossible to find anyone *not* wearing a red ribbon. The entire city had been "converted" to Bolshevism, or, as we now call it, Communism.

Actually, I felt then and I feel now that the nature of the average Russian is quite the antithesis of the Communist ideal. I had the pleasure of getting to know a goodly number of them in Vladivostok. I was invited to their homes and drank vodka with them out of the peculiar little corked cans which were used as containers for this fiery beverage in those days.

I found them open-hearted, hospitable, deeply religious, and so sentimental that they would almost cry at card tricks. I cannot think that any despotism, no matter how harsh or how ruthless, can drive these amiable qualities completely out of a race of people. These are bred in the bone, and the hope of the future,

[3] Maybe I got the decoration because I had worked on the Chinese Eastern Trans-Siberian Railroad.

peace of the world is to find an effective way of reaching through the wall of isolation which separates us and reactivating those qualities on a people-to-people basis.

We left Siberia's icy shores as a nonvictorious military expedition in March 1920, and sailed for the Philippines via Nagasaki. We were on board the U.S. Army transport *South Bend,* an all-steel ship, even to its decks. After having our physical thermostats adjusted to Siberia's sensationally freezing weather, the sudden change to subtropical and tropical weather was a little tough to take and I remember those steel decks with particular loathing. When they really heated up, they all but blistered the feet, and there was no place on board where one could escape discomfort.

In the Philippines I was given the responsibility of putting up the first radio station at Baguio, with the old umbrella-style antenna. I spent two years on Corregidor as chief radio operator until 1922, when my enlistment period expired and I was ordered home.

Naturally I was elated. I was weary of being abroad in uncomfortable places. I was sick for a sight of the United States. But most of all I wanted to see a telegraph operator in Cincinnati who signed her messages "GD."

Reassignment home was not that easy, however. We had been in the tropics so long, and before that in the none-too-healthy atmosphere of Siberia, that civilian authorities in the States, primarily on the West Coast, actually raised the query as to whether we were physically, spiritually or ideologically "fit to come back"! Every soldier faces disillusionment after the first flush of patriotic fervor fades and the citizenry grows bored with the sight of uniforms. But this was the first time any segment of the civilian populace wanted to keep their "soldier boys" from coming home at all! We had been engaged in a military expedition everyone wanted to forget. We had been doing obscure things in obscure places and nobody gave a hoot in Hades about us. Besides, there was a depression on and civilians didn't want any more competition for jobs from returning soldiers.

Common sense and decency finally prevailed and we were returned to the States where, at Angel Island, California, I received my honorable discharge in June 1922.

I rushed back to Cincinnati only to find to my dismay that I had been "blacklisted" in the telegraph industry because of the unsuccessful 1919 strike. As a twenty-year-old veteran I couldn't get my job back as a telegrapher with Postal Telegraph because of a strike I had participated in three years earlier, when I was seventeen years old.

It was an ironic turn of events. Blacklisting participants in a strike was made possible by the unfavorable climate in labor-management relations that had been created by the so-called "Bolshevik scare" of the early twenties. This hysteria in turn was originally created by the events in Siberia which, as part of the A.E.F., I had been trying to combat.

But this was no time for philosophical rumination. The bosses were back in the saddle. The termination of hostilities had caused an industrial depression and had necessitated a cutback in employment. Labor no longer was as necessary to management as it had been during the war. I considered myself fortunate to get temporary employment with the old Huenefield Stove Foundry in Cincinnati, operating a Boss oven pressing machine, a piece of equipment of the existence of which I had been singularly innocent until the date of my employment. I knew this job couldn't last long. So when someone suggested that I take the civil service examination for letter carrier, I took it. I passed the examination and started work in the Cincinnati Post Office as a substitute letter carrier on January 23, 1923.

The salary for a substitute in those days was sixty cents an hour. You had to pay for your own uniform and you had to show up for work every day, even if you were not used. If you were not used you received no recompense for your time and trouble.

Today a substitute letter carrier gets two dollars an hour. The government gives him a uniform allowance of one hundred dollars a year and if he is ordered to show up for duty and is not used, he is paid for two hours' work anyway.

The pay of letter carriers, substitute or regular, is far from adequate, but conditions are greatly improved over what they were in 1923. I am very proud of the fact that I have been privileged to play a part in achieving that improvement.

And certainly the green and somewhat apprehensive youngster named Doherty who showed up for work that first day as a substitute letter carrier at the Cincinnati Post Office had no idea of the role he would be playing in the development of the National Association of Letter Carriers. He had no way of knowing it, but he was entering into the happiest and most satisfying career a man could possibly have.

CHAPTER 11

THE WAY IT WAS

T HE old Cincinnati Post Office at which I showed up for my
first day's work as a letter carrier on January 23, 1923, was
not an attractive or a reassuring edifice. It was, in fact, a rather
forbidding architectural horror which had been erected genera-
ations earlier in a furore of civic zeal and artistic bad taste. It
was a Gothic study in dirty red granite, and generations of pig-
eons over the years had proved themselves art critics by express-
ing in their own way unmistakable opinions on the building's
architectural shortcomings. They did not enhance the structure's
appearance.

The training of a new letter carrier in those days was definitely
along lick-and-promise lines. The first day a substitute showed up
for work he was assigned to a regular carrier. He spent that first
day "off the clock" carrying the regular carrier's bag and observ-

ing everything he did. On the second day he was given his own bag and told to go out and distribute the mail.[1]

I was extremely fortunate in that I was assigned on my first day to a veteran carrier who was one of the most dedicated men I have ever known. His name was Herman Storch. At the time I met him he was a middle-aged man with a sandy mustache and the possessor of one of the most wholesome personalities I have ever encountered. He knew everyone on his route and he was loved by everyone he knew. Herman Storch took my indoctrination seriously and was intensely interested in my "starting off right." As long as he remained in the service he considered me a kind of special protégé, and the number of his kindnesses toward me is beyond computation.

As a matter of fact, I still keep in my desk the *Amended Postal Laws and Regulations in Relation to Free Delivery Service* (dated 1896) and the *Rules for the Instruction of Carriers at the Post Office, Cincinnati, Ohio and the Stations Thereof* (dated 1888), which Herman Storch inscribed to me and gave me on the first day I entered the Post Office. They are among my most cherished possessions. He also, I might add, signed me up that first day as a member of the NALC.

The Cincinnati postal team which I encountered was very special in its devotion to duty and its care and concern for postal neophytes. The postmaster, Arthur L. Behymer, was a career man (rare in those days) who looked a little bit like Adolf Hitler. He had formerly been a railway mail clerk and he lived by the book and expected everyone else to do the same. He was a strict disciplinarian, but his stop-watch type of management did not prevent the letter carriers in his office from paying attention to the special needs of their patrons even if it took a little extra time and meant the risk of a dressing-down. Among those whom I

---

[1] There is not much improvement in post-office training today. Personnel experts and training officers talk a good game, but actual progress has been slight.

remember most affectionately were Harry W. Knight and his son, Harry W. Knight, Jr., William Schorr, William Maderis, Walter Dunphy, William J. Wunderlich, Frank Roth, and Henry Schiller, all of whom are long since dead. And among those who are still at this writing, happily, among the living, there were Walter Heunefeldt, Christian L. Lang and his son, Francis, Edward Gleason, Harry J. Knight, William McClelland, and Ray T. Bryson. These sterling men, and many others like them, helped shape my postal life, encouraged me, and gave the hand of friendship and assistance whenever I needed it. I shall never forget them. They were real character builders.

Actually, a neophyte carrier entering the service in 1923 *needed* encouragement. Financially speaking, carrying the mail, at that time, was not a very attractive job.

Unfortunately, Postmaster General Hays had remained in office only a year. It was a memorable year, but the time was not long enough to make his progressive ideas permanent postal policy. His successors, Postmasters General Work and New, while a great improvement over those who had ruled the Department during the previous twenty years, were still not a patch on Will Hays. The Hays policy of "humanizing" the postal service had been watered down considerably by January 23, 1923.

Nonetheless it is true that conditions were far better than they were under Burleson. In the Götterdämmerung of the Wilson administration, the Congress, sensing what a political millstone Burleson and his policies were to themselves and to the Democratic party, voted into law several important improvements so far as postal employees were concerned.

One of these was a wage increase, the first one to be given postal employees since 1907! The financial condition of letter carriers at the time of the passage of this increase can be judged by the fact that Department of Labor statistics for that period show that union wages in private industry were more than a hundred percent higher than they had been in 1907, and that the

1920 dollar was worth only sixty-one cents when compared to the 1914 dollar.[2]

This postal wage increase contained in the Reclassification Act of June 5, 1920, which Burleson fought bitterly, squeezed through the House by a 344-0 margin and passed the Senate handily. It was inadequate but it helped. It raised the entrance wage of letter carriers to $1,440 per annum and the maximum wage to $1,800. (Previously, the maximum wage was $1,200.) The letter carriers had been asking for a maximum wage of $2,400.

However, there were certain fringe benefits which the Congress voted for postal workers which make 1920 an historic year.

The first of these was a retirement plan. For more than thirty years the National Association of Letter Carriers had labored unceasingly to secure enactment of a decent and humane retirement law. This had caused a great deal of friction with the various department heads, but the NALC had stuck to its guns. On August 20, 1920, the Stanfield-Lehlbach[3] Retirement Bill was enacted into law. This provided a retirement plan which, although inadequate in many of its provisions, was an epochal achievement when viewed in the light of those times.

As is true in so many similar cases, all opposition to the Retirement Act disappeared after its enactment, like hot breath from a looking glass. There were still people who disagreed as to what details should be included in the legislation, but there was no further vocal opposition to the principle of the law.

The National Association of Letter Carriers (and particularly its president, Edward J. Gainor) was instrumental in passing another tremendously progressive piece of legislation during the twilight hours of President Wilson's administration. This con-

[2] Economists talk about our modern monetary inflation as if it were a brand new thing. It seems inflation has been with us a long, long time.

[3] Authors of the Bill were Senator Robert N. Stanfield, of Oregon, and Rep. Frederick R. Lehlbach, of New Jersey. Both earned the eternal gratitude of letter carriers by their devotion to the cause of retirement.

cerned the inclusion of the principle of sick leave in the Postal Service.

Previous to this time the sick leave privilege had been denied postal employees despite its general observance elsewhere throughout the Federal service. The Reclassification Act of June 5, 1920, granted to postal employees ten days sick leave *per annum,* cumulative to thirty days within three years.

It is hard, looking at the labor-management picture in the light of 1960, to grasp completely the scope and significance of these legislative victories. These victories were accomplished by labor pioneers who were operating in a jungle controlled and dominated by skilled and wealthy anti-laborites who were obsessed with monolithic and archaic theories concerning the place of labor in the national economic scene.

Although the letter carriers and all other federal employees have come a long way since those days, all due credit must be given to these pioneers who risked their careers and the economic stability of their families in order to effect those original pieces of legislation upon which most of the fringe benefit legislation subsequently enacted has been based.

However, as I have said, by the time I entered the carrier force of the Cincinnati Post Office in 1923, much of the shining idealism which had been injected into management-labor relations within the Postal Establishment by Postmaster General Will Hays had become somewhat tarnished. In the sudden boom which followed the short depression of the immediate postwar period, the inadequate salary increases voted by the Congress in 1920 had become sadly obsolete.

Dr. Work and Mr. New, the Postmasters General who followed General Hays in office, were not imbued with quite the same idealistic philosophy as had motivated their illustrious predecessor. Although Mr. Hays had won popular favor with his fair administration and thus had made impossible an immediate return by postal authorities to the old tooth and claw philosophy which had characterized practically all postal administrations during the previous half century, there were unmistakable signs that the professional politicians within the Republican party were determined to effect a stealthy return to "politics as usual."

Postmaster General Work had in 1922 formulated a plan of holding what he called "conference conventions," on a large scale. These were to embrace all segments of the employee force. This plan was enthusiastically and joyously received by employee leaders as well as by the rank and file of their organizations. There were widespread hopes that a truly modern concept of labor-management relations would evolve from these conferences. However it seems apparent that a combination of the professional politicians and a dominant and nonprogressive element within the Postal Inspection Service sabotaged any good that might have come out of these conferences and they were soon abandoned.

In recent years, Postmaster General Arthur E. Summerfield has attempted to revive this idea, but only from a management point of view. He has held, sporadically, conferences of leading postmasters and supervisors, but has never included in such conferences representatives of the rank and file employees whom these worthy gentlemen must supervise. These conferences have accomplished a considerable amount as far as the education of newly appointed postmasters is concerned, but lack of adequate communication between management and labor has prevented them from being as fruitful as they should be. Postal management at the highest levels has always been hesitant to discuss its problems, on a shirtsleeves basis, with labor. This is a pity, because management could learn a great deal thereby if it did, and so could labor.

When I joined the National Association of Letter Carriers in 1923 the top leadership of our union had moved miles ahead in the area of free speech. The repeal of the "gag law" and the moral and political collapse of the Burleson administration had moved the leadership of the NALC to a point where they no longer thought that any criticism of the postal administration would automatically lead to the loss of their jobs and to a serious and perhaps permanent impairment of the strength of the Association itself. And though the columns of *The Postal Record* were suitably respectful at all times, there did appear now and then serious criticisms of certain policies of the Postmaster General and certain policies of individual postmasters. The *Record* more and more became a stalwart union journal, and there could be no further credence given to those jealous critics of the NALC who were wont to slander it as a "me too" organization.

And this new approach generated a great deal of enthusiasm among letter carriers throughout the country. When I joined the Postal Service there were 2,004 branches of the National Association of Letter Carriers throughout the country. The Association had 41,208 paying members. However, post office figures show there were only 39,693 letter carriers on the payroll at that time. So there were actually four percent more members of the association than there were working letter carriers.

Whenever I am inclined to become overenthusiastic about the progress that has been made during my administration as president of the National Association of Letter Carriers, I recall these tremendously impressive figures and I remember the great obstacles and discouragements under which my predecessor, President Gainor, had to operate during his twenty-five years as chief executive of our Association, and a proper degree of humility returns.

In any continuing operation such as a labor union, any man who, upon attaining a position of leadership, does not realize that his achievements are built upon the foundations constructed by his predecessors is not only very foolish but, in all probability, will soon be headed for oblivion.

CHAPTER 12

THE FIRST CRUSADE

A T THE time I entered the postal service one of the greatest campaigns of its kind ever to be staged by postal workers was being mounted. It was the first full-scale crusade to achieve a living wage for postal workers.

The Reclassification Act of 1920 was obsolete on the day it was passed and in the rapidly expanding economy of the early 1920s it was becoming more and more obsolete with every passing day.

The crusade, which was to last eighteen months, was spearheaded by the National Association of Letter Carriers. Although many leaders of the Association earned a full share of glory in the fight, special tribute must be paid to one man who was a tragic battlefield casualty, and whose loss severely hampered the efforts of the postal employees. He was Edward J. Cantwell, of Brooklyn, New York [1] who served as national secretary of the NALC for more than twenty-six years. Cantwell had been in impaired health for some while, but his devotion to his fellow letter carriers was such that he refused to retire to the rear echelons during the struggle. He remained in the foremost rank of the battle until, on October 13, 1924, he died, literally in the saddle, fighting, despite his fatal infirmity, to win a living wage for those whom he loved the most and for whom he had worked so tirelessly.[2] His determination and courage were typical of the spirit which permeated the entire NALC during this struggle.

The wage fight which took place in 1923, 1924, and early 1925 was in many ways memorable. After a long and arduous campaign, led by the letter carriers, to create a climate in which a wage boost could be successfully argued, Congressman Clyde Kelly [3] introduced, on May 2, 1924, a bill which would raise

---

[1] The inspiration of Edward J. Cantwell led to the first movement to erect a NALC Building in Washington, D.C. The plan to do this as a memorial to this valiant man failed, after a national referendum. However, this effort was an inspiration, in later years, to erect a headquarters building, and the present impressive NALC Building at 100 Indiana Avenue, N.W., Washington, D.C., is the result. The story of how this came about is told in Chapter 23.

[2] Two months later, the letter carriers lost another great champion. Samuel Gompers, president of the AFL, died on December 13, 1924. He had been a great friend of the NALC all during its troubled years of development. He had supplied the necessary urging when he felt it was time for the NALC to join the AFL, and he had seen that the letter carriers were welcomed and recognized when they did join the parent union. And, of course, his contribution to the cause of the working man of America is beyond computation. He was one of the truly great men of his, or any other, time.

[3] Rep. Clyde Kelly, of Pennsylvania, was one of the greatest and most effective friends the letter carriers, and the postal service generally, ever had. Not only was he the architect of much beneficial postal legislation, but his book, *United States Postal Policy,* which was published by D. Appleton and Company in 1932, became the bible for everyone involved in designing postage rate legislation. Like so many fine men, Congressman Kelly thought far more about others than he did about himself, and when he died, in 1935, it was found that there was not sufficient money in his estate to care for his widow and his two daughters. The National Association of Letter Carriers set up the Clyde Kelly Memorial Trust Fund and invested more than $26,000 in U.S. Government Bonds with the interest going to Congressman Kelly's widow. This

letter carriers' (and clerks') salaries to the level of $1,700 at entrance and to $2,100 maximum, with an increase in substitute letter carriers' salaries from sixty cents an hour to sixty-five cents an hour. (Since I was a substitute and engaged to be married, this five cents an hour increase was important to me, representing as it did an 8½ per cent increase in salary.)

The Kelly Bill passed the House by a vote of 250-14 and the Senate by a vote of 73-3. The conference report was approved by the Senate and was adopted by the House by a stunning majority of 361-6.

But President Coolidge justified his reputation for "keeping cool." In fact, he was downright glacial. Ignoring the overwhelming will of the Congress, he vetoed the bill. Not only that, he cannily waited until the day the Congress adjourned before he let his decision be known, so there could be no attempt to override his veto until the Congress reassembled after the national elections of 1924.

Coolidge gave the classical reason for his veto of the wage bill: the Congress had failed to provide the means of raising postal revenues in order to offset the extra cost of a wage increase.

This argument has been a sharp thorn in the side of postal employees for many years. It is the constant cry of postal management whenever postal salary increases are discussed, and while, on the surface, it sounds logical enough, it is totally fallacious because it ignores the fundamental differences between labor in private industry and labor in the Post Office.

In private industry there must be some correlation between wages and profits. A company cannot pay out in salaries more than it takes in and remain in business for any length of time. But in private industry prices are determined and profits are

---

arrangement went on until Mrs. Kelly's death in 1959 and helped her materially in bringing up and educating her two children. Other postal unions also co-operated in similar projects.

achieved (or at any rate they *should* be determined and achieved) through open competition in the market place.

This is not the case in the Post Office Department. It is a government monopoly. Its "profit" or "loss" is determined by comparing the Department's revenues with its expenditures. Its revenues come from the postage which the public pays, the rates of which are artificially set by the Congress.[4] Almost 80 per cent of the Post Office Department's expenditures are in wages, the rates of which are also artificially set by the Congress. There is no comparison between this situation and the situation which exists "outside the walls" in the free economy in which private industry operates.

The Congress is traditionally more receptive to postal wage legislation than it is to postage rate legislation. Increasing the salaries of half a million human beings makes political friends. Increasing the postage rates of 175,000,000 people can conceivably make political enemies. Ergo, the law of self-preservation causes many (but not by any means all) congressmen to view any attempt to raise postage rates with an extremely jaundiced eye.[5]

It is not necessary to comment on this situation beyond pointing out that it is not of the postal employees' making. Therefore, when a President refuses to grant a justified wage increase for postal employees because the Congress has refused or neglected to provide the extra revenue to cover the additional cost, he is making an innocent victim of every postal worker in the land. Postal employees are, in short, being penalized for someone else's action or, as the case may be, inaction.

It is curious that this question of supplying sufficient revenue

[4] Even this is not strictly accurate. All revenues from postage go directly into the United States Treasury. The Post Office Department must operate under congressional appropriations.

[5] The postage rate increase which the Congress voted in 1958 was the first major increase since 1932. In the intervening years the cost of running the Postal Establishment had more than doubled.

to cover the cost of a salary increase is never brought up in the case of other federal employees. The postal worker is made a special case simply because the Post Office Department charges postage rates which can be raised from time to time in order to produce additional revenues. The Post Office returns to the Treasury about 85 per cent of its operating expense, which, under the circumstances, is not bad. But since the costs of operating the Postal Establishment are so great, the 15 per cent difference between expenditures and revenues seems proportionately larger than it is.

This brings us to a second philosophical consideration which has vexed governmental thinking ever since 1789. Is the Post Office a business or a service?

I firmly believe it is a service to the American people. It should no more be expected to show a "profit" than should the Department of Agriculture, let us say, or the Department of Defense.

I do not advocate this as a monolithic, or even as a unilateral proposition. Certainly there must be a decent and due regard for economy. There must be an insistence on maximum efficiency. The actual *users* of the mail should pay a fair share of the allocated costs of the particular class of mail they use.

Unfortunately, no one has ever determined to everyone's satisfaction exactly what a "fair share" is, nor has anyone ever designed a universally approved formula for allocating the proper costs to each class of mail. In addition, the Post Office does perform numerous and necessary welfare services for the public at large which have little or nothing to do with the business of carrying the mail. The cost of these services, which is considerable, should certainly be borne out of general taxation and should not be thrust upon the shoulders of the users of the mail.

It is, admittedly, embarrassing for a Postmaster General to have to keep explaining to uninformed citizens that the half-billion dollar annual postal deficit is not the result of inefficiency in his administration but, rather, the result of congressional determination to keep the postal service exactly as the term implies, a *service,* to all the people of this country.

But, as a matter of fact, a great deal of this embarrassment could be eliminated if the post office accountants would swallow their pride and stop referring to the disparity between postal revenues and postal costs as a "deficit." It is really no deficit at all.

In any case, since both postal revenues and postal salaries are artificially determined by Congressional action, it is ridiculous to make the income of postal employees dependent on postage rates. Therefore, the concept of tying rates and wages together into a single piece of legislation is theoretically anathema to postal employees. But this is an imperfect world filled with imperfect people, of which I am certainly one.[6] There are times when a theory, no matter how valid, must be sacrificed on the altar of practicality. This was the case in 1924. Letter carriers and all other postal employees were in dire need of a wage increase, and a compromise had to be made. So the postal unions, under protest, eventually went along with the idea of a combined wage and rate bill.[7]

The reasons for this compromise were curious, to say the least.

In November, 1924, Calvin Coolidge, the greatest President ever to come out of Plymouth, Vermont, was triumphantly returned to office.[8]

However, the turnover among members of both Houses of the Congress was considerable.

Those were the days of "lame duck" Congresses, when senators and representatives who had been rejected at the polls by their constituents still remained in office and were free to participate in the operation of the people's business until the new administration came into power the following March.

[6] For verification consult my wife, Gertrude Dacey Doherty.

[7] The same thing happened in 1958, and for the same reasons.

[8] He was also the greatest President since Warren Harding.

Although the unfinished business of overriding the President's veto of the postal wage bill was taken up immediately after the Congress reassembled on December 1, 1924, the atmosphere on Capitol Hill was greatly different from what it had been in the previous June. Statesmen who had passionately and vociferously pleaded the cause of the postal worker were now indifferent or hostile. (To paraphrase the words of Jimmy Walker's old song, they did not love us in December as they did in June.)

Roadblocks were thrown in the path of a showdown on the veto. But the showdown did come at last, on January 6, 1925, and on that date the Senate failed by a single vote to override the President's veto. The final count was 55-29.

On the face of it, this was a remarkable reversal of form in a body which just six months previously had voted for an increase in postal wages by the overwhelming margin of 73-3. (Remember, almost exactly the same individuals participated in both roll calls.) But, if one looks below the surface, the reversal was not quite as surprising as it seems at first glance.

In the first place, the original vote was taken *before* the national elections. One-third of the senators and all the members of the House of Representatives were looking apprehensively toward the day on which they would be weighed in the balance by the electorate and they were eagerly courting the postal employees' vote.

But in December the election was over. Many of the members felt they no longer needed the postal employees, and so they deserted them. Furthermore, in the Senate, where the reversal took place, there were numerous "lame duck" members who were anxious to curry favor with Coolidge and thereby win from him a juicy political appointment after his inauguration in March. A vote to override the President's veto would, of course, be fatal to any such hope.

This point was amusingly brought out in a colloquy on the Senate floor on January 6, 1925 (the day on which the vote was taken) among Senator Tom Heflin of Alabama, the ineffable Senator Ashurst of Arizona, and "lame duck" Senator Sterling of South Dakota, chairman of the Post Office Committee.

Sterling, who had completely reversed his position on postal wage increases, had quoted in a particularly flatulent and self-serving speech, the words of the unfortunate Wolsey, in Shakespeare's *Henry VIII:*

> O Cromwell, Cromwell!
> Had I but served my God with half the zeal
> I served my king, he would not in mine age
> Have left me naked to mine enemies.

Heflin,[9] a very mean man in a debate, got to his feet at this point and the following dialogue took place:

MR. HEFLIN: Mr. President: the effort to serve the king here is what caused the change in the vote before the election and after the election. Last year senators were looking out for themselves. They were seeking to serve their country. They were trying to do justice by the postal employees. But the election is over and now they come to serve the king, he who holds the appointing power. There is a lake full of lame ducks swimming around, hobbling about the Capitol and they are looking wistfully toward the White House.

MR. ASHURST: And, Mr. President, many, if not most of the lame ducks are performing a strange miracle—singing swan songs.

MR. HEFLIN: Yes. But, Mr. President, since the election and during this session the senator from South Dakota has changed his position and made several speeches against the position he took last year. I think I can see dangling before his eyes a fine and luscious plum in the way of an appointment to some fat

---

[9] Although Senator Heflin was on the side of the postal employees on this occasion, I would not want it thought that I approve generally of his policies or his prejudices. I do not.

federal office and sometimes I can see him looking up anxiously at it and tiptoeing as he stretches forth his hands as if eager to take it in his grasp.

MR. STERLING: Mr. President, I simply wish to say that I wish I had the imagination even of the senator from Alabama.

MR. HEFLIN: I think the senator would much prefer to have the appointment. (Laughter on the floor and in the galleries.)

A few moments later, Senator Heflin had this to say about his lame duck brethren:

MR. HEFLIN: . . . What has become of these dear and beloved senators who voted before the election to increase the postal employees' salaries as they ought to be increased? Where are they now? Many of them are swimming in the lame-duck mill pond and are looking anxiously and imploringly, and some disgustingly, toward the White House, crooning softly the name "Coolidge! Coolidge! . . ." [10]

As I say, Senator Heflin was a mean man in a debate. Such outspoken talk is rare in the Senate today. The institution has become so gentlemanly, so much of a club, that when any member so far forgets himself as to speak disparagingly of the motives or the intelligence of another member, the words are swiftly expunged from the *Congressional Record* lest anyone's sensibilities be offended. (As a matter of fact, if such a colloquy as this were to take place in the Senate today, there would certainly be a request for "The Regular Order," which would force the senator offending either to sit down or to abandon that particular line of debate. Apparently the senators were a tougher breed in those days.)

As a result of this unexpected setback, the desperate postal employees agreed to the stratagem of linking wages to postage rates.

[10] See *Congressional Record,* January 6, 1925.

After a remarkable debate which consumed eight legislative days, a combined rate and wage bill which, it was felt, would be satisfactory to the President, was passed in the Senate by a vote of 70-8.

The joy of letter carriers at this turn of events, however, was short-lived. The House rose up in its wrath and accused the Senate of infringing on its exclusive revenue-raising prerogative. The bill was sent back to the Senate by a 225-113 vote.

The situation was getting desperate. A bill had to be passed before the current Congress adjourned and a new Congress came to Capitol Hill.

Since all legislation dies with each Congress, failure to pass the bill before adjournment would mean that entirely new hearings would have to be held and the whole cumbersome legislative process gone through all over again before action could be taken. This would have held up the pay raise for many months, and the postal employees were in truly serious need of immediate help. They and their families were bleeding.

On February 4, Congressman Clyde Kelly once more leaped into the breach. He introduced a bill asking for the same wage features which his previously proposed legislation had contained, and also for rate increases which would bring in an additional $61,000,000 to the U.S. Treasury. The wage increases were to be made retroactive to January 1. There was a great deal of squabbling and recrimination during the ensuing debate, but on February 25 this wage and rate bill passed the House by a vote of 368-8 and the Senate by a 69-12 vote. On February 28, the last possible day, President Coolidge, with a sour grin of triumph, signed the bill into law.

As far as Coolidge was concerned, monetary virtue had triumphed, but the innocent victims of all this by-play were the postal employees who had their sorely-needed wage increase delayed for six months by the Coolidge veto for reasons completely beyond their control. (As a matter of fact, the original

Kelly wage bill had been introduced in the House on December 20, 1923, fourteen months previously!)

Naturally, as a fledgling letter carrier, my part in this crusade was small indeed, albeit, as a private in the postal army I worked hard with my brethren in an organized effort to arouse public sentiment in favor of the faithful, underpaid postal employee. This concerted attempt by members of the NALC, carried out simultaneously and strenuously in every city in the land, did a great deal to influence congressional thinking.

The final passage of the salary increase had more than a theoretical interest for me, however, because on February 23, 1925, two days before passage of the wage increase and five days before President Coolidge signed it into law, William C. Doherty and Gertrude Dacey stood before Msgr. John F. Hickey in St. Matthew's Church, South Norwood, Ohio, and became man and wife.

There are two things about our courtship which, over the span of years, still impress me. One was my stamina. I lived in Price Hill, Cincinnati, and my intended lived in South Norwood, far at the other end of town. Three times each week, after a full day's work at the post office, I would take the long and unbelievably slow street-car ride all the way across the city so as to take Gertrude to a movie or, perhaps, just to sit and talk about our future together. Then I would catch the "Owl" street car each night and make the same long, slow journey home, so I could get a few hours' sleep before getting up to go to work at 5 A.M. Only a young man very much in love could survive a routine like that!

Second, on looking back I am surprised at the amount of Irish gall I showed. My wife, at the time of our marriage, was a star telegrapher for the stockbroking firm of A. and J. Frank Co., and she was making at least three times as much money as I was making as a substitute letter carrier. Yet at my suggestion she resigned her job on the day we were married.

I shall always be grateful for both my stamina and my gall. February 23, 1925, was not only the proudest but also the most fortunate day of my life. There never has been a moment of regret on either of our parts since the day we exchanged our vows and set up housekeeping on a salary of sixty-five cents an hour.

CHAPTER 13

PROSPERITY AND PANIC

AFTER a long and successful fight for higher wages such as that which the National Association of Letter Carriers and the other postal unions concluded in 1925, there follows almost inevitably a period of comparative legislative inactivity. Even though the postal employees had failed to get as much of an increase as they originally hoped for, there was clearly no point in returning prematurely to the legislative trenches. Both the Congress and the unions were too exhausted from the struggle, and any attempt to win further wage increases would have been foolhardy.

Therefore, for several years there ensued a period in which the NALC marked time and consolidated its gains. A kind of honeymoon between the unions and the Department set in. The average salary of a letter carrier in 1928 was $2,063.67.[1] Although this was far from munificent, it was as much as the Congress was

---

[1] Report of Postmaster General New, Fiscal 1928.

willing to grant, and the several attempts during the latter half
of the decade to increase the maximum salary to $2,500 were
more or less token efforts, undertaken with little fervor on the
part of the unions and with less than complete seriousness on the
part of the postal committees of the Congress.

This period of comparative contentment can be judged best
by the fact that the Department's figures for fiscal 1928 show that
only 421 letter carriers resigned from the service out of a total
carrier force of 51,293. This low level of resignations during a
period of unheralded national prosperity is an accurate barometer
of the relationship between the employees and postal management. The percentage of resignations today is almost twenty times
higher than it was then.

The legislative efforts of President Gainor and his universally
respected and invaluable secretary, Michael T. Finnan, were
mainly directed toward improving the provisions of the Retirement Law and agitating for a shorter work week in line with conditions prevailing generally in private industry.

However, it was during these years that certain young bucka-
roos in the NALC first began to shed their anonymity and to start
a climb up through the organizational "chairs" which can eventually lead to national office.

I know that in the Cincinnati Branch I was extremely fortunate
both in the loyalty and the patience of my friends, and in the fact
that my previous union experience, particularly in regard to the
ill-fated strike of the Commercial Telegraphers Union of America, gave me a head start in achieving recognition among my
brothers.

I am the first one to admit that I never could have gone anywhere if it had not been for the fatherly assistance of one of the
greatest leaders the letter carriers ever had, John T. Mugavin,
after whom the Cincinnati Branch (43) of the NALC is now
named. Mugavin, who died in 1932, served as Chief Clerk,
in charge of the Letter Carriers' National Sick Benefit Association,

for approximately twenty-six years. He was highly respected at the national level of the Union. And in Cincinnati, through the sheer force of his personality and his ability rather than through any desire to rule, he was absolute leader. If John Mugavin wanted something done in the Cincinnati Branch, it was done. If he did not want something done, it simply did not come about. It was as simple as that.

I shall always be grateful for his tolerance in those early days toward one William C. Doherty. I was, on looking back, a remarkably bumptious young man endowed with a somewhat premature ambition. While still extremely wet behind the ears, I ran for the position of local clerk of the Branch's Sick Benefit Association in 1924, just a year after I had entered the postal service, and tried again in 1925 and 1926. My opponent each time was the incumbent, William J. Wunderlich, and each time I was roundly and decisively trounced. The margin of Wunderlich's victory in 1926 was more than 3 to 1.

However, despite the fact that I was running against Jack Mugavin's friend and personal representative in the Cincinnati Branch, I managed to maintain the friendship of both Mugavin and Wunderlich. If these gentlemen had been less understanding or less tolerant of a young man's exuberance they could have put a permanent stop to my ambitions then and there. To their everlasting credit they actually encouraged me to keep trying.

Undeterred by a perfect record of political failure, I made the somewhat surprising decision to run for even higher office in 1927, and declared myself a candidate for the presidency of the Branch, challenging another fine postal leader, Raymond T. Bryson. When the ballots were counted, I got my ears pinned back so far that I could have tied them together in a bow knot behind my neck.

At this point the leaders of the Branch decided enough was enough, and when the office of financial secretary of the Branch became vacant in that same year because of a resignation, they gave me that appointment.

If this gesture was meant to keep me quiet for a while, it failed dismally. The very next year I once again announced myself a candidate for the presidency of the Branch. In retrospect I can imagine that the older local leaders threw up their hands in weary resignation at my obstinacy and decided to let me have my way. This time I won the top post in the Branch without opposition. I had lost every battle except the last one.

No sooner was I sworn in than my friends started a campaign to organize and consolidate support in the other local branches in the state. They performed wonders in the field and in 1932 I was elected Ohio state president of the letter carriers. I had barely warmed up this new seat when I had to resign because, out of a clear and very blue sky, I was appointed by President Gainor to national office as a member of the Board of Directors of the National Sick Benefit Association upon the death of Jack Mugavin. Shortly afterwards, when Walter R. Beavis, president of the N.S.B.A. Board of Directors, died, I had the good fortune to be elected to succeed him in that position. Thanks to the constant and enthusiastic support of my friends and, in a small part, to the Irish bullheadedness which prevented my knowing when I was beaten, I found myself, at age thirty, well on my way.

Meanwhile, up in Minneapolis, a new star was rising in the ranks of the letter carriers. His name: Jerome J. Keating.

Jerry Keating entered the Minneapolis Post Office as a substitute carrier in 1924 when he was twenty-one years old. He became active in NALC affairs immediately, and by 1927 he had attained considerable status nationally because of his work on behalf of substitute letter carriers.

During the 1929 NALC national convention, which was held in his home town of Minneapolis, he did a masterful job as chairman of the Publicity Committee. He served as president of his branch in 1932 and 1933 and in 1935 was elected to national office as a member and later as chairman of the Constitution and By-laws Committee of the NALC. In 1941 he went on the Executive Board of the NALC. He rose steadily in the union until, at our New York convention, he was elected vice-president of the NALC.

I might add that during his early years Jerry Keating managed to complete his education, receiving his B.A. from the University of Minnesota in 1930 and, in the following year, completing all the work for his Master's except for the writing of the thesis. He still swears he is going to get that M.A. before he is through.

It is almost impossible to explain how important Jerry has been not only to me but, particularly, to the letter carriers of the United States. He has played an indispensable role in all our successes, and because of his modest and self-effacing nature, he has always tried to give the credit to someone else.

I remember so vividly having a quiet cup of coffee with Jerry at the 1933 national convention in Atlantic City. It was right after my election to national office and new and enticing vistas were opening up before my eyes. I said to Jerry that if it ever happened that lightning struck me and I became one of the top leaders in the NALC, I wanted him by my side every step of the way. At the time that sounded like a romantic dream, but like so many dreams, it turned out exactly that way. And no man could have a more able or more loyal right-hand man. And nobody could have a better friend.

During these same years, a red-headed Irishman named Peter Cahill was cutting quite a wide swath in the Boston Branch of the NALC.

I heard about Peter long before I knew him personally. Because of his unshakable integrity and his devotion to justice, Peter developed the reputation of being somewhat of a stormy petrel. The Boston Branch was pretty well split in those days into two factions, the old-timers and the young Turks. (Or, as someone once put it, the chivalry and the shovelry.) Peter, as a leading light of the younger group, became vice-president of the Branch in 1933 and president in 1934. However, in 1937 he was defeated in his bid for re-election and, believing that his organizational life in the NALC was ended, he accepted promotion to the supervisory ranks. He remained a supervisor until 1944, when he voluntarily returned to the letter carrier ranks.

Peter did not know it, but his organizational future was just beginning. In 1945, the president of the Boston Branch, Joseph P. Considine, passed away and Peter Cahill was elected in his place. In 1946, at the Detroit convention, he was elected chief clerk of the National Sick Benefit Association. He held that position until 1952 when he was promoted by the membership, at the New York convention, to secretary of the NALC. Four years later, at Minneapolis, the offices of secretary and treasurer were combined and Peter was elected to hold down both jobs, which he does with brilliant efficiency.

In some ways Peter Cahill represents the Voice of Conscience in the NALC. Although at this writing he is at the retirement age, he has lost none of his youthful fervor and he continues to see postal matters through the eyes of the fellow who is delivering the mail. We all try to do this, naturally, and I devoutly hope we succeed, but it could be that national officers might get so engrossed in the big picture that they would lose their awareness of the needs and desires of individual members. Peter Cahill personally sees that this can never happen. If a single letter carrier in Pocatello, Idaho, is being discriminated against, Peter gets just as indignant, and works just as hard in the interest of justice, as he does when the welfare of the entire membership is threatened. His capacity is as great as his heart and, as Post Office Department officials have so often found out, he is a lion when it comes to debate.

A fourth national officer in our Washington headquarters is a man to whom I shall always be grateful because he was one of my original supporters when I ran for the national presidency. He is Reuben B. Kremers, the assistant secretary-treasurer.

Rube was born in the metropolis of Running Water, South Dakota, but eventually migrated to Seattle, Washington. He entered the service as a substitute carrier at the age of twenty, in 1919, and four years later, while still a substitute, became the branch secretary. His rise in the union has been a success story ever since. From 1931 to 1934 he served as Washington state president of the NALC and from 1935 through 1937 he was president of the Seattle Branch. He resigned that position in 1938 upon appointment to that organizational springboard for future national leaders, the National Sick Benefit Association. He served as president of the Board of Directors from 1939 until 1941, at which time he was elected to the Board of Directors of the Mutual Benefit Association of the NALC.

He was elected to the National Executive Board in 1943, at the Denver convention and was promoted by the membership to assistant secretary in 1946. A tremendous detail man, Rube Kremers performs the invaluable service of picking up the pieces the rest of us leave lying about and fitting them expertly into the NALC pattern of accomplishment.

So each of the four of us, Doherty, Keating, Cahill, and Kremers, was working his way separately toward the top of the NALC. And considering the difference in our backgrounds and our geographical environments, it is a kind of miracle that we all should meld together into an efficient and harmonious team.

I am proud of Jerry, Peter, and Rube because they are, in a very real sense, a direct reflection of the character of the membership that elected them to office. Unions, like nations, almost always get the kind of leadership they deserve, and when it comes to integrity, ability, and loyalty, I would confidently place the members of the NALC Executive Board in competition with the leaders of any other organization in the country. They are, in my opinion, unbeatable.

These were the years, also, when two other future national officers were beginning to show the signs of leadership that would mean advancement to the top. One of these was James Patrick Deely, of Philadelphia, one of the most delightful personalities in our association, and one of the ablest executives. Jim Deely is Director of the NALC Health Insurance program and is responsible for the distribution of more than a million dollars a year in health and hospitalization benefits. Largely because of Jim Deely's fervor and ability the nation's letter carriers today have by far the finest health and hospitalization program in government. Even Departmental officials and members of the Senate and the House of Representatives have sought to become associate members of the NALC in order to share in this insurance program.

The other national officer resident in Washington is George A. Bang, chief collector of our Mutual Benefit Association, which embodies the life-insurance program for the NALC. Bang, who rose to prominence after a career of carrying the mails in Omaha, Nebraska, is a quiet and highly efficient Scotsman who brings to this important function a fine combination of deep compassion and an acute business ability. Union insurance programs have grown to be big business and demand of their directors absolute integrity and broad vision. Deely and Bang possess these qualities to a tremendous degree, as well as many other qualities that have endeared them to me and, far more important, to the letter carriers of the country.

It so happened that I emerged upon the national level of the NALC at the most troubled period of its existence.

The trouble began on that dark day in October 1929, when the bottom dropped out of a spurious and meretricious world which the financiers and the average citizens of this republic had kidded themselves into believing was the realization of the "American Dream." As a matter of fact it was merely a period of wonderful nonsense, and when, at last, someone shot a phony Santa Claus and brought into being the Great Depression, the American people suffered a traumatic shock from which they have not entirely recovered to this day.

As soon as it became apparent that the depression was not an ephemeral phenomenon and that recovery was not just around the corner, all attempts at increasing postal salaries were abruptly abandoned and every effort was directed toward maintaining the *existing* levels of pay.

This was not easy. The job of the letter carrier, which had been very low on the employment totem pole during the years of inflation and prosperity, suddenly became infinitely attractive in the depressed economy of the thirties.[2] As the unemployment lines grew longer and grayer, and as the army of apple sellers swelled in numbers, the letter carrier, who had always been scandalously underpaid, found himself being accused of being a government parasite living off the misery of his fellow man!

People, stunned and embittered by the disastrous turn of events which had impoverished them, turned in blind rage against the federal government. Since the letter carrier, by reason of his uniform, was the most easily identifiable representative of the government, and, because of the nature of his job, the most accessible, he was subjected, particularly in the more depressed neighborhoods of the country, to considerable abuse and, at times, was threatened with physical violence.

---

[2] Ironically enough, the Post Office was and still is the major beneficiary of this state of affairs. During those years of panic and depression the level of ability and education of those who took the civil service examinations for Post Office jobs rose higher than it had ever been or ever has been since. Many of the recruits who joined the service in those days have survived to become the most respected postal professionals of today, and some of the greatest improvements in service techniques have been developed by the men who were forced by economic conditions to seek postal employment in the 'thirties.

The Administration and the Congress were, if nothing else, extremely sensitive to the moods and desires of a rebellious and often unreasonable populace and governmental emphasis was on "postal retrenchment," with a growing insistence on drastic cuts in government salaries.

Herbert Hoover's Postmaster General, Walter F. Brown, was up against the gun as postal revenues declined from $705,500,000 in fiscal 1930 to $588,100,000 in fiscal 1932, with no appreciable decline in postal expenditures. The postal "deficit" rose from $98,000,000 in 1930 to $206,000,000 in 1932 and, since 78 per cent of all postal expenditures go into salaries, and since most of the other expenditures are protected by long-term contracts, the pressure to cut the pay of postal workers grew by the day. This was the only apparent means of reducing postal expenditures.

The National Association of Letter Carriers took the quite logical position that the answer to the depression was not to *cut* salaries but to *raise* them, thereby increasing the purchasing power of the worker and repriming the nation's economic pump. Although I am convinced that, theoretically, this is the proper answer to any economic recession, I must admit in all fairness that during those days of blind panic nothing short of mass psychiatry could have done any good. The American people came very close to losing their faith in the American way of life. Those who did have a supply of money refused to spend it. They withdrew their funds from the banks, weakening the entire financial structure of the nation, and adding materially to the economic debacle which they were trying to avoid.

In such a febrile climate there was little chance of making the calm voice of reason heard above the terrified shrieks of a badly stampeded populace. President Gainor and his cohorts were forced to fight a purely defensive battle to protect the membership of the NALC from wholesale calamity.

The first step in the projected evisceration of federal employees was taken when the Congress, at the urging of President Hoover, inserted in the Appropriations Act for the fiscal year ending June 3, 1933, a section entitled "The Economy Act." This act was designed to save money in the government by taking it out of the hides of federal employees.

The legislation enabled the Postmaster General to instruct all postmasters to hold up all promotions, automatic or otherwise, in their offices except the few that were mandatory by law. This broke all the rungs on the career man's ladder of advancement. It also postponed indefinitely any hopes that substitute carriers might have of advancing to the ranks of regular letter carriers. They were expected to do the work of regulars at a wage of sixty-five cents an hour.

But, bad as they were, these were not the worst of the bill's provisions. The worst feature was the authorization of so-called "furloughs"—or lay offs without pay aggregating one month during the year. This, of course, amounted to an 8½ per cent pay cut for all postal employees.

While in this minatory mood the Congress also inserted in the economy bill provisions calling for reduction by one-half of the extra compensation for night work, and compulsory retirement immediately upon reaching the retirement age.

This legislation was based on a series of false premises. The first of these was that the postal service was operating inefficiently. This was simply untrue. According to the *Monthly Labor Review* of the U.S. Bureau of Labor Statistics for October 1932, the index of productivity of labor in the post office had increased from a base of 100.0 in 1908 to 171.8 in 1930. This is a remarkable increase in view of the scant improvements that had been made during those years in equipment and mail-handling techniques.

Another false premise was that postal employees were overpaid, and therefore could suffer a wage reduction without injury to themselves, to the service, or to their community. This was also untrue. The postal employee's salary had always lagged far behind the rises in the cost of living.[3] It traditionally compared unfavorably with that of civilian occupations demanding similar skills and responsibilities. From an economic point of view the main attraction of post office work was its security and regularity of employment. Postal employees felt safe in pledging their future incomes in order to buy homes as far as any surplus over living expenses permitted. This security was taken away from them by the Economy Act, and postal salaries were reduced at a time when they were, for the first time in history, reasonably comparable with those prevailing in private industry.

The third false premise was that the public demand for postal service had fallen off to a point where the work force could be greatly reduced. This was another misconception. The need for the service of postal employees does not diminish proportionately as the mail volume diminishes. Deliveries must still be maintained and the routes must be traveled even when the mail load is lighter. Schedules must be met. And because of the highly specialized skills of postal work, a trained employee force must be maintained to meet the requirements of the future.

The NALC protested vigorously against these measures. Secretary Finnan was particularly compelling in his arguments, but the effort was to no avail. The Economy Bill was signed into law, and on December 7, 1932, President Hoover, who had been decisively defeated in November by Governor Franklin D. Roosevelt, asked for an even further reduction in the pay of federal employees.

In his annual message to the Seventy-second Congress, Mr. Hoover pointed with alarm to the two-billion dollar national debt and urged sweeping retrenchment and higher taxes to meet the

---

[3] It still does!

situation.[4] He went on to say: "I will recommend that, after exempting the first $1,000 there should be a temporary reduction for one year of 11 per cent of that part of all government salaries in excess of the $1,000 exemption, the result of which, combined with the furlough system, will average about 14.8 per cent reduction in pay to those earning more than $1,000."

It is easy to be unfair about Mr. Hoover. In many respects he was the most maligned man ever to inhabit the White House.

There is no doubt of his nobility of purpose or his driving desire to serve his country. In normal times he would have been a great President. Indeed, if he had served in the place of either Harding or Coolidge, it is possible that the Great Depression might never have happened. But Mr. Hoover was a conservative traditionalist, and five minutes after the monumental crash of October 1929, every conservative traditionalist in the country was as out-of-date as the Conestoga wagon or the muzzle-loading rifle.[5]

There was in the Hoover Administration a surplus of timidity, an unwillingness to attempt the bold experiment. The traditionalist conservative economists were saying what they had always said, that the way to cure a depression was to batten down the hatches by cutting wages and reducing expenditures and then to wait out the storm. It occurred to very few people in or out of government that this depression was unique and far out of the area of reference of any practicing economist of that era. The storm

---

[4] There is a touch of irony in the fact that Mr. Hoover showed even more concern over a $2,000,000,000 national debt than Mr. Eisenhower shows about the present debt of approximately $295,000,000,000. The annual *interest alone* on the national debt today is about five times the entire size of the gross national debt of Mr. Hoover's day.

[5] Although I am a lifelong Democrat and never voted for Mr. Hoover, I rejoice in the fact that he has outlived both his calumniators and the calumnies they perpetrated against him, and that he has survived to become, as a senior statesman, one of the most respected citizens of the republic. Even those who, like myself, disagree with many of his basic philosophies cannot fail to be impressed by the dignity with which he bore adversity and with the good humor and moderation he shows in presenting his point of view.

was here to stay. It was not just a question of bad weather; it was a question of bad *climate*.

The traditionalists failed to learn from bitter experience. Every wage reduction they recommended just made matters worse. Each reduction meant that much less in the purchase of consumer goods. This inevitably led to layoffs in industry to such an extent that every dollar saved in wage reductions cost two dollars in unemployment relief. But the Administration continued to ask for more and more economies, more and more wage cuts, and thus succeeded in pouring more and more poison into an economic system that was already highly toxic.

Postmaster General Brown [6] at first tried to buck the trend within his own administration. In testifying before the House Appropriations Committee in 1932, he said: "Of course we could discharge people, but it has been our policy not to discharge regular civil service employees. By dismissing surplus personnel we would simply add them to the number of unemployed."

Eventually he caved in before Administration pressures and recommended a reduction in force of three thousand post office clerks and one thousand letter carriers.[7]

Although the Congress refused to tolerate dismissals of civil service postal personnel for economy reasons, it did go along with the administration's policy of reducing the force through mandatory retirements and failure to fill vacancies. During the years 1930 through 1932 the letter carrier force, for the first time since free city delivery was instituted in 1863, showed a sharp reduction in numbers. In December 1932 there were 1,577 fewer letter carriers than there had been in 1930. This represented a drop from 53,762 to 52,185.

---

[6] General Brown, a rather frosty individual, was widely known by the nickname "High Hat." He wore a silk hat a good deal and even wanted a custom-made government sedan constructed so he could get in and out without knocking his hat off.

[7] Cf.: *The Postal Record,* Vol. XLVI, No. 1 (January 1933), p. 1.

But, of far more importance, the lame duck Congress refused to follow the false economy proposals of their lame duck President and turned down every suggested further reduction in existing postal salaries.

The legislative history of the Hoover administration, as far as letter carriers were concerned, was not entirely one of gloom and doom. In 1931, just before the ceiling fell in, the Congress, mainly at the instigation of President Gainor of the NALC, passed legislation that gave postal workers, at long last, a forty-four hour work week.

The first eight-hour-day law (based on a six-day week) was passed in 1888. The second progressive step was taken in 1912 when the eight-in-ten-hours-a-day law was passed. It was not until 1931, nineteen years later, that the Congress reduced the working hours of postal workers to forty-four a week. This led the way to similar reductions in private industry, and earned Edward J. Gainor, the NALC national president, the accolade of "Father of the Shorter Work Week."

President Hoover signed the LaFollette-Kendall Bill into law on February 7, 1931.

This was the last major piece of constructive legislation for postal workers to be enacted for many years to come. The only victories of the immediate future were to be defensive ones, and there were to be precious few of those.

A long and difficult period lay ahead.

CHAPTER 14

THE THUNDERBOLT HITS

FEW people today remember that Franklin Delano Roosevelt was elected President of the United States on a relatively conservative platform. During his campaign he accused the Hoover administration of being "the greatest spending administration in peacetime in all our history" and charged it with piling bureau upon bureau, bureaucrat upon bureaucrat, commission upon commission. He promised the American people he would reduce government expenditures and, eventually, balance the federal budget.[1]

It is important to understand this background in order to comprehend what happened to federal employees in March 1933.

President Hoover, on the last day of his Administration, signed the Appropriations Act for fiscal 1934. Letter carriers and other federal employees barely had time to mop their brows after narrowly escaping a further wage cut at the hands of the Seventy-

[1] Speeches, Sioux City, Iowa, Sept. 29, 1932; and Albany, N.Y., July 30, 1932.

118

second Congress, as recommended by President Hoover, when, on the very next day, the sky really fell on them.

On March 4, in his inaugural address, President Roosevelt lowered the boom by announcing that he would "recommend measures that a stricken nation in the midst of a stricken world may require." He intimated strongly that far-reaching government economy would be one of those measures.

On the following day President Roosevelt called the Congress to convene in extra session on March 9, 1933.

Seldom has a Congress convened in such a spirit. Along with the Roosevelt landslide, a Democratic sweep of both Houses had also taken place. The mandate of the electorate was clear, and the Congress was not only prepared but openly eager to give FDR everything and anything he wanted. In most Congressional Districts of the country open opposition to the wishes of the President would have led to real trouble for a Congressman, perhaps even to a recall vote.

On March 10, in a special message to the newly assembled Congress, Roosevelt made the unprecedented request that he be granted, within certain wide limits, complete discretionary authority to prescribe the administrative details in the granting of pensions and other veterans' benefits and the fixing of wage rates of government workers in connection with certain economy legislation which he was recommending to the Congress.

Pointing to the accumulated national debt of five billion dollars, he declared that "for three long years the Federal Government has been on the road toward bankruptcy." [2] He continued:

> ... I request also the enactment of legislation relating to the salaries of civil and military employees of the Government. This would repeal the existing furlough plan, substituting therefor

[2] In later years, when FDR changed his mind on spending and economy, Republicans had a nasty habit of bringing up old statements like this. However, nobody listened to them much except other Republicans, and, in those days, they were hard to find.

a general principle and authorizing the Executive to make application of this principle. The proper legislative function is to fix the amount of expenditure, the means by which it is to be raised and the general principles under which the expenditures are to be made. The details of expenditure, particularly in view of the great present emergency, can be more wisely and equitably administered through the Executive.

This was a bombshell. It is inconceivable that the Congress at any other time in recent history would have acceded to such a sweeping request for an abrogation of its powers. But this was March 10, 1933, a unique moment in the nation's history. The Congress immediately rolled over and played dead.

The House on that same morning adopted a resolution unanimously authorizing the Speaker to appoint an Economy Committee of five members to consider and report on the President's message at any time by bill or message. Later on that day (March 10) Representative McDuffie, of Alabama, chairman of the Economy Committee, introduced a bill "to maintain the credit of the United States." Also on the same day, Senator Robinson, of Arkansas, the majority leader, introduced an identical bill in the Senate.

On the next morning the House, immediately upon convening, took up this extraordinary legislation under a rigid rule limiting debate to two hours. During the brisk interchange on the floor of the House serious doubts were expressed concerning the wisdom of granting such unheard-of powers to the President, but the steamroller was well oiled and moving inexorably in a direction the members were convinced was forward. Even the Republican floor leader, Representative Snell, of New York, advocated passage of the legislation, and the bill was approved without amendment by a vote of 266 to 138.

The Senate also took immediate action. Its Committee on Finance held a hearing on March 11 that was limited to just one hour. President William Green of the AFL, President Gainor of the NALC, and Secretary Thomas F. Flaherty of the Federation of Post Office Clerks [8] testified vigorously against the imposition of further wage cuts on government employees. They were arguing in a legislative vacuum. The committee took no notice of their testimony and reported out the Economy Bill in record time. The Senate took up the bill on March 13 and passed it, as amended, on March 15 by a vote of 65 to 13. It was immediately shot over to the House where the bill, with the minor Senate amendments, was approved, 373-19. On March 20 President Roosevelt signed the Economy Bill into law.

When one considers that it sometimes takes months for badly needed and almost universally approved legislation to wend its way through the congressional processes, it is amazing that this highly controversial and even revolutionary bill could progress from a mere gleam in the President's eye to full status as the law of the land in just nine days! The boys in the back room had obviously done considerable homework before coming to Washington.

The new law gave the President authority to determine an index figure of the cost of living for the first six months of 1928 which was called the "base period." After making this computation, the President was "directed" to compute an index of the cost of living during the last six months of 1932 and each six months thereafter. The percentage by which the cost of living index for any of these periods was found to be lower than the index for the base period would be the percentage of reduction in the salary to be paid federal employees during the succeeding six months. There was a stipulation, however, that such reduction would not exceed 15 per cent.

---

[8] Tom Flaherty, of San Francisco, California, was seriously ill at the time he testified, and died on June 3 of that year. He served for twenty years as legislative representative of the Post Office Clerks and was a man of great courage and integrity. He was widely respected by all postal employee organizations.

Roosevelt did not take long to determine the new basis of pay. He decided that the cost of living index for the six-month period ending December 31, 1932, was 21.7 per cent lower than the 1928 base period and ordered the maximum 15 per cent slash in the salaries of all federal employees.

Over and above the philosophical reasons that made this decision unwise, the cut was most unfair to postal workers because, (a) the "base period" used in the computation covered a period when the era of wonderful nonsense was at its height and living costs were comparatively astronomical, and (b) postal salaries during the base period were demonstrably low as compared with those in private industry, but the Roosevelt formula assumed that they had been adequate and in line with comparable salaries elsewhere.

However, the White House had made its decision and there was no appeal. Letter carriers took faint hope from the fact that the reduction would last only until June 30, 1934 (the limit originally prescribed by the law), and that remedial legislation would be forthcoming at that time. So they took another notch in their belts and, like all other good citizens, offered up their sacrifice on the altar of the commonwealth.

The role of President Gainor during the month of March 1933 was difficult in the extreme. The psychological effect of this setback on a membership accustomed to legislative victories was considerable. The fact that the legislative reverse came immediately after the defensive victory at the tail end of the Hoover administration merely aggravated the disappointment of letter carriers in the field.

There is no doubt that Gainor was taken entirely by surprise at the sudden action of FDR and the Congress. And once the legislative ball was rolling, he found himself caught between a rock and a hard place. As president of a large and important union whose members were about to be grievously hurt, he was morally bound to make a vigorous protest against the proposed legislation. Conversely, as an old Washington hand, he knew the cause was hopeless and that any attempt on his part to protect his members would arouse hostility in the Congress and could weaken the prestige and popularity of letter carriers throughout the country. This prestige, in the long run, is the most valuable asset the letter carriers have, since it is readily negotiable into public opinion which, in turn, is negotiable into congressional support.

Knowing full well the predicament he was in, Edward J. Gainor took the only course an honorable man could take. He buckled on his armor and sailed into the fight.

Unfortunately he was not prepared for the *degree* of hostility with which he was met by the Senate Finance Committee when he testified on March 11, 1933. The committee had given only twenty-four hours' notice of its one-hour long hearing, and there was not time to ascertain the precise temper of its membership. Gainor was accustomed to a warm and even affectionate atmosphere before Congressional committees. He was understandably nonplussed when he found himself unexpectedly sparring with a buzz saw. Things went very badly indeed and it must be admitted that this occasion, through little or no fault of his own, was not Ed Gainor's finest hour.

The following excerpts from the official record of testimony at the hearing will illustrate the temper of the committee and the treatment Gainor received at its hands.

MR. GAINOR: .... Therefore I submit, Gentlemen of the Committee, that for Congress to institute a policy based primarily upon a desire to restore prosperity by reducing wages is fundamentally an error. . . .

SENATOR BARKLEY: If we are confronted with the alternative of reducing government expenditures or increasing taxes, which do you think would have the more depressing effect upon the country?

MR. GAINOR: I contend that neither one is necessary. I quote your own statement made in the Senate, Senator Barkley, wherein you directed attention to the decline in national income from nintey billion dollars to forty-five billion dollars.

SENATOR BARKLEY: Yes, but you must remember—

MR. GAINOR: (Interposing) Therefore, the prime purpose of the administration is to stimulate the economic processes of the government so as to expand production, whereby you may have more money from production out of which taxes, in the last analysis, have to be paid. The difficulty now is—and according to recent reports, that figure has dropped to thirty-eight billion dollars—you are confronted with the anomaly that for every dollar in every governmental subdivision you have attempted to save by cutting expenses, you have expended two dollars in unemployment relief. And there is no escape from it.

SENATOR CONNALLY: Mr. Gainor, I take it you are on salary with your Association?

MR. GAINOR: Yes, sir.

SENATOR CONNALLY: Has your salary been reduced?

MR. GAINOR: No, sir.

SENATOR GORE: How much is your salary?

MR. GAINOR: It is $6,000 a year.

SENATOR CONNALLY: Don't you feel you ought to make some sacrifice along with everybody else in this time of depression?

MR. GAINOR: Speaking from a personal standpoint I would be willing to do it. But, as an example, I abhor it.

SENATOR CONNALLY: You have not reduced your salary any, have you?

MR. GAINOR: Well, I, of course, have the shining example of the Supreme Court judges.

SENATOR CONNALLY: Well, you understand that we have reduced our own salaries as senators and members of the House?

MR. GAINOR: Yes. And when we meet at our next convention we may do it. However, my opinion is that our organization, or our membership, will be opposed to it because of the example it would set. We have not reduced the salaries of our employees in our offices, and we have ten of them.

SENATOR CONNALLY: Well, you will not do it if you can prevent it, will you?

*   *   *

SENATOR CONNALLY: Why should federal employees be the only people in the world who do not take any reduction during these hard times?

MR. GAINOR: Because I think you ought to be convinced by now that the wage reduction policy is, as it has proven, a dangerous if not a fatal blunder, and you will have to reverse your policy before you can have any chance of starting prosperity again.

SENATOR CONNALLY: Then I take it you would rather have a few people drawing full wages and a large number out on the bread line?

MR. GAINOR: No. What we need is food and clothing and shelter. And we must expand into luxuries, and produce and sell automobiles, and get the country once more into a condition of enjoying purchasing power and using it. . . .

SENATOR GORE: Then you think the farmers of the country ought to produce and sell corn at ten cents a bushel and cotton at five cents a pound in order to maintain the government employees?

MR. GAINOR: The farmer is a manufacturer. He retains his individualism, and consequently he must take the vicissitudes that come from an individualistic business.

SENATOR CONNALLY: That is about all he has left, isn't it? Individualism?

MR. GAINOR: Yes, sir.

*   *   *

SENATOR GORE: You get a salary of $6,000 a year?

MR. GAINOR: Yes, sir.

SENATOR GORE: .... Don't you think you ought to be willing to take a reduction corresponding with the fall in the cost of living?

MR. GAINOR: If you want me to answer that question, let me say—

SENATOR GORE: (Interposing) Yes, I want you to answer it.

MR. GAINOR: I am going to answer it, but please don't make me answer it categorically.

SENATOR GORE: But, you have not answered my question, whether you think your salary ought to be cut from 20 to 30 per cent to correspond with the reduced cost of living.

MR. GAINOR: On a basis of equality?

SENATOR GORE: Yes.

MR. GAINOR: Yes, sir. I shall answer that by saying certainly. But on the basis of public welfare, I say certainly not.

SENATOR GORE: Well, that means nothing to me. That means an answer of yes *and* no.

MR. GAINOR: It means everything to me.

SENATOR GORE: Yes, it means $6,000 a year to you.

*   *   *

SENATOR GORE: Do you think that if salaries of government employees were cut from 20 to 30 per cent that a single one of them would resign?

MR. GAINOR: No—well, I don't know whether they would resign or not, but I would like to say—

SENATOR GORE: (Interposing) Don't you think there are several million Americans who would be willing to take their places if they did resign?

MR. GAINOR: Are you going to confine your observation as a senator to the *immediate* effect of a wage cut?

SENATOR GORE: I am asking you some questions in order to get your views, *if you do not object,* and I would be glad to have an answer to them. . . .

MR. GAINOR: Let me answer that question briefly.

SENATOR GORE: Well, can't you answer it yes or no?

MR. GAINOR: Are you going to insist upon an answer, yes or no?

SENATOR GORE: Yes.

MR. GAINOR: Well, I don't feel I can properly answer it that way.

*   *   *

SENATOR GORE: There is no need for you to make a speech. . . . I am asking you the simple question whether you will take a cut or not.

MR. GAINOR: I stated I was predicating everything I said on the ground of the public welfare. On that ground I answer no.

SENATOR GORE: Isn't it really on the ground of *private* welfare? Do you feel free to advocate a cut in salaries when your own salary depends upon the good will of those people whose salaries are about to be cut? . . .[4]

The brutal unfairness of this inquisition is still apparent, even through the cold photography of print, without the reproduction of the original inflections of the senators.

On reviewing this testimony across a chasm of twenty-seven years, one can point to certain tactical errors that were made and certain weaknesses that are particularly apparent because the senators simply would not give Mr. Gainor the running room to state his very logical case.

Although subsequent history vindicated Gainor's stand, in that the New Deal eventually came around to accepting and promoting the selfsame philosophy he was advocating in his testimony, this was clearly not the time to insist upon a point of principle. Public opinion had forced Congress to reduce its own salaries and the members of both Houses were sore as boils about this turn of events. It was extremely unwise to cite the case of the Supreme Court's refusal to cut its salaries, since the senators and representatives were very resentful of this decision by a body which consisted of men appointed for life and not answerable to the electorate.

I might also point out that Senators Gore and Connally came from states that were, and are, primarily agricultural in character. President Gainor, goaded as he was by the unreasonable unfairness of the committee, made a tactical error in arguing that the farmer was a manufacturer and, since he refused to become unionized, had to pay for his insistence on individuality. This was old-line union thinking and had been a constant source of irritation to the farmers and their representatives in Washington for many years. To bring the subject up in the hysterical and bitter atmosphere that prevailed in Congress at this time was

[4] Testimony was reproduced in full in *The Postal Record*, Vol. XLVI, Number 4 (April 1933), p. 2. The italics are mine.

extremely unwise. But then, hindsight is so very easy after twenty-seven years, and it must be remembered that Gainor was, above all else, a human being and his reaction to senatorial brutality was extremely human. He was right in his thinking, and the Congress was wrong. His error was in *insisting* he was right before a tribunal that was not open to reason at that particular time.

Edward Gainor was not the first or the last man to become rattled under the overbearing cross-examination of Senator Tom Connally. Senator Connally was a master of the *non sequitur*,[5] and despite the many great and statesmanlike contributions he made to the safety and welfare of his country, he could, when aroused, be as brutal and as intimidating as a barroom bully with a broken beer bottle in his fist.

When the debate was over, President Gainor knew he had failed to make a good impression before the committee and he was deeply depressed about it. However, with him intellectual honesty was a fetish, and he insisted on having his entire testimony reproduced in *The Postal Record* without comment.

From a political point of view this was a mistake. The membership was stunned and angry at the unexpected reversal of their fortunes and was in no mood to read the testimony with understanding or sympathy. For the first time since Mr. Gainor became president of the NALC in 1915, highly critical communiques from local branches began to appear in the columns of *The Postal Record*. One of the most vociferous of these critics, incidentally, was my friend John H. Rehring, the correspondent of my own Cincinnati local. Although I had nothing to do with Rehring's free expression of opinion, it placed me, as a newly created national officer, in a rather awkward spot. However, Ed

---

[5] His vicious and meaningless remark about full wages and breadlines was a classic example of his technique. Senator Gore of Oklahoma was one of the two blind men serving in the Senate and was known for his acerbity. As National Secretary Mike T. Finnan once said of him: "You could shave yourself with his tongue."

Gainor understood the situation and two years later proved his bigness of spirit by supporting me in my successful bid for election to the Executive Board, the policy-making body of the NALC.

Like a cloud on the horizon as large as a man's hand which eventually develops into a destructive thunderhead, the debacle of March 11, 1933, before the Senate Finance Committee had far-reaching effects. Although he served honorably and efficiently as national president until 1941, Ed Gainor's control over the letter carriers was never again as strong as it had been previous to that occasion.

And among those who knew him best there was a definite feeling that the unfair and uncalled-for verbal trouncing he took from the members of the committee on that day killed something inside him. He was, even at that time, an elderly gentleman with his well-deserved honors thick upon him, and he had been treated with insolence and disparagement by senators who should have known, and did know, better. It was a disillusioning and embittering experience and there is little wonder that it took its toll of Ed Gainor.

CHAPTER 15

AVE ATQUE FARLEY

JAMES A. FARLEY, who was President Roosevelt's Postmaster General for eight years, holds a position unique in postal history. Despite the fact that he held many views diametrically opposed to those generally held by postal employees and initiated many policies which most employees felt were inimical to their best interests, he was, and still remains, one of the most beloved personages ever to appear on the postal scene.

As far as letter carriers were concerned, this was due more to what he *was* than to what he *did*. As Postmaster General he was an official of absolute integrity and, like it or like it not, you knew precisely where you stood with him. He announced his philosophy boldly and succinctly at the very beginning of his administration and he left no doubt as to that being the way things were going to be. He announced that he was in favor of running the post office on a self-sustaining basis. While he did not succeed entirely in achieving this end, he never relented in his efforts and he did manage to reduce the postal "deficit" from $206,000,000 to $41,000,000.[1]

Also, it must be remembered that as chairman of the Democratic National Executive Committee in the midst of a depression, Jim Farley had a hungry party to feed. The Democrats had been kept away from the public trough for twelve years and demands for patronage were constant and insistent. Farley was always (and still is) an outspoken advocate of the spoils system and he practised what he preached. In his very first year in office he fired 1,500 Republican postmasters and replaced them with deserving Democrats. He was an outspoken and formidable foe in 1938 of the Ramspeck-O'Mahoney Act, which was designed to perpetuate Democratic postmasters in office in case of a change in administration. And yet he is still a welcome guest at every national convention of postmasters. (It will be interesting to see if Postmaster General Summerfield, who, in contrast to Mr. Farley, has been outstandingly tolerant of postmasters belonging to the opposite political faith, will retain the same affectionate regard for the same length of time after he retires from office.)

Jim Farley also held the line against postal promotions as long as the Economy Law was in effect and, when it was lifted, he saw to it that mostly Democrats were recognized when promotions were handed out. From a theoretical point of view, this was obnoxious to postal supervisors and rank-and-file postal employees, yet Farley was always received warmly at their

[1] Using the Kelly Law, which removes from postal accounting certain public welfare expenditures which should be borne out of general taxation rather than out of postal receipts, as a yardstick, Mr. Farley could and did claim a "profit" rather than a "deficit" during several fiscal years. The Kelly Act is still the law of the land. During the early years of his administration Mr. Summerfield chose to ignore its accounting principles because he thought the law charged too much money off to public welfare. However, since recent Congressional thinking has shown a tendency to charge much more off to public welfare than the Kelly Law allows, the Summerfield administration would probably be glad to settle for it now, anytime.

gatherings and is still regarded with real affection by most postal workers.

The fact that there was no hypocrisy about the man got through to every level of the employee force. His word was as good as his bond and he would make even the most unpopular decisions swiftly and unequivocally, without trying to pass the buck to someone else. And of course, he has always been an intensely warm human being who instinctively presented to almost all postal personnel a "father image" which they gratefully accepted. A family may disagree with the opinions and actions of the paterfamilias and still retain intact its affection for him. This was, by and large, the situation that existed in the Postal Establishment when Jim Farley was Postmaster General.[2]

Thus, when further legislation affecting adversely the pay of postal workers was passed into law, very little of the employees' resentment rubbed off on Farley, even though such legislation could never have been passed without his acquiescence.

And it was not long before another legislative body blow was aimed at the postal workers' vitals. On April 20, 1933, President Roosevelt submitted estimates to the Congress for the Independent Offices Appropriations Bill for fiscal 1934. This was necessary since this Appropriations Bill, because of a large supply item, had failed of passage during the Seventy-second Congress.

This seemed like a routine and innocuous business until Budget Director Douglas suggested, as an economy measure, that heads of departments be invested with authority, in cases where the number of their employees exceeded service requirements, to furlough employees on a rotative basis without pay, not to exceed ninety days, during the fiscal year beginning on July 1. Douglas also recommended that retirement of all federal employees be made mandatory after thirty years of service. This, according to

[2] Former Postmaster General Farley, a close personal friend, dedicated the NALC building in 1952, at my invitation. He took the place of Postmaster General Donaldson, who was not invited to participate.

Representative Buchanan of Texas, chairman of the Appropriations Committee, was part of a campaign to reduce the federal employee force by at least 25 per cent. (The fact that it would not only add to the unemployment rolls but would also automatically eliminate thousands of the most valuable and experienced employees in the prime of their lives and at the height of their value to the government apparently did not occur to Congressman Buchanan.)

The bill, with these provisions embodied in it, came up for consideration by the House on May 10. The Roosevelt steamroller was still in excellent condition and the legislation was discussed under a drastic rule which forbade any amendments save those emanating from the committee itself.

During the debate there was practically no mention of the compulsory retirement features of the bill either in the House or in the Senate. As a matter of fact, in the House an unprecedented and highly dangerous procedure was adopted whereby even the *reading* of the compulsory retirement provisions in the bill was waived. As a result, many members did not know what injustices they were perpetrating both on experienced postal personnel and on the postal service itself when they voted for the bill on May 12, 249 to 118.

The Senate made a half-hearted attempt to ease the retirement provisions of the bill but collapsed before the Roosevelt steamroller when the legislation went to conference. The furlough and compulsory retirement provisions were in the Independent Offices Bill when it passed both Houses on June 16, 1933. President Roosevelt, who had previously agreed to limit the wage cuts of federal employees to 15 per cent, signed the bill into law on the same day it was passed.

The unexpected furlough provision of the Independent Offices Bill was enthusiastically put into operation by the postal administration, which ordered rotative furloughs of nine days for the September quarter. This reduced the letter carriers' pay level to the level of 1916.

The 1933 NALC convention in Atlantic City was relatively stormy and President Gainor was forced at several points to employ his gavel and his silver-tongued eloquence somewhat lavishly in order to quell incipient mutiny among some of the more embittered delegates. However, the feelings of the letter carriers were somewhat mollified by the appearance of Postmaster General Farley at their convention. Farley's speech gave to the delegates more hope than they had received from the White House in nine months. Among other things, Mr. Farley promised that the hated furloughs without pay were on their way out, a statement of policy which brought down the house. However, he reiterated his intention to run the mail business in such a way as to reduce the "deficit" to "endurable proportions." This did not entrance the delegates, because every attempt thus far to make the "deficit" endurable had tended to make the job of letter carrier more unendurable. (The fact that President Roosevelt, after consulting the cost-of-living index, had extended the 15 per cent wage cut until December 31, 1933, did nothing to improve the delegates' spirits.)

When January 1934 rolled around, the orange blossoms had begun to wilt a little and the honeymoon between FDR and the Congress was beginning to show some signs of strain. There is no doubt that the country had been in dire need of a strong hand at the helm, and many of the revolutionary measures of the famous "first hundred days" would have been impossible if the President had been impeded by parliamentary bickering. But the ruthlessness of the Congressional steamroller had exacerbated the feelings of many of the members. The "hundred days," after all, were over, and the Congress was beginning to make plans for the recovery of some of the prerogatives it had so subserviently voted over to the Executive Branch.

The Administration, flushed by its almost unbroken string of victories in both Houses of the Congress, underestimated the growing spirit of independence on Capitol Hill.

In his message of January 4, 1934, Roosevelt had this to say about postal wages:

> I have recommended (for the fiscal year beginning July 1, 1934) a flat restoration of 5 per cent or one-third of the 15 per cent reduction. I have asked also for authority to restore such portions of the balance of the 10 per cent as may be warranted by a possible increase in the cost of living.

The NALC, through President Gainor and Secretary Mike Finnan, presented to the House Appropriations Committee, on January 7, a most compelling "Memorial" disputing the President's figures on the cost-of-living index and giving in detail all the reasons why a full restoration of federal employees' wages should be made immediately. This was a remarkable document, the first truly scholarly presentation ever made by a postal union in a wage dispute. Although it had almost no effect on the ultimate action of the House Committee, it was to serve a very useful purpose as far as senatorial thinking was concerned.

The House Committee reported out the Appropriations Bill with most of the Roosevelt recommendations intact. However, when the legislation was brought up for consideration on the floor, there was trouble. With their usual confidence the House leadership insisted on a "gag" rule which would deny members the right to vote directly on the economy measures (those which affected the pay of postal workers) in the bill. This stirred up the latent spirit of rebellion in many of the members who had begun to doubt the wisdom of allowing the constitutional rights of the Congress to wither away under the blazing heat of expediency. The debate on the "gag" rule was sharp and bitter and, when the vote was taken on January 10, the controversial and almost unprecedented provision was passed in the House by an extremely close vote of 197-192. This was the real battle on the issue. The Appropriations Bill was then passed by a voice vote.

The debate in the House was warmed up considerably by the fact that, on the day before the vote was taken, FDR announced that he was continuing the 15 per cent wage cut until July 1, 1934, the beginning of the new fiscal year.

This decision put the Administration in an impossible position. The controversial National Industrial Recovery Act (NIRA) had been signed into law on the previous June 16,[3] and the government was exerting enormous pressure on civilian employers to maintain high wages and to raise them even higher in order to prime the economic pump. Thus, the decision of the President to continue the 15 per cent salary *decrease* for federal employees was exploited widely as proof that the government was not following its own preachments. It was difficult, if not impossible, for the New Deal Administration to escape the charge of discrimination against its own employees and treating them as second-class citizens. What was sauce for the goose was definitely not sauce for the New Deal gander, or even its "propaganda."

The Senate did not prove as tractable as the House. On February 12, 1934, the Senate Appropriations Committee reported out the 1935 Independent Offices Appropriation Bill with some highly significant changes. The bill called for immediate restoration of 5 per cent of the 15 per cent wage cut, retroactive to February 1, and for an additional 5 per cent restoration to become effective on July 1. The bill provided for restoration of automatic promotions and authorized the President to restore more of the wages of postal employees if the cost of living rose any higher.

This bill passed the Senate by a 41-40 vote.

While this issue was in the balance, other troubles arose to plague the postal administration and the White House. On

[3] The Supreme Court declared it unconstitutional, May 27, 1935.

March 2, Postmaster General Farley felt compelled to issue an order calling for compulsory four-day furloughs without pay for all postal employees in the quarter ending on June 30. He also prohibited any vacations for employees in that three-month period.

This, understandably, did not sit well with letter carriers who had been given the joyous news at their national convention just six months previously that compulsory furloughs were a thing of the past.

General Farley's reasons were understandable from his point of view. The Post Office Department operates under congressional appropriations and must either live within them or get a supplemental appropriation to cover additional expenses. Failure to live within the budgetary limitations is a criminal offense and General Farley, wedded as he was to the economy principle, chose to live within what appropriations he had rather than to seek a supplementary sum from the Congress.

Two days after Farley's new furlough order was published, President Roosevelt threw the fat right smack in the middle of the fire. On March 5 he said: "The thing to do is to get more people to work. Every examination I make and all the information I receive lead me to the inescapable conclusion that we must now consider immediate cooperation to secure *increases* in wages and shortening of hours."

That did it. A roar went up in the nation's press from one end of the country to the other. The Administration had long since abandoned its budget-balancing philosophy and was pouring out money at a rate unprecedented in history in order to make reasonably paid work in other fields, and the only employees in the country who were expected to rejoice in peons' wages were the federal employees. Some newspapers went so far as to intimate that the Administration's indifference to the plight of government employees was based on the fact that they were forbidden to participate actively in pro-New Deal political activity. The fact that 26,000 postal employees had already been cut by New Deal economies from the payroll, thereby adding to the unemployment rolls at a serious cost to the efficiency of the postal service, underlined the double standard under which the Administration was operating at this point. Congressmen were hearing things from their constituents and, after all, 1934 was an election year.

When the bill as amended by the Senate was brought up for consideration by the House, the leadership wheeled out the steamroller once more and tried to introduce another "gag" rule which would, without debate, express House disagreement *in toto* with the Senate amendments and send the legislation into a conference among hand-picked members from both Houses. But this time the steamroller had run out of gas. The House was sick and tired of "gag" rules and White House dictation. It was sick and tired of seeing the Postmaster General sitting in the first row of the gallery keeping score, for future reference, of each man's vote. The "gag" rule was rejected by a whopping vote of 247-169. The House then agreed to send the bill to conference, after first going on record as favoring the pay restorations as voted by the Senate.

After considerable wrangling as to the provisions of the Senate and House versions of the bill, both Houses, on March 26, passed the legislation in virtually the same form as that approved by the Senate.

On the very next day President Roosevelt, in a sharply worded message, vetoed the bill.

FDR was fresh out of his usual magic that day. Just a couple of hours after the veto was received, the House overrode it by a vote of 310 to 72, and on the next day the Senate did likewise, 63-27.

This was a stirring victory for the NALC and the other postal unions and a sobering setback for the New Deal Administration in that it served notice that Congress would no longer be an automatic pushover for anything and everything the White House wanted.

There was one more victory to be won before spring that year was loosed from winter's traces. On April 14 the Postmaster General proved he could read the handwriting on the wall as well as, if not better than, the next man. On that date he issued an order rescinding the compulsory furloughs without pay which he had ordered six weeks earlier.

CHAPTER 16

CROSSING THE RUBICON

THE tide of events which started to favor the letter carriers and other federal employees in 1934 continued to flow their way in 1935.

President Roosevelt on January 7, 1935 submitted the federal budget to the Congress and, in his accompanying message, urged complete restoration of the pay cut, effective July 1. In their newly found spirit of independence the Congress did not think this quite good enough. The late Senator Pat McCarran of Nevada, a consistent champion of the postal employee, insisted that the restoration of wages be made retroactive until January 1. However, at the suggestion of South Carolina Senator Jimmy Byrnes, McCarran agreed to a compromise by which complete restoration under the 1936 Appropriations Act would be retroactive only until April 1. The Senate then passed the Appropriations Act as amended, adding extra funds to pay for the retroactive features incorporated by McCarran.

In the House, Chairman Buchanan of the Appropriations Committee fought desperately against the retroactive clause favored by the Senate but his opposition was crushed under the forensic attack of Representative Jim Mead of New York, who led the battle on the floor for federal employees. The House voted overwhelmingly to concur in the Senate's retroactive amendment and President Roosevelt, having learned his lesson in the preceding year regarding the temper of the Congress in these matters, signed the bill into law on February 13, 1935.

The Appropriations Bill contained some other features which were of vital importance to postal employees. It eliminated the right of the Executive Branch to set wages in accordance with the cost-of-living index. It also eliminated the suspension of automatic and other promotions in post offices and made the detested payless furloughs a thing of the past.

This was a great victory, and it was won through unremitting hard work on the part of many people, particularly President Ed Gainor, Secretary Mike Finnan, and Assistant Secretary Clarence F. Stinson.

But it must be remembered that this victory, important as it was, succeeded only in returning postal wages to the level of 1925. And there they were destined to stay for far too many years.

There was a final victory for Ed Gainor and that was one very close to his heart: the passage of the forty-hour week law.

This legislation was introduced in March 1935 by Congressman Mead, who pointed out, with accuracy, that the forty-four-hour week was no longer acceptable in private industry. The bill was passed by the House without objection or debate on June 3. The bill was then taken up by the Senate, and during the hearings before the Committee on Post Office and Post Roads President Gainor distinguished himself by his brilliant and compelling testimony. This was to be expected, since the forty-hour week was Ed Gainor's "baby." He had led the fight for the shorter work week in the American Federation of Labor and he obviously knew far more about the subject than anyone else in the hearing room.

However, the issue was still in doubt because both the President and his Postmaster General were in opposition, and the spirit of rebellion against the Administration did not flourish as luxuriantly in the Senate as it did in the House. However, the letter carriers' "educational committee" was in fine fettle when, at last, they approached Postmaster General Farley with their arguments. Farley listened with an open mind and was convinced. On July 3, with the candor which characterizes only men of superior stature, he boldly reversed his field and announced that both he and the President were withdrawing their opposition and now favored the legislation. After that, passage was almost automatic, and the forty-hour week for federal employees became law when FDR signed the bill on August 14.

The years that followed were, in many ways, painful to Ed Gainor. Although it is inevitable that there must be a hiatus in congressional activity after a substantial victory such as the complete pay restoration, any administration in any organization must perforce keep moving and thinking toward the future. There should be no marking time, no mere treading of the water. You must either swim strongly upstream or you will be carried backward by the tide.

There is no doubt that the Gainor administration was growing older. Ed Gainor himself had served as president of the NALC since 1915 and had held national office almost since the turn of the century. The victories of 1934 and 1935 seemed to exhaust him and many of the other members of the so-called "Old Guard" who surrounded him. The old fire began to flicker, the drive to diminish, and each year passed without any major legislative victories. War broke out in Europe, and as the United State began to prepare itself in case of involvement, the depression slipped into the past and the cost of living began a steady climb. Letter carriers who were being paid 1925 salaries

grew more and more restive with each increase in the cost of
living. They were grateful for the victories of yesteryear but the
remembrance of things past does not buy groceries. Among the
"Young Turks" in the NALC, who saw shipyard workers getting
wages which made the letter carrier look like a serf, the measured eloquence of their national president began to lose its
charm. Uneasy stirrings began to make themselves felt in the
hinterland.

There was a growing belief that Gainor and his cohorts were
losing their militancy, that they were more interested in basking
in the sunlight of departmental approval than they were in getting
the job done for letter carriers. Much of this criticism was unfair, but it did exist. Demands for new blood at the national
level became more audible, more frequent.

It would be pleasant to say that the Old Guard accepted this
display of critical vigor among the membership with good grace.
However, this cannot, in fairness, be said, for the latter years of
the Gainor administration were marred by outbursts of ill-will
and bad temper on both sides. The Young Turks pressed perhaps too strenuously for advantage, unmindful of the feelings
of their elders. The Old Guard, on the other hand, died hard
and bitterly.

Trouble for the Old Guard began to take serious form in 1938
and 1939 when twenty-seven branches, led by Branch 39, at
Indianapolis, succeeded in forcing a national referendum, which,
if successful, would amend the NALC constitution so that national officers would be elected directly, by mailed ballots, rather
than by convention.

This so-called "Hoosier Amendment," which was aimed
directly at the Old Guard, never had a chance, and was defeated
by 36,331 votes to 10,231. However, there were some significant features to the controversy. In the first place, the uprising
began in President Gainor's home state where, ordinarily, he
would be expected to have overwhelming support. (The refer-

endum vote was defeated in Indiana by a vote of 841 to 679, a ratio far less than that which pertained nationally.) In the second place, feelings in this referendum ran so high that a record vote was recorded, 72 per cent of all the members having participated. And third, the Old Guard, during this controversy, lost a good deal of its Olympian calm and responded to opposition with a kind of shrill anger which rubbed many of the rank and file members the wrong way. This was unnecessary and unwise, since the referendum was doomed from the start.

Actually, the direct election proposal, whenever it arises in any large organization, is a tricky one to handle. On the surface it seems to be reasonable, and it gives its proponents an admirable opportunity to talk about democracy in action. In reality, it is the very opposite of democracy, and there is no better way to wreck a union or any other national organization than by its adoption.

Here's why: Direct election of officers leaves the door wide open for demagoguery and irresponsible electioneering. It would make it possible for a cynical candidate with money (perhaps supplied by an outside source inimical to the best interests of the union) to cause havoc among the membership, while responsible officers or candidates would have no means of competing adequately with his campaign. If it were necessary to go to the political hustings in this manner every two years, the succession of inflammatory contests would cause irreparable rifts among the members and destroy the solidarity which is essential to successful and effective unionism.

It is inaccurate and misleading to cite, in support of the direct vote proposal, the method in which the President of the United States is elected. The candidates of both major political parties are nominated by convention, and this insures a solid element of responsibility in their selection. (As we all know, the ability of a candidate to win the popular vote in primaries has little effect on his selection as the party candidate.) The electoral college system also acts as a safeguard against a sudden hysterical outburst of sentiment on the part of the public resulting in an ill-considered popular decision which everyone would bitterly regret. However, the arguments against this type of proposal are more subtle and more complicated than the one big argument in its favor. This is what makes it so dangerous.

I bring this out to illustrate that the 3½-1 majority against the "Hoosier Amendment" did not necessarily reflect the ratio of pro-Gainor sentiment in the NALC at that time. There were many letter carriers who were ready to oppose Gainor, but who voted against the referendum because they felt the ends did not justify the means. The good of the order was more important than any feelings of impatience they might have felt against their leaders.

The referendum voting ended on April 5, 1939, and the wounded feelings which it created were carried into the NALC convention, in Milwaukee the following September.

To the average delegate, this convention was the most stimulating of all time, but to Ed Gainor and the Old Guard it was a nightmare. It was the Golden Anniversary Convention, marking the fiftieth anniversary of the NALC. Also, on the day before the convention opened (September 3, 1939), Great Britain and France declared war on Germany. When the convention was called to order, a spirit of tension prevailed.

No sooner had the first business session of the convention begun when an insurrection was ignited on the floor by a group of highly vocal nondelegates demanding to be heard. The convention hall immediately became a tumult of cheers, boos, and cries of "Throw them out," and President Gainor restored order only by threatening to call in the police to eject the troublemakers.

Several other occasions brought forth angry explosions, and the official report of the proceedings is studded with "boos" and other expressions of bad temper.

It must be pointed out that Ed Gainor's personality did not

help to quell these disturbances. He was always an exciting person, even in these, his declining years. His booming voice and his talent for the quick and appropriate phrase were a delight if you were on his team, as I was. But he did have a formidable capacity for the sharp and biting word, which wounded and sometimes antagonized those who sought to be his friends. During the 1939 convention we all felt that the president was inadvertently throwing gasoline on the smoldering fires. Certainly it is true that comparative calm would descend upon the gathering only when Vice-President William J. Gorman, a smooth and able diplomat from Brooklyn, took over the gavel.

The real fireworks broke out on the Wednesday afternoon of the convention when Resolution No. 70, which would have made it unconstitutional for any national officer to stand for re-election if he had reached his sixty-fifth birthday, was read to the delegates.

This was aimed directly at the Old Guard, right where they lived. If passed, it would have eliminated four of the top NALC officers, including Gainor, at one fell swoop, and would have numbered the days of several others who hovered around the proposed age limit.

A similar proposal had come up at the Oakland convention in 1931 and passage had been prevented only by the granting of certain concessions by the Old Guard. At that time two of the older national officers were jettisoned in order to permit the infusion of some new blood at the national level. In this way the other older officers were saved. However, the proponents of Resolution 70 in Milwaukee were in no mood to accept any compromise. It was all or nothing.

Brother Hugh Noonan of the Resolutions Committee no sooner had announced his committee's disapproval of the resolution, when clamor became endemic on the floor of the convention. The arguments were loud and angry, and there were ugly accusations that the Old Guard was monopolizing the only two microphones in the hall, so as to control the discussion. (Two other mikes were eventually set up in the rear of the hall, but they never did work efficiently.)

Amid some scenes of wild confusion the committee's disapproval was finally upheld by a voice vote and by virtue of the beleaguered president's fast gavel. As he finally banged the convention to order with his thunderous gavel, Gainor cried out in jubilation: "The old men are saved!"

And so they were—temporarily. However, the storm clouds were gathering fast and the sands in the Old Guard's glass were swiftly running out.

All of us on the national board felt relief when the convention was adjourned *sine die* on Saturday, September 9.

I might add that I was very much of a Gainor man, and although, like everyone else at the national level, I was aware of the toll that old age and years of devoted service had taken of our president, my loyalty did not waver. Certainly when I responded to a request to sing "God Bless America" to the convention in its waning moments I had no idea that in the next two years I myself would be catapulted into Ed Gainor's place as national president.[1]

Gainor was more of a fighter than he was a diplomat, and after the convention he scorned to mend his fences. He treated the unsuccessful attempt to oust him contemptuously, almost as if it had never happened, and he would not stoop to any attempt to conciliate those who had opposed him. It is always a mistake to underestimate the opposition, and nobody ever was beaten by overestimating it. This was no exception. The fires that had broken out in Milwaukee had not been quenched. They continued to burn in the field and no one at the national level was trying to put them out.

[1] If I had been politically ambitious at that time I would have refused the request to sing a solo. I don't sing that well.

Meanwhile, no progress was being made on the legislative front. The Old Guard desperately needed a victory of some kind but they could not produce anything that would convince the membership that they were still vigorous and enthusiastic. Salaries became more and more inadequate with each passing day, and dissatisfaction became rampant.

And I must sadly admit there was reason for such dissatisfaction. All of us at the national level had taken it for granted that Ed Gainor would prepare to retire before the 1941 convention. After his vindication in Milwaukee he had the opportunity to retire in a blaze of glory. I am convinced that he wanted to resign, but some members of the Old Guard, knowing their own organizational futures were intertwined with Gainor's, insisted that he keep on. They took the attitude that the national presidency should be considered Gainor's lifetime possession and, of course, that this right should be extended to themselves. In response to the Old Guard's goading, Ed Gainor made it abundantly clear that he had no intention of resigning, then or ever.

This caused a situation of great delicacy. We were all, as I have said, loyal Gainor men, but we owed an even greater degree of loyalty to the National Association of Letter Carriers and its 65,000 members.

There was no doubt that Gainor was reaching the end of his rope. He had served at the national level for almost four decades and he had spent his vigor lavishly in behalf of his beloved letter carriers. He could look back pridefully on a long list of achievements, including shorter labor hours; higher wages; retirement benefits; old age, injury, illness, and accident protection; increased promotions from the ranks; and liberalized Sunday and more widespread holiday observance. But the responsibility to serve the membership is a constant and a continuing one. Past achievements earn a man gratitude but they do not, of themselves, earn him indefinite continuance in high office. Ill health and old age had ravaged Ed Gainor until he was no longer able to serve the best interests of the letter carriers as their president. This was a bitter fact but it had to be faced. We would have been less than loyal to the membership if we did not face it.

When we would gather together at headquarters in Washington we found we were all too loyal and too discreet to bring the subject up. The tension became almost unbearable as we watched each other in silence, wondering what the next step would be, and who would take it.

Vice-President Bill Gorman finally broke the ice. As second in command, he was the logical choice to succeed Gainor as president. He finally called me in from Cincinnati for a conference and, in a tone almost of regret, announced that he felt compelled to make the race against the boss. He asked me to support him.[2]

I had to pray over that one. I was fond of Bill Gorman. He was a kindly person, a man of great talent and tact, but somewhat lacking in forcefulness. However, there was no doubt of his ability to serve as president. There was also no doubt that a change had to be made, and plans for that change had to be laid very soon. But it was tough to take a step that would hurt Ed Gainor, a man whom I loved like a father. However, the loyalty to the good of the order prevailed over every other consideration. I finally agreed to go along with Bill Gorman.

This put me out on a limb, since it was I who had to incur the wrath of my friends of the Old Guard by going out openly and helping to build up an organization among the branches for Bill Gorman.

However, an unexpected turn of events occurred soon after I had made my first extensive forays in Bill Gorman's behalf. The Old Guard considered Gorman one of themselves, and they

[2] Gorman was at that time in his fifties. There were four national officers who were over sixty-five years of age. They were President Gainor; Secretary Finnan; Charles D. Duffy, chief clerk of the NALC Sick Benefit Association; and L. E. Swartz, chief collector of the NALC Mutual Benefit Association.

immediately began to put pressure on him from every conceivable angle. He collapsed without warning.

At the semiannual meeting of the National Executive Board, which was held in Washington in January 1941, Gorman arose and, out of a clear blue sky, announced that he was withdrawing his candidacy. He added that he had been poorly advised and that, after due reflection, he found that he could not find it in his heart to oppose Ed Gainor.

I was stunned. I had been out leading a parade and suddenly found that it had turned down another street and that I was all alone, baton in hand, leading a bandwagon that had disappeared into thin air.

I looked around me. The members of the Old Guard seated around the table were looking at me with what seemed to me a bitter amusement. I was convinced that if someone took the trouble to explore the broad expanse between my shoulder blades at that moment he would have found protruding the nicely-tooled handle of a stiletto.

I decided then and there to cross the Rubicon. I looked them squarely in the eye and said: "Gentlemen, this is a painful statement to make but I feel it must be made. If Brother Gorman will not make the race for national president then I, here and now, announce my own candidacy for that position."

There was a dead silence as I got up from my chair and walked out of the room. When, at last, I turned around, I found that I was being followed. Six junior members of the Board had walked out with me: Rube Kremers, of Seattle; Jim Langan, of Pittston, Pennsylvania; Charles F. Fleming, of Baltimore; William F. McHale, of New York; Valentine J. Wells, of Milwaukee; and Ben Sparks, of Rushville, Indiana. We were known thereafter as "The Unholy Seven."

It took guts to take that walk with me and I shall forever be grateful for the action of those six men. After all, fifteen members of the Board stayed in their seats and remained on as members of the Gainor team. In walking out of the room the other six members of "The Unholy Seven" were laying their organizational futures on the line just as much as I was.

With that decision the die was irrevocably cast. First I rang up my closest and best adviser, Gertrude Dacey Doherty, and told her what had happened. (She was just as surprised as I was.) Then I sat down with my six supporters and started to map out a national campaign.

CHAPTER 17

END OF AN ERA

ONCE a man crosses the Rubicon he has to keep moving ahead or he will be ambushed from behind. Having made the decision to run for national president I decided to give it everything I had. There is no point in running unless you expect to win.

The first thing I did was to ask my friend, Francis J. Lang, president of the Cincinnati Branch of the NALC, to act as my campaign manager. This was a tremendously happy choice on my part, and Franny, who is now superintendent of delivery and collection in the Cincinnati Post Office, did a brilliant job of organizing branches all over the country. My young friend, John T. Donelon, also of Cincinnati, volunteered to act as my campaign secretary. I owe a great deal of my success to his devotion and ability.[1]

[1] John Donelon claims to be the direct descendant of Brian Boru, first king of all Ireland. I wouldn't be surprised. I have long since stopped being surprised at anything about John Donelon. When I was elected president of the NALC I took him with me to Washington as my administrative assistant and no one could have a more loyal or a more able friend and associate. However, it *is* funny how many Irishmen claim descent from kings. At times I think I am the only Irishman in America descended from the working classes.

Once the campaign came out into the open, there was a feeling akin to relief in almost every branch in the country. Letter carriers were being torn between their love for Ed Gainor and what they sincerely believed was best for the NALC, and breaking the ice with a frank declaration of candidacy snapped the tensions in the field.

Although nothing overtly antagonistic against me was said or done in the Washington office, I found myself placed very much in a deep freeze as far as the Old Guard was concerned. I had sinned against the light, and had stepped beyond the limits of forgiveness.

It must be said that, although Ed Gainor was at first wounded by my opposition, he never became bitter against me personally. He often said that if he had had the opportunity of choosing a successor he would have selected me. I think he meant this sincerely. I am proud of the fact that I never lost his friendship.

As the campaign gathered in strength and scope, however, opinion in the field began to solidify behind the Doherty campaign. The more I traveled around the country the more it became obvious that we were going to win. And, the more this fact became obvious the more I hoped and prayed that something would happen to persuade Ed Gainor to announce his retirement. I loved and respected the man and I did not want to subject him to the embittering experience of a defeat in a hand-to-hand political battle.

Meanwhile, things were indeed happening.

In December 1940, more than two hundred branches, led by Branch 1 (Detroit), and its able president, Ray Lieberman, signed a petition for a referendum demanding that the sixty-five-year-old age limit be placed on the candidacy of all national officers.

This was the same proposition as that which had been brought up and defeated at the Milwaukee convention in 1939. At that time Ed Gainor had shouted that the old men were "saved." Now the sands of their salvation were really running out.

Although I had no part in the planning of this referendum, I was, quite naturally, relieved that it was brought up at this particular time.

It gave Ed Gainor and the Old Guard their last opportunity to bow out of contention gracefully. They refused to do so, choosing rather to go down with the ship, with all guns blazing and with their tattered ensign flying.

It was obvious from the start that the referendum movement had enormous popular support. The Old Guard fought back with everything it had. The campaign was the most extensive and the most violent ever waged within the Association. There were no neutrals. You had to be either a Gainor man or an anti-Gainor man, and the choice was forced on the members by Gainor and the Old Guard itself. If a man proved to be anti-Gainor, no matter how high-minded and impersonal his reasons, he was condemned forever to outer darkness. In this contest, everything was placed squarely on a personal basis. To the Old Guard, Ed Gainor and the good of the order were one and the same thing. In their opinion anyone who disagreed was an ingrate, a scoundrel, and a traitor to the NALC.

It is the custom to turn over the columns of *The Postal Record*, the official NALC magazine, to arguments on both sides of every referendum question. Each side is supposed to have an equal opportunity to argue its case. *The Postal Record* was controlled by the Old Guard, however, and this rule was pretty thoroughly disregarded. The columns of the *Record* thundered against the referendum with unremitting vigor and with no pretense at fairness. For instance, there were sixty-nine letters concerning the referendum in the January and February issues. Fifty-one of those printed were strongly *against* the referendum, and only eighteen were for it. And those eighteen were invariably buried in the inside columns.[2] Anyone reading those letters would, quite naturally, surmise that the referendum was in for a decisive and humiliating defeat.

But, of course, this was only a reflection of the indignation and hysteria which had seized the Old Guard in the face of mutiny. When the votes were counted on April 5, 1941, it was found that the referendum had won by a vote of 26,583 to 23,838.

The result was close, but decisive. Just about ninety per cent of the members voted in the referendum, an all-time record percentage of participation.

Perhaps the most embittering result in the election was from Ed Gainor's home state of Indiana, which cast its vote against him, 723 to 658.

Looking back objectively on the decision of twenty years ago, I can say unhesitatingly that it was eminently wise. It is human nature for men in power to try to hang on to that power. It is also human nature to reject any suggestion that one is growing old. Furthermore, it is essential that ambitious young men have the incentive to work hard for their Association in the hope of some day succeeding to its highest positions. This incentive is killed when the old cling tenaciously to high offices. Every organization is invigorated by infusions of new blood, and if a union is not vigorous, it is nothing. I know I shall feel exactly the same way as I do now in 1967, when (God willing!) I shall reach the age of sixty-five.[3]

---

[2] Most of the letters created more heat than they did light. It was that sort of a campaign. However, one of the most reasoned arguments *against* the referendum, and therefore by inference against Bill Doherty, came from Jerome J. Keating who is now national vice-president of the NALC. As much as I would have liked Keating's support on this issue, his opposition did not affect my feeling for him in the least. Anyone who knows Jerry Keating knows that he always calls them as he sees them, and once the shouting died down, he became my closest friend and adviser and my most valuable source of support.

[3] Last January I was talking about this subject with Peter Cahill, secretary-treasurer of the NALC. Pete is scheduled for retirement at the 1960 national

The referendum, of course, amounted to my election, since it prevented President Gainor from seeking re-election at the Los Angeles convention which was scheduled to take place five months later. It left the Doherty campaign a virtually clear field, since there had been no other candidate opposing the Old Guard before the referendum vote was taken. Under Franny Lang's skillful direction, and with the devoted assistance of scores of friends and supporters, the campaign train kept chugging away.

The Old Guard had been in power so long that they were accused by many of operating a political machine within the NALC. It is a truism in politics that a machine is never defeated by a close vote. When reaction sets in to an extent sufficient to overcome the machine in power, it gathers momentum and finally overwhelms it. Those who had been timid before recognize the bandwagon when it rolls down the street and jump on it. This happened in 1941 in the NALC.

Naturally enough, feelings ran high during this historic Los Angeles convention. The Young Turks were feeling their oats; the Old Guard was licking its wounds. The Old Guard's attitude toward the Doherty forces was hostile, but when attempts were made to circumvent the wishes of the membership, as expressed in the April 1941 referendum, Ed Gainor was fair. He insisted on observance of the moral obligation to abide by the will of the majority. His intellectual honesty invariably prevailed over his personal feelings when the chips were down.

Although conditions at Los Angeles were not as riotous as they had been two years previously at Milwaukee, there was a considerable amount of indiscriminate blasting, and not a little determined sharpshooting during the proceedings. As chairman of the Resolutions Committee, Jerry Keating had an exhausting

---

convention, even though he has the vigor and vision of a youngster. Pete's reaction was typical of the man: "It was the smartest thing the Association ever did. Let the youngsters come into their own!"

time of it, but his good sense and calm personality rode through a constant storm.

The Doherty-for-President campaign came to its successful conclusion on the morning of September 6. I was elected president without opposition.[4]

But just before I was sworn in as national president there was a little surprise in store for me. My good and great friend, Dan Sullivan of San Francisco, the national treasurer, reported to the convention on the financial condition of the NALC. It seems that, through no fault of his own, the financial condition of the Association, to use a euphemistic expression, was none too good.

To put it quite bluntly, the frantic struggle to "save the old men" during the April referendum campaign had cleaned out the till.

This was news to me. President Gainor, in his biennial report, had insisted, as he always did, that the National Association of Letter Carriers was in excellent condition. Its membership was at an all-time high. There had been no reason to suspect incipient insolvency.

As I say, Dan Sullivan made this announcement almost immediately before Bill Riley, the installing officer, began to swear me in as national president.[5] It is hardly remarkable that I gulped a little nervously as I raised my right hand and took the oath of office.

---

[4] It was my great good fortune to be surrounded by a fine team of officers. William F. McHale was elected vice-president; Bill Gorman stepped down from vice-president to secretary; Dan Sullivan was re-elected treasurer; and Clarence F. Stinson was re-elected assistant secretary.

[5] Ohio has been called the "Mother of Presidents," and this applies to the postal service as well as to the White House. I am the second resident of Cincinnati to serve as national president of the NALC; in 1894 C. C. Couden also occupied the top position in the NALC. From 1901 through 1905 James C. Keller, from Cleveland, Ohio, served as president. The present president of the National Association of Postmasters, incidentally, is Hobart A. Wehking, postmaster of Cincinnati and, I might add, a good friend and a great leader.

So the Old Guard had the last laugh, after all. I had won the national presidency, but the union was stone broke. There was not even enough money to meet our financial commitments for the final quarter of the year.

It seems I had quite a job ahead of me.

CHAPTER 18

NEW MAN ON THE JOB

WHEN the Doherty family moved to Washington it represented just about the largest mass movement of humanity since the westward trek of the Mormons. When I say that we "moved to Washington," I am exaggerating. The capital city was in extraordinary turmoil because of the military emergency existing in October, 1941. Finding housing space for Mrs. Doherty, nine children, and me was an almost insoluble problem. The nearest we could get to bulging Washington was Catonsville, Maryland, about forty miles away. Since I did not own a car it was necessary to commute by train each day.

The day that I sat at the desk of the national president for the first time I had a very nasty shock. Awaiting my arrival was a letter from William Green, George Meany, and John P. Frey, trustees of the old American Federation of Labor Building in which we had our offices, asking us to vacate the premises as soon as possible!

160

So on the first day I showed up for work as national president I found that not only was the NALC broke, but it looked as if we were going to be thrown out in the street as well.

There were rumors at the time that this request by the leadership of the AFL was punitive against us because of the action of the Los Angeles convention. Nothing could be further from the truth. The fact of the matter is that the AFL was growing at a prodigious rate and the building was bursting at the seams. They simply needed the room.[1]

As a matter of fact, nobody could have been more considerate than Green, Meany, and Frey. The NALC had been among the original tenants of the building when it had been opened twenty-four years previously, and our relationship with the parent union was close and cordial. Bill Green often said that the AFL would never have been able to pay for the building during those early years of its existence had it not been for the rentals which the National Association of Letter Carriers and other postal unions were paying. As it turned out, it was absolutely impossible to find office space in Washington at that time and, when this situation became apparent, the AFL leaders were most tolerant of our predicament. They let us stay on until 1948, when we moved into another building owned by the AFL, at 1525 H Street, N.W. We remained there until January 1953, when we occupied our present building at 100 Indiana Avenue.

But in that October of 1941, the threat of being evicted from our quarters was a considerable worry, particularly since it arose at a time of financial insolvency.

I am an optimist by nature and I felt confident that we would be able to borrow the money to tide the NALC over until the per capita tax of $2.80 per member started rolling in during January. In this I was sadly mistaken. I had been accustomed to the comparatively warm and friendly banking atmosphere of

[1] The AFL membership at that time was over the four and a half million mark and had been increasing at a rate of 350,000 a year.

Cincinnati, and I did not realize that the banking fraternity in Washington ordered their affairs somewhat differently.

I went to see the bank with which the NALC had been doing business for more than half a century. I explained the situation facing us and told them we needed to borrow enough money to meet our payroll during the months of November and December.

To my surprise and consternation a chill descended so swiftly that I felt quick frozen, like a Birdseye steak. I was told in quite acid tones that the anticipation of a per capita tax could not in any sense be considered collateral, and that the loan was therefore refused.

On looking back over nineteen years with more objectivity than I could muster at that time, I still think this was a stupid decision. I might add that, once the per capita tax did come in and the crisis was averted, we changed banks. Since the NALC has prospered and grown, the original bank has made constant but unsuccessful overtures, seeking our business.

We were all stunned by this development. The five top officers, McHale, Gorman, Stinson, Sullivan, and I, sat down for an emergency conference. It was obvious that extraordinary austerity measures had to be undertaken immediately. Unanimously we decided to forego our salaries as national officers and return home to carry the mail along our respective routes until the crisis was relieved. This was a grim moment. Never was the NALC in more perilous shape. We were literally on the brink of bankruptcy, and the emergency measure we were contemplating, while necessary to our survival, would be extremely damaging to our prestige and influence.

I was in my office drafting a notice to the membership, outlining this emergency plan of action, when one of the most beautiful miracles of my life occurred.

Through the door came Mike Finnan, who had just retired as national secretary at the Los Angeles convention after serving twenty-four years in that position.

Mike, who was seventy-five years old at the time of his retirement, was one of the great gentlemen of the labor movement. He had been a member of the Old Guard, and he had opposed my candidacy, but he never became bitter against me. He was always a helpful friend despite our political disagreements.

Mike Finnan sat down and said: "Bill, I have an idea you may be needing some money."

I told him that this was the understatement of the year. I outlined the desperate situation to him. He nodded his head sympathetically. After all, he knew the situation even better than I did. "Bill," he said, "maybe I can be of some assistance. I have a little money laid aside—my life's savings, as a matter of fact. It's yours for the asking. Would $25,000 help you?"

I almost kissed him. His question was somewhat like asking a man in the condemned row whether a governor's reprieve would be useful to him!

Somehow I got the message over to Mike that $25,000 would indeed be very useful. The loan was negotiated on the spot, and through it the financial situation of the National Association of Letter Carriers was saved.

I am proud to say that the loan was repaid within three months, and that the NALC has never looked back since that day. We have grown in numbers and prosperity, but it is very doubtful if we could have made that progress—or even have survived at all—if Mike Finnan had not come forward as he did on that day.

Mike died seven months later and I am not ashamed to admit that I cried like a baby when I followed his body to the grave. There is so much good to be said about Mike, but to me he is the man who loved the letter carriers so much that he risked his entire life's savings to help them when the banks refused to risk as much as a penny. I can think of no better epitaph.

I shall always be grateful, too, for the wonderful loyalty and cooperation I received at that time from the NALC headquarters employees, particularly Harry J. Coffman, who was the office manager, and Mrs. Amy Sigourney. These people had known no other president but Ed Gainor, and at first I was worried about the reception I would receive at their hands. A disloyal office staff can be ruinous to a new man on the job. I found, to my delight, that my fears were unfounded. No one could ask for a more devoted team than the one I inherited when I assumed office.

I did find, however, that these people were overworked and underpaid. The National Association of Letter Carriers had been in the forefront of the successful struggle to win a forty-hour week for the working man, but they had neglected to enforce the rule among their own employees. There had not even been a provision for overtime pay, and the employees, almost without exception, were working extra hours. Therefore one of the first orders of business was the installation of the forty-hour week in the Washington office. The second order of business was to insist that all our employees join the Office Employees International Union, a move that had been discouraged by the Old Guard.

It's an old saying that the shoemaker's children have to go barefoot, and during my lifetime I have had several other opportunities to observe cases in which union employees were not treated as well as the members of the union insisted upon being treated themselves. These instances have been few and far between, but whenever they have been brought to my attention I have had no patience with those responsible. Unions have a solemn duty to set an example in these matters. If they are not themselves ideal employers, how can they expect management to treat their members fairly? We had a commitment to begin a strenuous crusade in the Congress for a wage increase, but before embarking on this enterprise we first put our own house in order. It has stayed in order ever since.

Before the salary campaign could get off the ground, however, the Japanese perpetrated their devastating sneak attack on Pearl Harbor, and the United States was precipitated into World War II.

From a postal point of view the war created unique and all but insoluble problems. As letter carriers were called to the colors, depleting the postal ranks by the thousands, the mail volume soared to undreamed of heights.[2] Tremendous shifts in population concentrations and the tightening of transportation restrictions all combined to complicate the problems of running the postal establishment.

And of course, letter carriers had a serious salary problem of their own. They were still being paid (if they were in the top level) an average of $2,100 a year, or $38.40 a week. This was the same salary they were being paid sixteen years previously, in 1925, and compared to the $150 a week being paid tool and die workers and the $67.50 a week being paid stenographers in war plants, it was outrageously inadequate. Since substitute letter carriers were paid sixty-five cents an hour, recruitment was impossible.

Naturally, the Department was sorely troubled by this state of affairs, since the temptations being offered by private industry were becoming too enticing, and the tendency of skilled, experienced postal workers to quit the service so they could get triple the wages in war plants was growing steadily.

During World War I, as a result of Postmaster General Burleson's neolithic policies concerning postal pay, the mail service was demoralized by the wholesale exodus of experienced men going into war industries to secure higher wages. In 1942, although the general attitude of management was much more enlightened than it had been under Burleson, the wage differential

---

[2] Previous to 1941 the annual increase in postal volume was averaging around half a billion pieces a year. The total volume in 1941 was twenty-nine billion; it was thirty billion in 1942, thirty-two billion in 1943, thirty-four billion in 1944, and thirty-eight billion in 1945. See Annual Reports of the Postmaster General for the years cited.

between government and private employment was even greater than it had been in 1917, so, of course, the danger of mass separations was correspondingly greater.

Roosevelt's attempts to control wages and prices met with only partial success as far as private industry was concerned, but the control of government salaries was a comparatively easy matter, since they were set by the Congress.

As a matter of fact, Chairman William H. Davis, of the War Labor Board, to whom the President had left the job of settling labor disputes, declared in early 1942 that FDR had not intended to "freeze" wages, but rather, to adjust them to the cost of living. He told a press conference in April 1942 that, in his opinion, the President did not intend to prohibit necessary wage increases; he merely wanted to prohibit those that were not necessary, as a means of halting the galloping inflation which was sweeping the country.

In July 1942, more than 157,000 workers in "Little Steel" received a substantial wage increase from the War Labor Board. The vice chairman of the WLB, George Taylor, announced as a reason for the increase the fact that the cost of living had increased 15 per cent during the sixteen-month period, January 1941–May 1942.

However, the Congress had the right to interpret the President's message as they saw fit, and most members were too busy struggling with defense legislation to be bothered with the starving condition of the letter carrier. It was simpler for the Congress to ignore the plight of postal employees as a "patriotic" duty.

The 1941 NALC convention at Los Angeles had instructed us to seek an increase in salary up to $3,000 a year, and had demanded that we take our case to the court of public opinion. Although the war had complicated conditions unbelievably, we were prepared to do this. Congressman Martin Sweeney of Ohio, on January 28, 1942, introduced legislation in the House which would have given postal employees an increase in wages up to $3,000. Support was building up behind this bill when FDR dropped a bombshell. On April 2, he vetoed a federal employees longevity bill on the grounds that it "provided for a permanent increase in compensation," and would therefore be unfair to workers in private industry; and because he felt it was discriminatory in that it gave something to postal workers and nothing to other federal employees.[3]

The letter carriers thoroughly disagreed with the President on this issue. The longevity features of the bill in question had never been considered a permanent wage increase, so far as we knew, by anyone. And we felt there was a palpable fallacy in demanding the continuance of grievous injustices against postal employees in the interest of preventing the possibility of offending civilian workers who were already being paid several times what postal workers were being paid. But with this veto message, illogical and unfair as it was, FDR temporarily slammed the door shut on any postal salary increase. He was, after all, the Commander in Chief. The country was at war and in dire peril. No one could oppose a decision such as this at that particular time. The only way to relieve the situation was through persuasion at the very top level, which, of course, was FDR himself.

I might say that the role of a union leader in time of war is a difficult and a delicate one. Naturally, the welfare of the country and the success of its aims are of prime importance at all times. Nevertheless there is a tendency on the part of some employers to exploit patriotic sentiments and to perpetuate injustices in the name of the war effort. It is necessary to be watchful and alert at all times lest bad practices develop in wartime which can set a peacetime precedent. A union leader, if he insists upon justice for his members in wartime, can often be

---

[3] The bill would have given postal workers an increase of $84 a year after ten years' service and another $60 after sixteen years. Only $144 a year was involved in all.

vilified by "superpatriots" who want to see labor trodden in the dust.

I had several conferences with the late Frank Walker, who was Postmaster General in those years. I found him sympathetic but ineffectual. Walker was a very decent man who was more or less forced into the postmaster generalship against his will. He had gone into politics in the way most people go into half-mourning, and I always received the impression that he would have much preferred to be doing other things. He agreed that letter carriers' salaries should be increased, but he was loath to disturb his chief with postal problems when the weight of conducting a global war was on his shoulders.

In this respect Walker was a perfect Postmaster General for President Roosevelt. There is no doubt that FDR, great man as he was, had much more interest in the showier aspects of government than in the workaday aspects. He loved postage stamps, but he had little interest in the uses to which they were put. Walker was completely loyal to him and completely trustworthy. He could be relied upon to keep the post offices open without scandal, and without unnecessarily diverting the President's mind from enterprises which were more colorful and more intriguing.

President William Green, of the American Federation of Labor, joined me in one of these direct pleas to General Walker, and tried eloquently to explain that an increase of postal wages would be accepted cheerfully by civilian union members because every working man in the country was aware of the economically disadvantageous situation in which postal employees then found themselves. At our urging, Walker finally agreed to see the President in an effort to persuade him to support a pay raise. However, his heart was not in it and he got nowhere.

Various attempts were made in the Congress to salvage something out of the wreck that the President's veto had made of our hopes for a salary increase. Congressman Bob Ramspeck submitted a bill calling for a temporary three hundred dollar a year increase. When this ran into trouble, our old and constant friend, Jim Mead, who was now a senator from New York, introduced a makeshift bill calling for a compromise increase of 10 per cent.

However, Congressional indifference to the plight of the postal employees was so widespread that progress was impossible. The committees in both Houses were sympathetic but, as a general rule, members who were not on the committee refused to bestir themselves on any subject not connected directly with the war effort. Meanwhile, the cost of living was rising month by month and letter carriers were struggling to support their families on between $1,700 and $2,100 a year. In 1942 this was not easy.

The Congress adjourned on December 16, 1942, without accomplishing anything constructive about salaries. Although all the national officers of the NALC had done everything possible to relieve the situation, I, more than anyone else, realized that my first year in office had not been a particularly auspicious one. My constituents were still hungry, and some of the more unreconstructed members of the Old Guard were saying "I told you so" in increasingly loud tones. Some of the letters I was receiving from letter carriers should have been written on asbestos. I knew I had to deliver a wage increase somehow, and deliver it fast.

I immediately called for a Washington meeting of 164 top NALC leaders from all over the country. We worked out an eight-point wartime policy for the NALC and planned our strategy for the coming session of the Congress.

During this meeting, Ambrose O'Connell, First Assistant Postmaster General (Operations) assured us that the Department was fundamentally in favor of a temporary three hundred dollar a year increase in salary. This was hedged in from several directions, but it was the first indication of official support from the Department, and despite the fact that three hundred dollars was a ridiculously small sum, in view of the low wages postal employees were receiving and the stratospheric cost of living, we all knew that it was the maximum we could expect in the immediate future. It was just twenty-five dollars a month better than nothing.

When the Seventy-eighth Congress convened on January 6, 1943, we were ready to operate. Public opinion was building up in our favor and, thanks to the devoted efforts of letter carriers over the country, newspaper editors were given a course of indoctrination which resulted in hundreds of editorials supporting us in our demands. The Congress was in a far more amenable mood after being exposed to the opinions of the home folks.

Congressman George D. O'Brien of Michigan and Senator Mead introduced wage increase bills almost immediately and this time the sailing seemed reasonably clear, for a change.

In the House hearings, William H. McReynolds, the Administrative Assistant to the President for Personnel, unconsciously helped our cause when he boldly stated that he would be glad to recommend that the President veto any bill granting a three hundred dollar increase to postal employees, permanent or temporary. It was a silly thing to say, even for a man who, like McReynolds, had once been a post-office inspector. Arrogance on the part of the Executive Branch invariably arouses hostility in the Legislative, and usually backfires.

It so happened in this case. Even such comparative conservatives as Representative Fred Hartley of New Jersey joined in the movement to teach the bureaucrats their manners. The O'Brien Bill calling for a three hundred dollar annual increase temporary to June 30, 1945, passed the House by a vote of 381-4 and passed the Senate unanimously. If Mr. McReynolds did recommend that the President veto the bill, his suggestion was ignored. The bill was signed into law by President Roosevelt on April 9, 1943.

Even though this three hundred dollar a year temporary increase was approximately seven hundred dollars short of what the 1941 convention had requested as a permanent raise, it was all the traffic would bear at that particular time, and it gave me, as national president, at least something to point to when I faced my first national convention in Denver in September 1943.

There was another development which made that year memorable. On January 18, former NALC President Edward J. Gainor resigned as a national vice-president of the American Federation of Labor. Three days later, on January 21, William Green supported me for vice-president in Gainor's place. This was important to us all. It was a tribute, not to me, but to the National Association of Letter Carriers. And I might add that it came when the NALC membership was in the hollow of an economic wave, three months before relief was forthcoming in the form of a pay raise.

It had been a somewhat experimental act when the AFL convention in San Francisco, in 1934, elected the president of the National Association of Letter Carriers to a national vice-presidency. After all, the NALC, while very much a part of the national labor movement, must be recognized is some ways as being outside the main stream of organized labor, since Federal employees are forbidden the right to strike or to bargain collectively.

But the experimental act of 1934 had turned out very well, and Ed Gainor, particularly in the campaign to obtain a shorter work week for the working man, made a permanent and signficant contribution to the cause of all organized labor, in and out of government.

To tell the truth, I was definitely a dark horse candidate, and my election as a vice president surprised me as much as it did everyone else. It would never have come about had it not been for old Dan Tobin, president of the Brotherhood of Teamsters, who insisted that the NALC was the only true labor union in the government service, and who would not hear of any other postal organization being honored with an AFL vice-presidency. Dan Tobin was very much the strong man in the inner councils of the AFL, and his insistence carried the day for us.

CHAPTER 19

ANNUS MIRABILIS

BECAUSE of the war and its restrictions on travel, the 1943 national convention, held in Denver, Colorado, was an austerity affair. Usually the letter carriers' conventions are among the most colorful and spectacular in the country, with about five thousand delegates and visitors in attendance, and with as many as twenty brass bands from every section of the land. Such luxuries, of course, were prohibited during the war. The 1943 conclave was strictly business. There were only nine hundred delegates, and the only band available was that of the local post office. The convention lasted only four and a half days instead of the usual six.

On looking back, it was perhaps just as well for all of us at the national level that we did have a small convention. The nine hundred delegates in attendance represented the top leadership in the Association. Most of them were men who had been tested in the fire of many years of unionism and they were more understanding than men of lesser experience might have been of the problems which the war had created for us.

It was an amicable convention. There was none of the organizational scuffling and skirmishing which had characterized our meetings at Los Angeles and Milwaukee. The proceedings were carried on briskly and in the spirit of absolute fraternalism. The Old Guard had become resigned to the Doherty regime, and they offered the utmost in cooperation. Though the country was at war, the letter carriers were at peace.

Of course, the salary question was uppermost in everyone's mind. The temporary three hundred a year increase which the Congress had granted earlier in the year was a stopgap affair which satisfied no one. It was scheduled to go out on June 30, 1945, and even while it lasted it fell short of providing a *living* wage, let alone a *saving* wage for postal employees. And although the convention was most tolerant of our inability to get more out of the Congress than we had got, its mandate made it abundantly clear to us that a solid legislative achievement was expected before another convention rolled around.

There were other things to worry us, in addition to wages. Fifteen thousand letter carriers, or just a little less than one-quarter of our entire membership at that time, were in the armed services. Their rights had to be preserved in their absence. The question of replacements was a difficult one. With wages so low, it was almost impossible to induce anyone to enter the postal service. Anybody of reasonably sound mind and body who was not snatched up by the armed services was grabbed by the war plants. As the wartime mail volume skyrocketed, letter carriers were expected to assume an extremely heavy work load, as well as to perform a hundred and one additional tasks of a nonpostal nature, such as the distribution of 120,000,000 ration books and of other material vital to the war effort. As a matter of fact, during these years the letter carriers were not only the major instruments in the job of seeing that the mails got through despite all obstacles, but they were also the principal medium of contact between a wartime government and the civilian population.

We decided to begin the fight for higher wages in 1944, and we spent the declining months of 1943 in conducting a well-organized educational campaign, informing the general public as to the plight of their mailmen, and instructing the Congress as to the proper interpretation of President Roosevelt's so-called "wage freeze" of 1942. One of our worst problems lay in the fact that most congressmen preferred to believe that the order called for a freeze of all wages, whether they were adequate or not. We talked "Little Steel Formula" to them until they had our arguments running out their ears. And on the public support front our members did so well that some senators said they received as many as fifty thousand letters demanding a salary increase for postal employees.

As the pressure built up we sat in our offices in the AFL Building in Washington, singly or collectively drumming our fingers on our desks, awaiting the "break" that would provide the most dramatic and propitious moment to move into high gear.

The break came on January 25, 1944, when the President's Committee on the Cost of Living announced that, despite all the efforts of the Administration to combat inflation, the cost of living had leaped upwards by 43.5 per cent since January 1941. The Bureau of Labor Statistics hotly disputed these figures,[1] claiming that the increase had only been 23.4 per cent. A lively skirmish between the two governmental groups was set off, and with each barrage the letter carriers made more hay. After all, no matter which set of figures was correct, it was an incontrovertible fact that the letter carriers had received only one 12½ per cent increase in the previous twenty years, and this increase was a temporary one at that. We were therefore at best (from

[1] Determining the cost of living is by no means an exact science. It all depends on which items are selected for building the index.

the point of view of argumentation) 31 per cent behind the cost-of living increases and, at the very worst 11 per cent behind, depending on which set of figures you wanted to believe.

We determined to seek legislation not only to make the temporary three hundred dollars a year increase permanent, but to add an extra one hundred dollars onto postal salaries as well. On May 1, 1944, Congressman George D. O'Brien of Michigan, at the urging of the NALC, dropped into the hopper a bill calling for a flat across-the-board increase of four hundred dollars a year for all postal employees. On the next day, that constant and courageous friend of the postal employees, Jim Mead of New York, introduced a companion bill in the Senate.

At this point there ensued one of the weirdest legislative struggles of the century. Despite the fact that the most industrious search could smoke out only a small handful of congressmen and senators who were opposed to a postal pay raise, the wage campaign was to drag out for fourteen interminable months before it was crowned with victory. The Department, as usual, dragged its feet and attempted a series of diversionary gambits, and with the war entering into its final victorious stages, it was hard to get the Congress to pay any serious attention to a postal wage bill. You would start out talking about the suffering letter carriers and, before you knew it, you would find yourself in a deep discussion of the Hitler bomb plot, or V-E Day. Nobody in or out of Washington in those days wanted to talk about anything except the prospects of victory and peace. This was the most natural thing in the world, and I'm not complaining. I merely mention it to indicate how hard it was to carry out the mandate of our membership in those days. There were times when I felt like the frustrated little man in those ads which proclaim that "in Philadelphia almost everyone reads the *Bulletin.*" I did a terrible amount of talking but nobody was listening very much.

However, on December 14 the bill came up for a vote in the

House under a special rule, and it passed by a vote of 133-1. It was dispatched posthaste to the Senate.

The Seventy-eighth Congress was drawing to an end and time was very much of the essence. So far as we could ascertain, there were only two senators out of the ninety-six who were opposed to a pay raise. Unfortunately, they proved to be more than enough to thwart the majority.

The two stubborn men who ruined our hopes were Senators Bailey of North Carolina and Reed of Kansas. During the short debate on the bill, Bailey made a particularly windy address in which he quoted from Pitt, Frederick the Great, the Empress Elizabeth of Russia, and a number of minor Hohenzollerns. Under the barrage of verbiage that he threw up, the only discernible argument was that under this bill the postmaster of New York City would get a four hundred dollar increase just like anybody else, and the senator was against any such thing.

When Bailey's arguments fell upon deaf ears, he came up with a legislative gimmick which, on the final day of the session, surprised his colleagues and temporarily sealed the doom of the postal employees. Senator Tom Connally of Texas was in the chair at the time and, whether he wanted to or not, he had to go along with Josiah Bailey's technical point.[2] It was a cruel and shameful performance, but Bailey had the law on his side. So, despite the fact that only one member of the House of Representatives and two members of the Senate were opposed to the pay bill, it was ceremoniously strangled on the floor of the Senate.

We were weary and angry at this unexpected and unfair turn

[2] Although the actual date of the debate was December 19, the "legislative day" was November 21. Since the "legislative day" had been November 21 when the bill had come over from the House (though the actual day was December 15), Bailey made the technically valid claim that it had not been in the Senate for the required time and was therefore ineligible for consideration. This technicality is rarely invoked. It is almost impossible to describe the pain and disappointment Bailey's action provoked throughout the postal service.

of events. Victory had seemed within our grasp and then was snatched away from us. However, like good soldiers, we immediately returned to the fight and started to map out our campaign for 1945. Although this campaign was destined to be blessed with success, there were two events which intervened, both of which were of such magnitude that they dwarfed the struggle for economic justice for letter carriers.

The first of these was the death of President Roosevelt on April 12, 1945. It is impossible to say anything about the death of FDR that would not seem banal and presumptuous. There are a few events in the century which stand out with such brilliant clarity that one remembers precisely what one was doing at the exact time one heard the news for the first time. My own recollection of such events includes the news of the armistice on November 11, 1918, the news that Lindbergh had been sighted over Ireland, the news of the attack on Pearl Harbor, D-Day in Normandy, and the death of President Roosevelt.

Nobody was neutral about Roosevelt when he lived, and nobody is neutral to this day. The American people seemed divided, albeit unequally, between those who wished he would never die and those who wished he had never been born. I am proud to be among the vast majority who made up the first group.

It can be argued that FDR was no great friend of the postal employee. He did oppose our pay bills with such consistency that it almost looked like prejudice and discrimination. But it would be ridiculous to judge him in such a superficial and subjective perspective. He was one of the really few great men of this or any other age. It was a privilege to live in the same century with him.

The other intervening event was V-E Day, which at long last brought the first assurance of peace to every American heart.

On the first day the Seventy-ninth Congress convened, January 3, 1945, Congressman O'Brien and Senator Mead introduced postal pay bills identical with those which they had sponsored in the Seventy-eighth Congress. The legislative maneuvering began all over again but, in the end, we prevailed. On May 15 the House passed the bill by a vote of 360-1.[3] On June 26, the Senate passed the bill unanimously and on July 6 President Truman signed the legislation, making it Public Law 134.

I have condensed and simplified the story of this struggle because its complications, while interesting to the student of parliamentary procedure, are less than fascinating to the general reader. Suffice it to say that the bill as passed called for a classification of postal salaries, with the addition of certain longevity provisions for which letter carriers had been fighting for many years. The salary range of carriers and clerks was placed from $1,700 to $2,700, with three additional grades for longevity and exemplary service in first-class post offices. These additional steps, which were highly controversial at the time, enabled big city letter carriers to receive as much as $3,000 after twenty-five years of service.

I say the steps were controversial because, as far as the NALC is concerned, a letter carrier is a letter carrier no matter what the size of his office. A big city letter carrier works no harder than a small city letter carrier, and in reality he deserves no more pay than does his colleague in a smaller community. But although the Congress refused to extend these three extra grades to village-delivery carriers, we went along with the bill. Because these provisions did benefit a sizable proportion of our membership, it would have been stupid to oppose them just because they did not benefit everyone.

The jubilation among letter carriers of course was considerable. They had waited since 1925 for a permanent wage increase

[3] The persistent objector in the House was Congressman Frederick C. Smith, of Ohio, who had also cast the sole dissenting vote against a pay raise in the Seventy-eighth Congress. His administrative assistant, incidentally, was Harry Brookshire, who later became the lobbyist on Capitol Hill for Postmaster General Summerfield.

and, after a long and tortuous struggle, they had been given a measure of economic recognition.

Because of war regulations, our biennial convention, scheduled for Detroit in September 1945, was called off. The Federal War Committee on Conventions said that we could go right ahead and hold a convention just as long as no more than fifty out-of-town delegates attended! Since this was impossible, our meeting was postponed for a year.

This postponement of the convention took the heat off the national officers and, after such a long and harrowing fight, there was a great temptation to go fishing for a while and forget about any further wage increase.

But I am a stubborn man. Despite the four-hundred-dollar-a-year increase that the Congress had granted, letter carriers were still underpaid. The years of inactivity in the area of postal wages during the last half of the thirties had left postal employees so far behind the rest of the economic parade that they had a tremendous distance to catch up. The fight for Public Law 134 had lasted so long, and the cost of living had soared so high in the meantime, that the salary finally granted by the Congress was obsolete the day the bill was signed.

Anyone who remembers 1945 at all will recall that $2,500 a year (which was the top salary of letter carriers after Public Law 134 was passed) was a far from adequate wage for a family man, and most of our members were heads of families. They were better off than they had been, but they were far from being adequately paid.

There were two other events which spurred me on to further activity. First of all, on June 30 Postmaster General Walker had resigned, and he was succeeded by Bob Hannegan, of St. Louis. There could not be a greater contrast between two men. Walker was a decent man, and a sincere one, but he was a conservative businessman with his eye constantly glued to the accountants' reports. Hannegan was a forty-two-year-old extrovert and a natural politician who wanted to keep everyone as happy as possible. He was a liberal with a pro-labor background and was very favorably disposed toward letter carriers. Obviously, I reasoned, the chances of getting a further pay raise with Hannegan as Postmaster General would be considerably brighter than they had been under Mr. Walker.

Then, on August 14, Japan surrendered and the shooting war stopped. Ever since December 7, 1941, every attempt to get a pay raise had been seriously impaired because the opposition had used the war as a potent weapon against us. That weapon was now inoperative.

I conferred with my colleagues on the national executive board, and proposed that we embark on a wage campaign immediately. To begin a new campaign so soon after the old one had been won sounded at first like a wild Irish dream. Such a thing had never before been attempted in all history. But the more I talked, the more my revolutionary plan made sense to the board. At last I got unanimous approval of my plan to move ahead boldly.

We all decided that the dramatic approach was the best. The proposal had to come like a bolt out of the blue. We had to catch the reactionary forces completely unawares.

We did. On August 29, just six weeks after the enactment of Public Law 134, I appeared before a regular meeting of the AFL Government Employees' Council in Washington and, pulling out all the stops, offered a resolution calling for an immediate increase of 25 per cent in the salaries of all federal employees. The resolution was passed with a whoop and a holler, and we were all in business again.

I might add that the resolution of postal employees to man the trenches once again was strengthened by the fact that the Department, upon the conclusion of the war, issued instructions that postal employees should be returned "in orderly fashion" to a forty-hour week. This was a euphemism for cutting out almost all overtime, particularly on Saturdays, and reducing the take-home pay of postal employees by as much as three hundred dollars a year. In other words, the ruling tended to wipe out all the gains achieved under Public Law 134. Even after the salary increase, a letter carrier could make ends meet only if he was able to work extra hours each week at time and a half. Now even that was denied him. "The Lord giveth and the Lord taketh away" is a Biblical admonition subscribed to by all postal administrations. As soon as the Congress gives the postal employee something, the Department tries (and usually with some success) to find a way of taking it back.

However, President Truman's attitude toward federal employees was more liberal than Roosevelt's had been. First he made the statement that, in his opinion, federal salaries were "pitiful and inadequate." That was helpful. Then he released a report made by his economists to the effect that almost all salaries in private industry could and should be increased 24 per cent without necessitating an increase in prices. Since salaries in private industry were already miles ahead of those in government, this statement was useful indeed as far as our campaign was concerned.

Congressman (later Senator) Thomas G. Burch of Virginia introduced a bill, on December 19, 1945, calling for a three-hundred-dollar salary increase, plus fifteen cents an hour more for substitute letter carriers. "Old Faithful" Jim Mead introduced a similar bill in the Senate two days later.

Although I was not quite satisfied with these proposed increases, I decided to bide my time while sentiment for the bill solidified in the Congress. I found, somewhat to my surprise, that the Congress was weary of struggling with postal salaries and, now that the war was over, was very much inclined to go along with us on our proposed pay raise. A committee amendment in the House raised the increase to four hundred dollars a year, and on April 2, under a special rule, the bill was passed by a vote of 368-1.[4]

However, there was a slight snag when the bill came up before the Senate committee. Some wildcat delegations of postal employees, not understanding the temper of the Congress or the careful groundwork that had been so carefully laid for a reasonable wage increase, stormed the committee hearings "demanding" a thirty per cent increase in salaries, or nothing! These people represented no one, but they made an intolerable amount of noise and aroused considerable resentment among those senators who were most eager to be of assistance. These foolish enthusiasts even singled out Senator McKellar, chairman of the Senate Post Office Committee, for abuse, just at the time when McKellar was making an all out effort to get a pay bill reported out of committee which would be acceptable to the entire Senate!

I admit that I was mad as a hornet at this turn of events. As president of the National Association of Letter Carriers I had been in the position of kicking off the new wage fight, and I did so at a time when postal employees had not dreamed of entering a new campaign. Admitted, I did originally ask for a 25 per cent increase, but it had soon become obvious that this request was in excess of what the Congress was in a mood to grant. So we all had trimmed our sails accordingly, and we were just about to achieve final victory when these wildcatters stormed Washington demanding the impossible. I spent a busy week, blasting away at these insurrectionists on the one hand, and soothing ruffled senatorial feelings on the other. On May 9, Senator McKellar finally introduced the bill on the floor of the Senate, assisted by Senators Barkley and Mead. It was passed unanimously.

Federal employees not only got their additional four hundred

---

[4] Guess who the one dissenter was? Congressman Smith, of Ohio, again. It should also be mentioned that in the behind-the-scenes discussions Congressmen Tom Murray, of Tennessee, and Ed Rees, of Kansas, were invaluable to our cause. We would never have got a bill without them.

dollars a year, but the Congress made the pay raise retroactive to January 1, 1946. When President Truman signed the bill into law on May 21, it was a happy day for everyone on a federal payroll.

It was also a proud day for the National Association of Letter Carriers. We had spearheaded the fight every inch of the way and, in winning two pay raises within eleven months, we had achieved the equivalent of pitching a no-hitter and bowling a perfect 300 game on the same day.

To anyone who knew the long and bitter history of postal salaries, the disheartening struggle for economic justice forced on postal employees by such tyrants as Burleson and Hitchcock, this was indeed the *Annus Mirabilis,* the Miraculous Year, for the National Association of Letter Carriers.

Although all federal employees benefited from these two bills, and all postal employees played a part in achieving their passage, it was the National Association of Letter Carriers that led the fight and was principally responsible for the double victory.

Of course, it was a team effort and success was achieved through the hard work of seventy thousand dedicated men in the field. Tremendous recognition must also be given to the Executive Board of the NALC. We had a wonderfully effective group of men working at the national level at that time, and they performed some legislative miracles. However, I would have been less than human if I did not also feel a considerable degree of personal satisfaction at the results. After all, a national president invariably gets the blame when things go wrong, so it is only fair that he should take a little credit when things go right.

Although even after this double triumph letter carriers were far from being economic royalists, still we had accomplished something that had never been accomplished before in all postal history. As a result, I faced my first postwar national convention that year with a considerable amount of confidence.

My confidence was not misplaced. The letter carriers, after many years of starvation, were eating a good deal higher off the hog than they had been during the years previous to my election as president, and they convened in a spirit of triumph and fraternal cooperation.

The convention also marked the end of whatever differences still existed between the Old Guard and the Doherty forces. Secretary Clarence F. Stinson and the chairman of the Committee on Constitution and Laws, Solomon Worthington Berry, both retired from national office at this convention because of the sixty-five-year age limitation. They both asked to be permitted to act as installation officers at the swearing in of the new national officers of the NALC. As they administered the oath of office there was many an eye that leaked at this show of sportsmanship and solidarity. The old animosities were buried on that day.

We had come a long way. We still had a long way to go.

CHAPTER 20

FURTHER SUCCESSES

THERE is a saying to the effect that some things are akin to getting olives out of a bottle; when you maneuver the first one out, the rest, by comparison, come easily.

This pretty well describes the position of the letter carriers after the unprecedented legislative triumphs of 1945–46. There was a subtle but significant change in our relationship with the Congress after our double victory, and for the last fifteen years the sledding has never been quite as rugged as it had been previously.

By this I do not mean that the Congress has ever been unfairly partisan in our behalf, or willing to give us anything we did not deserve. The years between 1946 and the present have seen us fail in some cases, and fail badly, though our victories have by far outshadowed our disappointments.

But, in 1945–46 we showed a new kind of aggressiveness, and ever since that time there has been a deeper understanding of our problems and a more general willingness to help us out.

There are many reasons for this, none of them accidental. The NALC was growing and growing fast. Membership had, by 1947, climbed over the 85,000 mark and it was still climbing. We were becoming a definitely potent political factor. Again, ever since my administration began there had been a growing tendency in the NALC to move even further away from the role of the tame "company union" that the Association had been forced to play for too many years, and to become, instead, a more active and integral part of the overall labor movement in the United States. We were just as much an association as ever, but we were also very much more of a *labor union* than we had ever been. This was a role which the average congressman understood more readily, and one which he appreciated and respected.

Many factors contributed to this evolution. I think part of the change can be attributed to my own background, which was deeply and passionately involved in the labor union movement long before I joined the postal service. Part, also, can be attributed to the fact that the new leadership of the NALC came into office with fresh vision in an age when labor unions were for the first time seeking and achieving their rightful place in the political and social life of the nation. The psychological brutality which certain postal administrations had imposed on the working force of the Postal Establishment had left scars on those who had resisted the brutality the most. One cannot fight a Burleson for eight years and emerge from the struggle unscathed, and those who had led the fight in those bleak years had been almost completely unequipped for combat with an adversary who, as a matter of course, used brass knuckles and a loaded truncheon in even the least important skirmishes. The relentlessness of the calendar had removed these ancient gladiators from high office, and their places had been taken by young men who were instinctively less impressed by titles than their elders had been. We were all properly respectful, but we did not automatically cringe and tug at our forelocks at the mention of a postmaster general's name.

Part of the mounting ascendancy of the letter carriers during these years can also be attributed to the characters of the two Postmasters General who followed Frank Walker in office.

Bob Hannegan, as I have said, was a young and ambitious extrovert who in his forty-two years had traveled very far, very fast. He was a delightful personality and a great, instinctive friend of labor. But, for many reasons, he was not an outstanding Postmaster General. He was very ill during his entire term of office. This, combined with his natural inclination to look toward the next step of his career rather than to pay attention to the step on which he was standing, caused him to become pretty much of an absentee manager of the Establishment. I really do not believe Bob Hannegan ever took the time during his seventeen months in office to learn the price of a special delivery stamp. The business of running the postal service bored him and he could not be bothered with it. But his heart was in the right place, for all that. He was the only postmaster general in recent times who ever requested a pay raise for postal employees on his own initiative.

Frank Walker, a highly conscientious man, had been appalled by the fact that he was supposed to run the United States Postal Establishment, the largest business in the world, more or less during the spare time he had left over from his principal duty, which, in the view of the Administration, was the chairmanship of the Democratic National Committee.

This was a qualm which would never have occurred to Bob Hannegan. Hannegan was quite content to run the Democratic party from the office of the Postmaster General and to let the Department run itself.

This was for years the tradition in the Post Office Department, and it is a major reason why it has always lagged behind private industry in efficiency and progress. The top jobs were always given for political reasons rather than for professional merit. The political appointees who headed each bureau were much more interested in the care and feeding of their party faithful than they were in running the Postal Establishment.

This meant that the actual operation of the postal service was left to the highest-ranked career civil servants in the Department. Most of these resident mossbacks had achieved senior status through never sticking their necks out, and thus postal improvements had always come slowly and infrequently.

Worse still, most of the career men running the Department were alumni of the reactionary and Gestapo-like Inspection Service, in which they had been rigidly trained to resist change and preserve the *status quo*.

Although the NALC has had many bitter differences with Arthur E. Summerfield, it must be admitted that he has tried to break this ruinous pattern. It is a sad commentary on the operation of the postal service, which is the largest business in America, to have to point out that Summerfield was considered revolutionary in insisting on the selection, as assistant postmasters general, of men who had had extensive civilian experience in the fields for which they were to be responsible in the Department.[1]

Hannegan's tacit abrogation of leadership created a vacuum at the top which, if it had been filled by the professional reactionaries who cluttered up the Department at that time, would have caused a situation most inimical to the best interests of the postal employees. As the most aggressive and most influential of all postal organizations, we were forced to turn constantly to the Congress for help and protection while this situation existed. Bob Hannegan was personally a great friend of labor. Unfortunately, as Postmaster General, he could not find the time to work at it with any consistency, and most of the postal profes-

---

[1] As an example, when John C. Allen, who had been head of all traffic for Sears-Roebuck, was appointed Assistant Postmaster General for Transportation, it was announced that he was the first man with a background in transportation to hold that job in fifty-five years! The post office buys more than $400,-000,000 worth of transportation every year.

sionals who surrounded him were hopelessly and vindictively anti-labor.

Then, when Hannegan retired, President Truman made a decision which turned out to be catastrophic for the letter carriers; he chose Jesse Donaldson as Postmaster General.

On paper the appointment looked good. There is no doubt that, as a result of managerial inattention, the postal service had deteriorated alarmingly during the Hannegan administration. It was natural therefore for the President to reason that too much attention to politics and too little attention to post office affairs had cost the service dearly, and that, therefore, the best remedy lay in the appointment of a career man to the top job.

Jesse Donaldson was by far the most prominent career man in the Department, having risen from substitute letter carrier to First Assistant Postmaster General, in charge of all postal operations. He was the obvious choice for the job—on paper.

But there was one fatal flaw in Jesse Donaldson's career which prevented him from ever being an acceptable administrator. He was a post office inspector. In fact, no one ever was *more* of a post office inspector. He had been one of the most effective inspectors the service ever had, and his feats of bravery and cunning are part of the postal legend. But the police mentality seldom, if ever, can adjust itself to executive tasks. This was eminently true in the case of Donaldson. He had dealt with thieves and other miscreants for so many years that his attitude was permanently warped.

Naturally, such a man took a dim view of any and all postal organizations. In his opinion, they existed only on sufferance, and any assertion of rights on their part amounted to something very close to treason. In any dispute between a post office inspector and a letter carrier, the inspector, in Donaldson's opinion, was almost inevitably in the right. He had been an inspector so long that he forgot he ever had been a letter carrier.

As president of the NALC, therefore, I had to resist this attitude with all the vigor at my command. Rather than recognizing this resistance as a natural and necessary activity of a legitimate union, Donaldson looked upon it as if it were subversion, and he attempted reprisals.

This forced the NALC, in self-defense, to assume an attitude of aggressiveness, which, it turns out, has been a godsend to its development. We had to turn more and more toward our friends in the Congress for help and protection, and in doing so we were not disappointed. We still depend heavily upon the Congress, and we are almost always blessed with understanding and cooperation whenever we turn to Capitol Hill for help.

It is ironic, but if Bob Hannegan had been more of a Postmaster General, and if Jesse Donaldson had been less of an inspector, the NALC during those years might never have gone so far so quickly.

But I am getting ahead of my story. I have mentioned these matters merely to provide a background against which the developments of the last fourteen years are more easily understandable.

Between the time of the Detroit NALC convention in 1946 and the Miami convention in 1948, ten major pieces of legislation favorably affecting letter carriers were enacted into law, including an additional salary increase of four hundred and fifty dollars a year![2] The Eightieth Congress has been branded a "Do-Nothing Congress." As far as postal employees are concerned, this is a canard. Few Congresses have done as much for

[2] Legislation included a bill to provide for the promotion of substitute employees, and other matters; a bill to provide for the return of deductions of any employee separated from the service before completing ten years of service; a bill liberalizing the Retirement Act; a bill to ratify administration promotions of employees on military furlough; a bill to eliminate discrimination against the physically handicapped; a bill to pay salaries to government employees from the period of their separation from the service when they have been improperly removed; a bill to allow credit to postal employees for promotion eligibility when transferred; a bill to preserve seniority rights of certain ten-point preference employees; a bill further liberalizing the Retirement Act; and the salary bill mentioned above.

postal workers, and we have a very warm spot in our heart for
Bob Taft, who was the Majority Leader in the Senate, and for
Joe Martin, who was Speaker during these years. Both men
always gave us the warmest consideration when we went to them
with our problems.

The fact that we asked for and got a further increase from the
Congress in 1948 does not indicate any unnatural greed on our
part. Prices were being decontrolled, the Office of Price Administration was discontinued, and the cost of living was zooming
upward again. Adjustments were being made in all industry
wages. Usually these adjustments were made quietly, with no
fussing and no fanfare of national publicity. But with the letter
carriers and other federal employees there can be no quiet
adjustments. Negotiations, such as they are, are carried on with
the Committees on Post Office and Civil Service in the House
and Senate, and if a pay bill is agreed upon, it is then reported
out and voted upon by the entire Congress. There is a further
difference, and it is one of great importance. In private industry
wage negotiations are carried on by two sets of people, representing labor and management, who know exactly what they are
doing. They know the background, the need, the current situation, the reasonable expectations of the future. On both sides of
the bargaining table sit informed experts representing their own
points of view. But, aside from the Post Office Committees there
are few congressmen who know even the basic facts about postal
pay. This is inevitable, since a congressman usually becomes an
expert only in those fields in which his own committee operates.
So with each wage bill an educational program must be attempted
in the Congress, and extraordinary pressures must be developed
to get priority on the congressional agenda for legislation to
improve the lot of postal employees.

For some reason or other the Committees on Post Office and
Civil Service are considered minor committees in the Congress.
I have never understood why this is so. These committees regu-

late the activities of the largest and most vital business in the world, a business that touches almost every citizen in the country, almost every working day of the year. The work of either committee represents a tremendous challenge to any congressman with imagination and zeal. Nonetheless, most freshmen congressmen seek to avoid assignment to the Post Office Committee, and those who are placed on it usually spend most of their time trying to get off it. This attitude has a doubly deleterious effect on postal business.

First of all, the attitude of the Congress toward its Post Office Committees is so patronizing that, almost invariably, decisions on postal matters are delayed until every other kind of matter is disposed of. The chairmen rarely can induce the leadership to give postal bills any kind of priority. Congressional action on postal matters, when it does occur, is often taken hurriedly at the end of the season. And even then it is usually taken as a result of public opinion which has been solidified by postal employees in the field.

Second, the tacit derogation of the Post Office Committees results in a quick and constant turnover among the newer members. This means that a continuing educational program must be undertaken to acquaint each new flock of junior members with the postal facts of life. Thus, the committees always suffer from a lack of experienced personnel.

This complicates the work of everyone who must do business with these committees. It also complicates the work of those dedicated members who have devoted their congressional lives to postal matters.[3]

All these elements also tend to complicate the lives of postal

---

[3] There is a small but effective group of such postal professionals in the Congress today. And of course, many congressmen in the past have gone into the history books because of their devotion to the post office. I need mention only "Sunshine" Cox, Clyde Kelly, and Jim Mead as examples of what can be done by men of courage and vision.

employees. Every gain we make must be achieved in an atmosphere of strenuous publicity, and through the hardest kind of work at the grass roots level.

Achievements come with painful slowness. Often, in this age of monetary inflation, a bill that is adequate when it is dropped into the hopper is obsolete and inadequate by the time the Congress gets around to passing it. As even the ultraconservative Senator Barry Goldwater, of Arizona, said to me one day last year, postal employees are almost always at least two years behind the national economic parade. There have been times when they have been a quarter of a century behind the parade.

The wage campaign of 1947–48 was a classic example of what we are almost always up against. From the point of view of wooing and achieving congressional support it was comparatively easy. Yet winning the battle eventually became a harum-scarum affair with a climax as breathtaking as any cliff-hanging sequence in an old "Perils of Pauline" serial.

It all started when President Truman announced, on April 10, 1947, that the cost of living was 52.8 per cent higher than it had been in 1939, and that unless prices dropped, wage increases all around would be in order. The median average salary of letter carriers at that time was $2,700. Despite the three recent pay raises, it was only 42 per cent higher than it had been in 1939. (And it must be always remembered that the 1939 salary was a miserable pittance when compared to salaries in private industry.) During the years when postal salaries were rising only 42 per cent, wages in industrial manufacturing plants were rising by 76 per cent, and in durable goods industries by 61 per cent.

In contrast to the advice the economists gave Herbert Hoover during his administration, Harry Truman's advisors were urging the federal government to take the lead in raising wages "lest a forthcoming business readjustment develop into a collapse such as followed World War I." At first the Republican-led Eightieth Congress refused to listen to this Democratic advice. They had been elected in part because of charges of alleged waste and extravagance in the Truman administration and they were determined to keep federal expenditures at a minimum. However, the NALC carried out an intensive educational campaign back in the congressmen's districts. Letter carriers told their patrons about their problems and the patrons were impressed and sympathetic. Congress adjourned on July 27 without having taken any action on postal salaries. However, when they went home they found their constituents very much on the side of their mailmen. When they reconvened in November for a special session, their attitude had altered greatly. As one Washington newspaper remarked: "Committee members were especially concerned about the salaries of postal workers, an indication that the highly effective postal-employee unions have done yeoman work in the last few months in getting their cases across to hometown Congressman."

On December 4, Congressman John C. Butler, of New York, introduced a bill calling for a flat across-the-board increase of eight hundred dollars for all postal employees. Shortly after the beginning of the year, Senator Raymond E. Baldwin of Connecticut introduced a similar bill in the Senate.

Meanwhile, I had issued a call for a special legislative conference of letter carriers to meet in Washington on January 12-13, 1948. This was, at the time, a unique move. More than seven hundred carriers, representing forty-four states, came to Washington and participated in hammering out a "suggested program" for the second session of the Eightieth Congress. While in Washington they also visited with their congressmen. Seven of the ten legislative victories we achieved during the Eightieth Congress came during 1948, and they could be attributed in whole or in part to the recommendations and activity of this special conference of letter carriers. Legislative conferences have become almost commonplace among letter carriers ever since that time.

Our trouble in 1948 was that everybody wanted to get into the act. The congressional hoppers became literally stuffed with bills to improve the lot of letter carriers.[4] We found we were being encumbered by help, and the proliferation of legislation, with its attendant hearings, was causing dangerous delay. The Congress was running out of money. Appropriations were inching dangerously close to the budget limit the leadership had set on government expenditures. In fact, the Senate Republican Policy Committee decided on April 21 that an eight-hundred-dollar raise would be much too costly and that the increase, if any, would have to be in the neighborhood of four to five hundred dollars.

Even this increase was in danger, unless someone took action fast. So, on April 28, I went out to Canton, Ohio, and had a very friendly tête-à-tête with Senator Bob Taft. He could not have been more cooperative, and after hearing my arguments he shook my hand and promised that the Senate would pass a pay bill during the session then in progress. On the same day that I was with Taft, the NALC assistant secretary, Rube Kremers, visited with Speaker of the House Joseph W. Martin, Jr., and got from him the same assurance.

Both proved to be men of absolute honor. They labeled the postal pay legislation "essential" and started to push it through on a top priority basis.

This was necessary because the wage increase had to be included in appropriations for the fiscal year which would begin on July 1. The Congress was planning to go home on June 20 so as to get ready for the national party conventions. The Congress usually shunts postal pay legislation around interminably, and its final passage is generally a "Hairbreadth Harry" last minute thriller. This happened in 1948.

Congressman Ed Rees on June 15, introduced a bill in the

[4] Among others, major pay bills were introduced by Congresswoman Katharine St. George, Senators Langer and Chavez, Congressman Dingell and Congressman Ed. Rees.

Committee calling for a permanent $450 increase, which was the maximum the traffic could bear at the time.[5] The Rules Committee agreed to a suspension of the rules and, under the parliamentary procedures involved, there could be no amendments offered on the House floor. There were some bitter complaints from members that the wage increase was too low but, since half a loaf is better than none, the House passed the pay bill unanimously.

On June 19 the bill went over to the Senate where it was blocked at the very doors by a bitter filibuster which was being waged against the military draft bill. Bob Taft, once again, was true to his word and induced the Senate to leave off filibustering long enough to give the wage bill immediate consideration.

However, Taft, to his eternal credit, was a stickler for principle. The House bill contained provision for an increase in some postage rates. Furthermore, it failed to provide a wage increase for federal workers other than postal employees. Taft proposed an amendment striking out the rate increases and providing for a $360 a year wage increase for all non-postal federal workers. This reworded bill passed the Senate unanimously, but since this was the last day of the session it created all but intolerable difficulties. It meant that "managers" had to be selected from both Houses of the Congress for a conference, out of which a compromise bill would have to emerge which would then have to pass both Houses that same day before it could be sent to the President for signature. It was agreed to stop the clocks in both houses short of midnight until the job was completed.

The conference began at 11:30 P.M. on the night of the final day of the session. The conferees from both Houses agreed on the Taft version of the pay bill at 1:00 A.M. on Sunday morning.

[5] It was Speaker Joe Martin who was mainly responsible for the increase being as high as it was. It was he who put the decisive pressure on the Committee. However, he was materially assisted by Congressman John McCormack, of Massachusetts, who lined up the Democratic minority in our behalf. Postal employees have no more faithful friend than this great leader.

Both Houses remained in session, waiting for the bill. Since it was a revenue bill it had to go to the House first. It was passed at 2:20 o'clock in the morning and was hustled over to the Senate. The senators passed the bill at 3:14 A.M. on that Sunday morning. They sent the bill to the White House and wearily adjourned. President Truman signed the bill into law on July 3, 1948.

This is an illustration of how a postal pay bill can just barely squeak through the Congress even when everybody is for it. As I have said, the Congress, unfortunately, gives almost everything priority over postal matters. In 1948 the postal bill that everybody wanted would have been lost in the shuffle if Bob Taft and Joe Martin had not been men of great integrity and in positions of great power in the Congress.

CHAPTER 21

DONALDSON

DURING those early days of my tenure as president of the NALC I had been particularly fortunate in that we won our pay increases just before our biennial national conventions. This had happened in 1943, 1946, and again in 1948. The timing in each case was accidental, but I must, in all frankness, admit that when you can face a national convention of your constituents on the crest of a fresh legislative victory, "it *do* make it nice."

When the NALC met in Miami in September 1948, I could point with great satisfaction to our record of legislative achievement.

In 1941, when I was elected president at the Los Angeles convention, the beginning salary of a letter carrier was $1,700 a year and the top salary was $2,100 a year. These salaries were the same as they had been in 1925, sixteen years previously. Since that time letter carriers had received one temporary increase and three permanent increases. When the 1948 convention assembled, the beginning wage of a letter carrier was $2,550, or $450 more than the top grade had been in 1941 when I first became president. The top grade in 1948 was $3,550 (with meritorious increases going as high as $3,850 per annum). In 1941 substitutes were still getting paid at the 1925 rate of 65¢ an hour. In 1948 substitutes were getting a starting wage of $1.29 an hour and a maximum wage of $1.79 an hour. In addition, there had been many fringe benefits gained during the years, and in these too there was cause for satisfaction. Although all other postal employees, and almost all other federal employees, participated in these benefits, it was the letter carriers who had spearheaded each fight. It was we to whom postal employees looked for leadership in each campaign, and we had not let them down.

When the gavel banged to open the 1948 convention there had been two changes which affected postal employees directly: Ed Gainor was dead and Jesse Donaldson was Postmaster General.

Ed Gainor died on November 10, 1947, at the age of seventy-seven, and with him passed an era. He had fought the good fight for so many years, and he had fought it with honor and with such skill and courage that he burned out his great human machinery. The solemn requiem Mass for the repose of his soul was sung by his nephew, Father Leo Gainor, and I had the privilege of escorting his wonderful widow during the ceremonies. We buried a great deal of postal history on that gray day in Muncie, Indiana, and we buried it with a choking sorrow in our hearts.

Jesse Donaldson had succeeded Bob Hannegan as Postmaster General on December 17, 1947. Like many others in and out of the service, I originally rejoiced in his appointment, and I had reason to do so. Donaldson had started out as a letter carrier. He knew our problems and presumably would be a boss sympathetic to us.

By the time of the Miami convention in 1948 I was beginning

to have some niggling little doubts about Donaldson's philosophy, but I was still convinced that his appointment had been a significant step forward. I gave him a tremendous sendoff at the convention, using some phrases of fulsome praise which were to haunt me later. I even went so far as to say that his appointment was the greatest thing to happen to the postal service since the institution of city delivery service. That was, without a doubt, the most inaccurate remark of 1948.

One thing about Jesse Donaldson: he was not a politician. I remember an incident at our national convention in September 1948. He called me over to the Presidential Suite of his hotel in Miami on the night before he was to address our convention. "Bill," he said, "I know letter carriers are under the Hatch Act and are not supposed to engage in partisan politics, but the election is only two months away, so do you think the boys would mind if I said a few nice things tomorrow about Harry Truman?"

I gulped a little. Never in my life had I heard of a Postmaster General being so dainty about politics. In my time I had heard and seen Departmental officials not only violate the Hatch Act but ravish it.

I assured him that the delegates of our convention would not blush furiously if he made a favorable mention of the President of the United States. "As a matter of fact," I said, "considering that the polls show that Harry Truman can use all the nice things said about him that he can get, I think it would be highly expedient for you, as his Postmaster General, to squeeze a few favorable references into your remarks. It could be that if you *don't* mention the President you might not be Postmaster General very long."

This, of course, was no exaggeration. Harry Truman was, above all, a realistic politician who believed in rewarding the faithful and punishing the disloyal. Failure by Donaldson to support him publicly on such an important occasion would almost certainly be interpreted in the White House as disloyalty. Too many people who had reason to be loyal to Harry Truman were at this time trying to disassociate themselves from him, and the President, quite understandably, was inclined to get hotheaded about it.

Mr. Donaldson evidently agreed with my reasoning. In the final ten minutes of his speech he mentioned the name of President Truman *eighteen times!* When Harry Truman won his startling victory two months later, Donaldson was reappointed Postmaster General.[1] It is interesting to conjecture that, if Donaldson had not put in a plug for Truman in his talk, subsequent postal history might have been quite different.

During the first year of his term of office Donaldson's executive limitations began to become increasingly apparent. His long experience as a postal inspector had so conditioned his mind to universal distrust that he was psychologically unable to delegate responsibility even to his top assistants.

Despite insistent mutterings about nepotism, he brought his son, Jesse, Jr., also a member of the Inspection Service, into the Department so he could have someone in whom he could confide. Jesse, Jr., was known as his father's right-hand man during his tenure at headquarters. Almost every postal matter, large or small, passed over the Postmaster General's desk and thus created the largest bureaucratic bottleneck in postal history.

Donaldson was a prodigious worker but inclined to operate like a sewing machine, very fast up and down but always in the same place. But, be that as it may, nobody could have handled the prodigious and unnecessary workload which he insisted on assuming. Even the smallest matters had to be brought to his personal attention. Decisions were intolerably slow in coming,

---

[1] It is not generally known that the appointment of a Postmaster General is unique in that it is for four years only, and not for an indefinite period. Each Postmaster General, therefore, has to be reappointed or replaced at the beginning of each presidential term.

and as a result thousand-dollar problems were sometimes permitted to grow into multi-thousand-dollar catastrophes.

For many years thoughtful observers had pointed out that the Postal Establismment had to decentralize its operations or strangle to death in its own red tape. As early as 1908 a Congressional commission, after studying postal operations carefully, recommended that decentralization be undertaken immediately. Forty years later, the Hoover Commission also made this recommendation, pointing out that greater efficiency and economy could be effected if decisions could be made by responsible persons out in the field, where the actual operations take place.

To a man of Donaldson's temperament this was heresy. Delegation of authority to persons in the field was hardly palatable to a man who would not delegate it to his own deputy, who occupied the office next door to him! Donaldson refused to decentralize,[2] and the confusion and delays in the Department mounted by the day. In fact there was a rumor in the Department, which may or may not have been apocryphal, to the effect that there was in existence an official memorandum stating that all correspondence that had not been answered within two years should be considered "dead" unless it had been followed up by a second letter. Whether or not this is true, a wait of two years for an answer to a simple request was not impossible. And too often the answer, when it did come, was composed by some obscure person who had never been in a post office in his life except to mail a package, and based on a rigid interpretation of Postal Laws and Regulations.

This procedure was as unsatisfying as it was mindless, since the person making the request could, presumably, read Postal Laws

[2] Postmaster General Summerfield did decentralize operations, beginning in November 1953. While the present system is not perfect, it is a vast improvement. However, Summerfield, in decentralizing, committed the blunder of overloading his regional staffs with post-office inspectors. This negated much of the good that should have come from the move.

and Regulations just as well as the person answering the request. Requests are made when some relaxation of the rigid laws is needed to meet a specific situation. Under Donaldson there was no such relaxation. Rigidity was a way of life, and to make such a request was, in his inspector's mind, similar to walking into a church and suggesting a sweeping revision of the ten commandments.

Although these managerial shortcomings were becoming more and more apparent, postal employees were slow to realize just how great they were and how damaging they were to become.

For instance, great propaganda effect was made from the fact that Donaldson was no politician and that his administration would therefore be free of politics. It did not work out that way. Donaldson was certainly no politician. He considered politics some arcane mystery, and the politicians as specially anointed high priests of that mystery. He did not interfere with the politicians, but according to his critics, he simply let them have their way. As a result, the politicians took over in the Post Office Department to an extent seldom attempted in the past.[3]

As a career man who had once carried the mail on a city delivery route, it was presumed that Donaldson would understand the problems of the rank and file postal employee. It turned out that he had apparently forgotten all about that earlier part of his career. Although he kept at home his letter-carrier boots, bronzed in the way some proud parents preserve baby shoes, his policies seemed to be influenced only by his years in the Inspection Service. He became more and more anti-employee in his administration until, by the time he had retired, he had built up the worst anti-labor record of any Postmaster General since Burleson.

[3] This happened even in Donaldson's beloved Inspection Service. All post-office inspectors are obliged to list their political affiliations when they join up. Under the law the inspectors' jobs must be divided between the two political parties on a fifty-fifty basis. When Donaldson left office, 80 per cent of all inspectors were Democrats.

The postal employees were slow to believe all this because they did not want to believe it. The Truman administration was dedicated to the advancement and welfare of the so-called "little man" and it was unthinkable that Truman's Postmaster General, the leader of half a million working men, should be the absolute antithesis of what the President stood for. But then again, it had been unbelievable that a great humanitarian like Woodrow Wilson should have and keep a Postmaster General like Burleson. But he did!

The disenchantment of the National Association of Letter Carriers began to grow in 1949.

Donaldson opposed our attempts to get a wage increase. This is standard operating procedure for all Postmasters General so it did not surprise us greatly. However, we did expect a more sympathetic response from a career man and former letter carrier than we got from Donaldson. Despite all his previous protestations that his door would always be open to the representatives of the postal unions, he became almost impossible to see. As a matter of fact, it became a kind of bitter joke in the NALC that, whenever we tried to discuss a grievance with the Postmaster General, we were told he was busy with the "boo-jet," which was his singular way of pronouncing budget.

Consternation grew as he continually found ways to thwart and circumvent the wishes of the Congress in labor-management relations. When the Congress passed a law, for instance, providing special delivery messengers with ninety cents an hour, or seven cents a mile, for use of their own cars, Donaldson decided to lease automobiles in many large cities from private contractors. The law, when passed by the Congress, had emboldened many special delivery messengers to buy new automobiles. Donaldson's action left these employees holding a very large and empty sack, but when approached on the subject, he simply refused to discuss it any further.

He also, in 1949, devised ways of achieving "economy"

through assigning certain duties which had always been performed by post-office clerks to mail handlers who were lower paid and unskilled in clerical duties. This was done, of course, in order to cut down the clerical force, not to upgrade the pay of mail handlers. Like so many such moves it caused more confusion than economy.

This action led us to protest directly to President Truman, after we found it impossible to discuss the matter with the Postmaster General. President William Green, of the American Federation of Labor, President Leo George, of the National Federation of Post Office Clerks, President Bill Thomas, of the Postal Transportation Association, and I did this in person.[4] Truman was sympathetic, but refused to override his Postmaster General. Donaldson, despite the fact that we were merely trying to protect the rights of postal employees, considered our action a direct and personal affront.

He had also, on several occasions, resisted successfully Congressional attempts to establish proper labor-management regulations in the postal establishment. He thought such a move would give undue recognition to postal unions, and he fought against it ferociously.

Donaldson, with an inspector's lust for economy and an inspector's misunderstanding of management, raised havoc with postal transportation employees by a series of downgrading orders which reduced their morale to a minimum.

All these actions were hurting the service and achieving almost nothing in the way of economy, and as president of the National Association of Letter Carriers I found my temperature mounting with each passing month. The comparative inaccessibility of Donaldson added to the irritation. Farley and Walker, both of

[4] I had not been alone in my overestimation of Jesse Donaldson. Leo E. George, president of the National Federation of Post Office Clerks, had hailed Mr. Donaldson just previously as a world postal statesman! His opinion, by the time we made this trek to the White House, had undergone considerable alteration.

whom had achieved tremendous success in the outside world before entering the Post Office Department, and both of whom were national chairmen of their party as well as Postmasters General, were far more accessible than was this man who had risen from the postal ranks.

Although at the time I attributed Donaldson's aloofness to arrogance, I think now that I was being a little too harsh. It stemmed, in my opinion, from his own lack of self-assurance. The average postmaster general in the past had been an enormous success in private business before he entered the postal service and therefore was bursting with self-confidence. Donaldson did not have this self-confidence, and he tried to hide the fact through barricading himself behind his big oak door.

Despite many provocations, I was able to contain myself with reasonable success until April 18, 1950. On that day lightning hit the cow barn, and the resultant explosion caused reverberations which are still echoing through the Department's corridors.

On April 18, 1950, Jesse Donaldson raped the postal service.

It was on this day that he issued the infamous order reducing mail deliveries to one a day in residential areas and to two a day in most business areas. The order also drastically curtailed street collections and window service, cut in half parcel post deliveries to business firms, and completely eliminated service on particular days for certain portions of almost every city delivery route.

This order was issued in the interest of economy. It created havoc, hardship, and widespread delay. The second delivery in residential areas has never been restored to this day and the service has never recovered from the blow which the first "career" Postmaster General gave it at that time.

I was given a copy of the order (never mind how!) on the day *before* it was to be released. When I read it, the steam started jetting out of my ears! Here was an order that would cause hardships for every letter carrier by increasing his load and lengthening his route, and it was being issued without warning and without any pretense of consultation with the representatives of those who would be most adversely affected by it, the officers of the NALC.[5] Such an action would have been expected in men like Hitchcock and Burleson, but times had changed. This was 1950, and such high-handed action on the part of a "career" postmaster general was intolerable.

It was at this point that I took the step that made peace between this particular postmaster general and the NALC impossible from then on. Since the order amounted to a declaration of war against the letter carriers of the United States, I decided to get in the first shot. I let loose a blast against the order *on the day before it was published,* explaining in angry detail just what its effect on the American public would be!

This completely undercut Donaldson's strategy. He had been prepared to announce the service curtailment along with a lot of soothing syrup designed to delude the public into believing it would not be adversely affected.

Instead, he found himself, to his great surprise, on the defensive. He had to try to defend himself from the barbed and indignant questions of newspapermen who had been given the letter carriers' and the public's point of view first.

Although nothing could or would prevent his going through with his sneak attack upon the letter carriers and the postal patrons of the United States, he had lost any chance he might have had to woo public support of his rash and unprecedented measures.

Donaldson was furious at me, and in all fairness I cannot say I blame him. My action was not intended to please him.

The angry exchanges which followed caused a permanent change in the relations between the Department and the NALC. In the past, when we had disagreed with departmental policies,

[5] Since the American people were also adversely affected by this order, the Post Office Committees in the Congress were also enraged at Donaldson's autocratic action.

our disagreement, when it appeared in *The Postal Record,* was couched in language so polite that it would scarcely have brought a blush to the cheek of a novice in a cloistered order of nuns. Even our disagreement surrounding the unfair pay cuts which we suffered in the 'thirties was expressed in terms of sorrow rather than of anger. But on this occasion all the mounting, pent-up indignation we had been feeling, as Donaldson's performance as an administrator deteriorated, burst through its dam and flooded the pages of *The Postal Record* with some prose so colorful and forthright that I am sure it caused some of our predecessors to gyrate violently in their graves. We were mad clear through, and many of the ancient editorial taboos and inhibitions were quickly and unceremoniously discarded.

This was a good thing. *The Postal Record* ever since has been a faithful barometer of the feelings of the nation's letter carriers. It has also been, ever since, a far livelier organ of opinion. When we are angry (and we have had many occasions to be angry in recent years), we say so in no uncertain terms. We do not pull punches. This new freedom dates back to April 1950.

This service curtailment order had elements of "public be damned" and "labor be damned" in it to such an extent that it would have given pause to even such a rugged (but honest) individualist as Postmaster General John Wanamaker.

Under the one-delivery system (which still pertains) millions of letters every day are held up by at least twenty-four hours. It used to be that a local letter mailed early in the day could be delivered in the second delivery on that same day. This is now impossible. Since letter carriers must distribute all the mail available on their one trip, including magazines, newspapers, and advertising circulars, they must leave the post office earlier than they used to. Thus they cannot wait for some out-of-town dispatches of value which otherwise they would be able to deliver on the day of their arrival at the post office. Many letters arriving at a post office from out of town, which might have caught the first delivery or, at least, would certainly have caught the second delivery, now must wait twenty-four hours in the post office before being transmitted to their destination.[6]

Every day there are a number of letters misthrown (assigned to the wrong letter carrier) in a post office. The number, percentagewise, is small, but in sheer numbers it is large. These human mistakes will occur, no matter how dedicated the personnel. It used to be that such errors were corrected in time for the second delivery. Now, these mistakes are left uncorrected until the next day and a full twenty-four-hour delay in delivery ensues.

All the mechanical and electronic devices in the world will not alter this situation. No matter how swiftly the mail is processed in its journey through a post office, it will not reach its destination faster unless it is placed more quickly in the bag of the letter carrier.

When mail is permitted to lie around a post office overnight, just because there is no way of delivering it on the day of its arrival, all the mechanical advances in the world are fruitless. The mail service today, as a result, is hasty but not speedy.

Of course, because all the postal eggs must now be put in a carrier's one basket each day, deliveries at the end of a carrier's route get later and later. A carrier's "office time" has been drastically slashed and he spends as much as six and a half hours pounding the pavements. If you live at his route's end you are fortunate if you get your "morning's mail" by three o'clock in the afternoon. This is a ridiculous situation in the year of Our Lord 1960 in the United States of America.

At the time that Donaldson reduced residential deliveries from two to one, English postal patrons were getting as many as five deliveries a day. They still do. We were far behind most Euro-

---

[6] Donaldson's answer to this was typical: "Let them get post-office boxes." Any similarity to Queen Marie Antoinette's suggestion for the poor people of France, "Let them eat cake," is purely coincidental.

pean countries in service before the order was issued. Ever since the order, we have had a second-rate mail service. Big, but slow; slower even than in some small countries which we are inclined, somewhat smugly, to call "backward."

Postmaster General Donaldson claimed that the curtailment action would save a minimum of $80,000,000 a year. This was a fantastic figure computed by public relations people rather than accountants.

All such theoretical computations claiming enormous "savings" should be taken not so much with a grain as with a *stalactite* of salt. They seldom show up in the final accounting.

Thus, postal expenditures for fiscal 1951 (the first full year during which the curtailment order was in effect), were up 5.33 per cent over the previous year. In fiscal 1952, postal expenditures jumped by another 13.9 per cent! [7] It is hard to see where the savings were made, if they were made at all.

As a matter of fact, although Donaldson was perhaps able to sweat some savings out of the letter carriers and the public, there is a limit to what can be accomplished. As the population explodes into new areas, patrons must be served, and this requires manpower without direct relation to volume or to the number of deliveries involved.

This time there was no necessity for letter carriers to stir up public opinion. The public and the nation's press took care of that situation spontaneously. Even the foreign press, delighted at the opportunity of making fun of the United States, had a field day at Donaldson's expense.

Conditions in post offices became chaotic as the mail piled up on workroom floors. Small businessmen in residential areas were hit hard by the order. So was every other businessman who de-

---

[7] The expenditures for fiscal 1950 were $2,200,000,000 and the "deficit" was $545,000,000. In fiscal 1951, when the curtailment was in full effect, the expenditures were $2,300,000,000, and the "deficit" was $565,000,000. In fiscal 1952 expenditures were $2,670,000,000 and the "deficit" was $720,000,000.

pended for his livelihood on the swift and certain delivery of the mails.

Six months after the order was issued a survey among 357 business organizations conducted by the Commerce and Industry Association of New York showed that the curtailment order had slowed down trade appreciably and added to the operational costs among the firms queried.[8] The chaos created by the order had resulted in delays, particularly in out-of-town mail (which represents about 80 per cent of the total volume) of from two to five days, with some examples of mail being held up by ten days. The press took up the hue and cry to such an extent that Donaldson was forced, almost surreptitiously, to modify and adjust his order, but despite these involuntary improvements, one delivery a day remained in effect in residential areas and still remains in effect.

The furore in the Congress was considerable, and a bill to rescind the order, introduced by Representative Jimmy Morrison of Louisiana, passed the House by a vote of 264-108. However, the Korean War had broken out by the time the bill got to the Senate, and Donaldson, playing hard on the theme of what a highly conjectural $80,000,000 a year could mean to the war effort, was able to have the bill defeated there by a single vote.

And there the issue has rested ever since. The American people have been lulled to sleep. They have actually forgotten what really good mail service can be like, and they have taken second-class mail service for granted, almost as if such a thing as first-class service were unattainable.

However, if any postmaster general ever wanted to really win the heart of the country he could, by a stroke of his pen, reestablish the second delivery in residential areas and he would become a hero overnight. He would find that the American

[8] See *New York World Telegram and Sun*, p. 15, March 24, 1951.

people would respond to good mail service a great deal more favorably than they do to imaginary post office savings.

As far as the post office is concerned, the best politics is good service. The American people want their post office to be a service, not a cold-blooded business concern or a public utility. They do not want the service to be operated with wild extravagance, but they do want to see it operated with the emphasis on service rather than on penny-pinching. No administration ever won a single vote by presenting to the people a balanced postal budget. As a matter of fact, Burleson lost votes by trying to do this. His policies became a major issue in the 1920 presidential elections, and were a contributing factor to his party's defeat. But votes can be won by giving the people the kind of postal service they have a right to expect.

The bitterness between the letter carriers and Donaldson was so great that in 1950 we did not invite the Postmaster General nor anyone from his staff to attend our national convention in Seattle. As it turned out, they were not missed.

Donaldson's failure as chief executive of the postal service cast a new light on the entire question of the desirability of career men in top postal jobs. Certainly his performance makes it most unlikely that a career man will be appointed again for many years to come.

Like almost all questions, this one, if it does not have two sides, has at least a side and a half. Certainly a brilliant professional career in the postal service should give a man an advantage over a newcomer from outside the establishment who has to learn his job from the very beginning.

But it all depends on the individual.

Some postmasters who have come up from the ranks have been brilliant successes. There have been just as many who have been dismal failures, and who have turned out to be petty despots over those who had formerly been their brothers.

Contrariwise, there have been some brilliant postal executives

who came into the establishment from the outside and there have
been just as many who should have remained outside. There can
be no hard and fast rule about these things.

If a man has been forty years in the service, it does not necessarily mean he has had forty years' experience. He may have
had only one year's experience forty times.

Then, too, it is often the wrong kind of professional postal
worker who rises high enough to be considered for the top jobs.
Although the Hatch Act prohibits and penalizes partisan political
activity, there are many communities in which the only way to
reach the top of the heap is through judicious and continuous
violation of the Act. When this is the case the man who is advanced knows less about postal operations than he does about
political operations and, if selected, will almost certainly be a
worse postmaster than an outsider who brings to the office a fresh
outlook and the business know-how of the workaday world.

Often a career postal employee on his way to the top develops
obligations among his colleagues in the post office which hinder
him from doing the kind of job that is needed. Also, a man can
become so encrusted with the traditions of the postal service
that he refuses to consider new methods, new techniques, new
ideas. This certainly was true of Donaldson.

As the president of the largest employee union in the postal
service I would love to give a *carte blanche* endorsement of the
idea of confining all promotions to top jobs to career professionals. However, out of concern for the welfare of our members
and as a result of so many bitter disappointments from career appointments in the past, I cannot, in all honesty, do any such thing.

A career man, when he is good, is almost unbeatable; when
he is bad he is almost unbelievable.

Napoleon once said that every private in the French army
carried a baton of a Marshal of France in his knapsack. This
should be true in the postal service, too. But it is very important
that only the right men be permitted to get to use those batons.

CHAPTER 22

THE DISCHARGE
PETITION

IT IS often said that the chairmen of the committees run the Congress. This is substantially true. The chairmen wield tremendous power over legislation, not only because of their seniority in an organization substantially be-nimbused by long service, but also because of their privilege of convening (or failing to convene) their committees when they see fit, and of ignoring any legislation of which they do not personally approve.

There was a time when the chairman of a committee in the House of Representatives was all-powerful and there was no possible appeal from his decisions.

However, in the early part of this century a revolt took place in the House against the tough and tyrannical Speaker of that time, "Uncle Joe" Cannon. The rank and file members, who were treated as serfs by an overbearing leadership, combined their forces to overthrow Speaker Cannon and to change the rules of the House in such a way as to weaken some of the dictatorial powers of the Speaker of the House and his committee chairmen.

One of the results of this palace revolution was the institution of the discharge petition.

The discharge petition, which was initiated in 1910, was aimed at forcing a bill out of committee and onto the floor of the House for consideration, when that bill is being "bottled up" by the chairman.

When more than one-half the total membership of the House signs such a petition, the committee is thereby discharged of its obligation to consider the bill any longer. This is fancy and polite congressional language meaning that the committee can no longer sit on legislation it wants to kill.

However, successful discharge petitions are few and far between. There have been only thirty-one such during the half century in which the rule has been in effect, and many of these occurred soon after the institution of the rule and were an immediate result of the anti-Cannon uprising.

The reason for the unwillingness of most congressmen to sign discharge petitions is obvious. The leadership hates them. Committee chairmen and the elder statesmen who hope to become committee chairmen consider discharge petitions a violation of their proper prerogatives. Their disapproval is communicated to ambitious members who hope to gain further prominence in politics. As Speaker Sam Rayburn once said: "The way to get along is to go along." The approval of "The Establishment," the top brass of the House, is almost essential for congressional success, and their disapproval can be ruinous to a man of ambition.

Therefore, there are in the Congress many elder members who would not sign a discharge petition, no matter what its intention, even if one were to hold their feet to the fire from now until doomsday. There are also many younger members who will not, through fear of reprisals, sign a petition, no matter what it may be for.

Of course, when a discharge petition does get the necessary signatures, passage in the House of the bill discharged is practically automatic. There is no discharge machinery in the Senate. The committee chairmen in that body enjoy unabated powers and their word is law.

Ever since 1949, postal employees, and particularly the National Association of Letter Carriers, have become the chief and most successful initiators of discharge petitions. We have been responsible for six successful petitions and we have never failed in an attempt to get a bill discharged. This is a unique record, and it reflects the mutual esteem existing between the Congress and ourselves.

Our first involvement in a discharge petition was over a pay bill, introduced on May 3, 1949, by Representative George P. Miller, of California,[1] one of the most reliable friends of the postal employee in the Congress.

This bill, which finally became Public Law 428, Eighty-first Congress, gave, among other things, an increase of $120 a year in postal salaries and an increase of two and one-half cents per hour for substitutes. It also provided for three meritorious grades after thirteen, eighteen, and twenty-five years of service, with a hundred-dollar a year award for each step.

Our determination to seek a further wage increase was based, once again, on that elusive will-of-the-wisp, the cost of living. Our increase in wages in 1946 had placed us within rifle shot of the cost of living. However, official figures showed that the cost of living had risen 33.6 per cent between 1946 and 1949. Our wage increase in 1948 had lifted our incomes by about 14.5 per cent, leaving a gap of 19 per cent to be filled. We originally asked for a $650 increase in 1949, and, if granted, that would have filled the gap. We got, instead, less than a quarter of what we

[1] A companion bill was introduced in the Senate by Senator Langer, of North Dakota, for himself and for Senators McKellar, Frear, Humphrey, Baldwin, Ecton, Kefauver, and Hendrickson.

should have received. And we had to move a lot of congressional furniture around to get that much.

The chairman of the House Post Office Committee in 1949 was Representative Tom Murray, of Tennessee.[2] Murray is a stalwart conservative who comes from an area where living costs are low and where letter carriers are few. He is also a veteran of the Post Office Department, having served some time as one of its lawyers, and his attitude toward pay legislation is likely to reflect Departmental attitudes. He is also a great admirer of the Postal Inspection Service.

I have no desire to be unfair toward Chairman Murray. He is a thoroughly honest man who sticks to his principles through thick and thin. Although we have disagreed with him many times, we have found that he has never hesitated to support an unpopular cause. In fact, he seems to relish such causes. Chairman Murray has almost always opposed our pay requests in his committee, but he has usually voted on our side when our pay bills have come up for final passage.

In 1949 Tom Murray was adamant against a pay raise, and he refused to budge from his position. Despite widespread sympathy for us in the Congress, it was obvious that we did not have a prayer when it came to getting our pay bill out of committee in the usual way. Murray simply refused to call the bill up. Extraordinary methods were very much in order.

On April 30, 1949, I happened to be out at an NALC district meeting in the Fifth Congressional District of Indiana, which was at that time represented by a very personable freshman Democrat named John R. Walsh, a member of the Armed Services Committee. I fell into conversation with Walsh's administrative assistant and told him of the troubles we were having in getting the bill out of committee. Out of a blue sky the idea of a discharge petition came to me, and right there and then I tried it out on

[2] He still is.

the administrative assistant for size. He bought it on the spot.[3] When I returned to Washington I pursued the matter with the congressman himself, who was a very courageous friend of labor in general, and of the letter carriers in particular. He had already been briefed by his aide and was most receptive to the idea.

However, when I discussed the proposal at a subsequent meeting of the Government Employees Council (AFL) I was confronted with massive and almost universal resistance.[4] The idea was too revolutionary. It would merely embitter Tom Murray against all postal employees, my opponents said, and it would be in a hopeless cause. Discharge petitions were doomed to failure before they got started.

I hate negative thinking. If someone tells me a thing is impossible, a perverse reaction starts up in my brain and I begin to work up arguments to the contrary. Besides, I had a good old Irish hunch about this idea, so I boldly announced that the letter carriers would go it alone in sponsoring the petition. I was called some rather unpleasant names by a few of the more recalcitrant brethren at that time, but before the battle was over even the most vocal oppositionists had joined up with us, and a few of them were even taking bows for having thought up the idea in the first place.

On July 14, Congressman Walsh introduced this historic discharge petition.

We had a well thought out plan of action. Immediately upon presentation of the petition, letter carriers from nearby areas started walking the halls of the House Office Building on their time off the job, buttonholing congressmen and urging them to sign the petition. Tens of thousands of other letter carriers who could not come to Washington personally, as well as the mem-

---

[3] Anyone who knows the Congress knows how much influence a good assistant has with his boss. Some assistants are literally their boss's *alter ego*. (Occasionally the congressman is the administrative assistant's *alter ego!*)

[4] The mail handlers were the only group to support me and they went all out in backing me up.

bers of our very effective Ladies Auxiliary, wrote letters to their representatives. We put on a kind of legislative *blitzkrieg* and it had a stunning effect on the House.

Naturally, it was most important to me that this effort should be successful. I had, in a moment of bravado, stuck my neck out very far indeed, and a failure would have proved very embarrassing to me.

Success, however, came with astonishing swiftness. The last of the required 218 signatures was affixed to the petition on July 21, just one week after its introduction.

But our troubles were far from over. Despite our apparent success, there were an awful lot of things that we did not know then about the mechanics of discharge petitions.

One of these was how to write such a petition. Congressman Walsh, who also had no experience, wrote the petition in such a way that when the required number of signatures was secured on the petition, only he, and no one else, could make the motion which would make the petition operative.

There is another technicality involved in these things. A petition that has acquired the requisite number of signatures must be called up on a specifically designated day, or else it cannot be called up at all.

On the day on which the petition had to be called up, Walsh, the indispensable man of the hour, was completely out of pocket. He had been fulfilling a speaking engagement in the Midwest and was leisurely driving home to Washington. No one knew what route he had taken or where he was.

Our good and loyal friend, Congressman Bob Corbett, a ranking member of the Post Office Committee, brought us this distressing news. He also set out to find a remedy.

Corbett, who comes from Pittsburgh, was for a number of years the sheriff of Allegheny County, Pennsylvania. On this occasion he used his police experience and connections to great advantage. He figured out that Walsh was somewhere in Illinois by this time, so he telephoned the Illinois state police and asked them to put out an all-points alarm for the errant congressman. He gave them Walsh's license number, his description and the description of his car. The word was that Walsh was to telephone Washington immediately.

And thus it came to pass that Congressman Walsh, completely oblivious of the panic his absence was causing in Washington, was scared out of his wits while driving on the Lincoln Highway, about two hundred miles out of Chicago, by a sudden and determined convergence of screaming police cars. "Pretty Boy" Floyd never got more enthusiastic attention from the gendarmes!

The troopers, of course, did not know who Walsh was or why he was wanted. Corbett, perhaps out of a sense of mischief, neglected to supply that information. All the troopers knew was that they had orders from Washington to hustle their captive to a telephone immediately. In their insistence on carrying out their orders they handled the confused young Congressman with somewhat less than the deference to which he was accustomed.

Naturally, Walsh, when he heard he was to call Washington immediately, was scared witless. He envisaged, as anyone would, a family disaster. His hand and voice shook as he put through his call.

Now, Bob Corbett is a jovial man with a very jovial voice. He fairly bursts with good cheer. So when he answered the telephone in Washington and told Walsh the reason for all the excitement, the cheerful quality of his voice touched off an emotional explosion in the frightened congressman. Walsh was furious, and his first reaction was to consign us all to one of the more unpleasant circles of Hell and be damned if he would move a muscle to get to Washington any faster than his car would ordinarily carry him.

It took all of Bob Corbett's persuasiveness (and he has plenty of it) to talk him into a more cooperative frame of mind.

Walsh finally agreed to drive the two hundred miles to Chi-

cago, escorted by police car. Reservations were made for him on
the first possible flight to Washington.

So, with sirens screaming, Walsh was rushed to Chicago's Mid-
way Airport.

Just as he arrived, however, the grandfather and grandmother
of all summer storms broke loose. Lightning filled the skies, the
thunder rolled out its awesome diapaison, and the rain started to
fall in sheets. All commercial air line flights were canceled.

It looked as if the discharge petition was cooked.

But never sell Bob Corbett short. He responds to a crisis the
way a fire horse responds to an alarm bell. He started in on an
explosive series of telephone calls and finally determined that the
Air Force just happened to have a B-25 in Chicago that simply
had to get to Washington on that particular day, weather or no
weather.

Since Walsh was a member of the Armed Services Committee
of the House, this made everything peachy-dandy for everyone,
with the possible exception of Congressman Walsh.

Brave and fine man that he is, I imagine that Walsh, as he
was whisked out to the waiting bomber in a wind-driven down-
pour, wished that Bob Corbett had not been *quite* so ingenious
and persistent.[4]

He flew in the bubble, next to the pilot, through some of the
roughest weather imaginable. The sturdy plane did the roller
coaster bit all the way to Bolling Field, just outside of Washington.

I met him with my car at the airport and sped him to Capitol
Hill.

The House, of course, was quite cognizant of all the drama
that was taking place. So when freshman Congressman John
Walsh, green in the face, rubbery in the knees, and vastly dishev-

[4] John Walsh stayed in the Congress only one term. He is now Indiana's
secretary of state, a job which, I hope, he finds less hectic than that of congressman.

elled, walked down the aisle, he was met with a standing ovation seldom matched in congressional history. All it needed was ticker-tape hanging from the galleries to make it a reasonable facsimile of Lindbergh's reception in New York City in 1927!

Walsh made the necessary motion and the day was saved. The whole business on the floor of the House took about ten minutes. In an hour's time, the weather having cleared, Walsh was flying back to Chicago to reclaim his car. (That was the only item Bob Corbett had failed to take care of.)

Since committee chairmen do not like the record to show that their hands had been forced in this manner, Chairman Murray suddenly had the pay bill reported out of his committee before the discharge petition could take effect. This is a routine gesture, however, and undoubtedly it would never have happened if Congressman Walsh had not made his historic flight.

But our troubles were far from over. As a result of sheer in-experience we had neglected to include the Rules Committee in our discharge petition. This meant that the legislation which we had blasted out of the Post Office Committee was merely trans-ferred to the Rules Committee, out of the frying pan into the fire.

If there is anything the Rules Committee hates (and there is), it is a disruption of the orderly processes of the Congress. The Committee is usually dominated by senior statesmen, veterans of the House whose reaction to a discharge petition is suggestive of the devil's rumored reaction to holy water. Certainly there was no chance of getting the Rules Committee voluntarily to report out a bill that had been discharged so unceremoniously out of the Post Office Committee.

So there was nothing left but to go through the whole business once again. Corbett, ever our friend, introduced on August 18 a petition to discharge the Rules Committee from consideration of the bill, and the necessary 218 signatures were affixed within five days.

Chairman Adolph Sabath of the Rules Committee followed

the same procedure as did Chairman Murray of the Post Office Committee, by having a rule granted to the pay bill before the discharge petition became operative. The bill was passed by the House by a vote of 333-2. The Senate added some amendments to the bill which were subsequently approved by the House, and President Truman signed the bill into law on October 28, 1949.

This experience came in handy within a year's time when Congressman Walsh once again initiated a petition, this time to discharge the Post Office Committee from further consideration of a bill rescinding Postmaster General Donaldson's order curtailing city delivery service. This petition was introduced on July 10, 1950, and received the necessary number of signatures on July 24. As recounted in the previous chapter, it passed the House handsomely, but was eventually defeated in the Senate by a single vote.

Thus the seldom used discharge petition became the potent secret weapon of the letter carriers and postal employees generally. We performed the incredible feat of inspiring three of these petitions within one year and seeing each of them brought to a successful conclusion.

We have used this technique three times since then, and on each occasion we have been successful. On June 30, 1954, our late great friend, Harold Hagen, of Minnesota, introduced a petition to discharge another pay bill from the Committee. Despite a most spirited defense, spearheaded by Postmaster General Summerfield and his able and energetic executive assistant, former Congressman Ben H. Guill, the necessary number of congressmen signed the bill by July 21.

In 1957 an outstanding friend of the letter carriers, Congressman T. Ashton Thompson of Louisiana, initiated still another discharge petition to shake loose a pay bill. The petition was introduced on May 15 and was completed on July 11.

Just this year Congressman Thompson initiated another discharge petition to blast a Federal employees' pay bill out of the

Rules Committee. In just two days (June 2, 3) the petition received the required signatures.

So out of the total of thirty-one successful discharge petitions which have been initiated during the past half century, we have been responsible for six.

And this entire sequence came into being because I had a brainstorm one April night at a letter carriers' salary meeting in the Fifth Congressional District of Indiana.

CHAPTER 23

UP TO IKE

AS A result of the strife between Donaldson and the National
Association of Letter Carriers, almost all direct communication between the Department and our organization came to a
standstill. This meant that we had to lean more and more heavily
on the Congress in all our activities.

Actually, the Congress and we were brothers in distress. As a
result of the curtailment of service, letter carriers found themselves not only being overworked but also being made to bear
the brunt of their patrons' complaints about bad service. This
was only natural. If a patron has been accustomed to getting his
mail at 9 A.M. every day and suddenly finds himself getting it
twenty-four hours late and in the middle of the afternoon, to
boot, he gets angry, and the letter carrier is the most available
person to be blamed. It is the same way with bus drivers. When
a bus fails to arrive on schedule, it is the driver of the next bus,
who does arrive on schedule, on whom the passengers' wrath
is expended. Letter carriers were getting sick and tired, however,

of being lambasted by their patrons for service deficiencies for which they were not responsible and which they were trying to correct.

The Congress, particularly the Democratic members, was having troubles of its own. The nation's press was up in arms about the deteriorating service, and the public was writing angry letters to congressmen. Since Donaldson was a Democrat, his fellow party members in the Congress were being inundated with communications asking why they did not do something about him.

Actually, there was precious little that the Congress could do about the Postmaster General as long as President Truman kept him in office.

Donaldson remained stubborn and unperturbed by all the fuss.

He even, with great earnestness and obtuseness, told the House Post Office Committee that, unless a postage rate increase were passed by the Eighty-second Congress, he would be forced to make even further curtailments of service.[1] By this time the service was such a laughing stock that any further deterioration would have meant a reversion to smoke signals and tom-toms.

Meanwhile, Donaldson's boastful claims about the savings his curtailment order was making were arising to haunt him. He began to engage in a numbers game similar to that made famous by the late Senator McCarthy. Since April 18, 1950, he had at various times estimated savings from the curtailment order at fifteen million, twenty-one million, seventy million, and eighty million dollars. Then, on February 13, 1951, in a letter to Senator Ives, of New York, his first assistant said: "It would be difficult to accurately estimate the actual savings and no records have been maintained from which actual figures might be furnished." Each of the preceding estimates which Donaldson had made had been given publicity on the presumption that he had known what

[1] Cf. Hearings, House Committee on Post Office and Civil Service, March 6, 1951. Congress did *not* increase the rates and Donaldson did *not* curtail the service any further.

he was talking about. It was surprising to find that the figures had been more or less grabbed out of thin air and then released as authentic. Even the few newspapermen who had been friendly to Donaldson felt they had been "had," and the uproar in the Congress grew in intensity as the Democrats sought to disassociate themselves from the policies of the Postmaster General, and the Republicans sought to make political hay out of the disintegrating mail service.[2]

Donaldson's discomfiture was increased at this juncture by the defection of a one-time ally, James J. Doran, a former chief of post office inspectors. Doran, unlike most inspectors, believed the postal service should be, above all else, a service. This did not please Donaldson, and made Doran somewhat of a *persona non grata* in the Department. He was given jobs of lesser importance until October 1, 1950, when he felt he could no longer live with the existing policies of Donaldson's administration and voluntarily retired. He then spoke his mind in a series of brilliantly informative articles that blasted the manner in which the service was being dragged in the dust.

In the midst of this turmoil, we embarked on still another wage campaign. The increase we had won in 1949, despite all the drama that accompanied it, was a relative fleabite when compared to the need. We were determined to close the yawning gap between letter carriers' wages and the cost of living.

Once again, mainly because of the dilatory tactics of Chairman Murray of the House Committee, the process of getting a pay bill reported out and then voted into law was lengthy and involved.

A pay bill was introduced in November of 1950, but, despite widespread sympathy in its favor, it was killed when the Eighty-first Congress adjourned on January 3, 1951.

When the Eighty-second Congress convened, our friends in

[2] It is significant that *both* parties, in their 1952 campaign platforms, promised to reform and improve the postal service if they won the presidential election.

both Houses lost no time in introducing bills in our behalf. Ten months later President Truman approved Public Law 204, which gave us a four-hundred-dollars-a-year raise in pay.

In that ten months' interval the jockeying was intense and sometimes brutal. There would be no point in giving a play by play account of all that went on,[3] since there is a certain sameness to these legislative struggles, but the skirmishing was both brisk and constant.

We were helped indirectly in our campaign by Postmaster General Donaldson, however. The congressional committees asked him in January 1951 for official comment on the proposed pay legislation. He did not reply to the request until June 27,[4] and his reaction was, of course, unfavorable. The Congress was so teed-off at Donaldson by this time that his opposition won many members, previously lukewarm, over to our side. In the Congress at that time the feeling was that if Donaldson was against something, the members were for it, and vice versa. Donaldson wanted a postage rate increase and the Congress would have none of it; Donaldson did not want a wage increase and the Congress gave it to us.

Donaldson did eventually come out for a 10 per cent increase, but that was very late in the game when it had become obvious that the Congress was going to do better than that for the postal employees. It mattered little at this point what the Postmaster General favored or did not favor. The Congress was not listening to him very attentively.

The wage bill was passed in another typical "photo finish," on the day before adjournment. It was our sixth such victory in the eleven years I had been president of the National Association of Letter Carriers. It gave every full-time postal employee

---

[3] Students of the legislative processes can get the full story by reading my biennial report to the membership of the NALC in the September 1952 issue of *The Postal Record,* pp. 40-46.

[4] That old bottleneck in the PMG's office, no doubt.

an increase of four hundred dollars a year, and every substitute an increase of twenty cents an hour. The bill also provided a kind of reclassification of postmasters and postal supervisors with a ceiling of eight hundred dollars a year on any increase they would receive.

The pay bill, which was signed by the President after the Congress had gone home, was made retroactive to July 1, 1951. As a result of its passage, letter carriers were now receiving a starting wage of $3,270 (as opposed to $1,700 in 1941) and a top wage of $4,070 (as opposed to $2,100 in 1941).

Substitute letter carriers were getting a minimum wage of $1.61 and a maximum wage of $2.01, after our 1951 pay raise. In 1941 they were getting sixty-five cents an hour.

The years 1951-52 gave the Association further cause for self-congratulation, in that we saw our dreams of a new home of our own come to fruition.

The dream of a letter carriers' building came into being as early as 1924, when an abortive movement was started to erect one in memory of Edward J. Cantwell, a long-time great secretary of the Association. Although this particular project came to nothing, the germ of the idea remained in the minds of many letter carriers.

The need for action became pressing in 1941, when we were asked by the American Federation of Labor to vacate the space we had occupied in their headquarters for twenty-four years. Since this request came just one month before our involvement in World War II, we were unable to comply with it.

The AFL was most generous in its treatment of us. We remained in their building until 1948, when we moved to another building owned by the parent union, a beautiful and historical converted mansion on H Street, almost across the street from the White House.

This move had been undertaken only as a temporary measure. As early as five years before, at the 1943 convention in Denver,

I had broached the subject of building our own headquarters and had received from the delegates in attendance an enthusiastic green light.

At the 1950 convention in Seattle National Treasurer Charles H. Dillon, of Brooklyn, in a ringing and eloquent speech recommended that the NALC be given permission by its membership to borrow a million dollars and proceed with the construction of the building. The membership gave us unanimous approval. Dillon's remarks on that occasion have gone down in our annals as "the million-dollar speech." Eventually I was able to put Jerry Keating, who was by then national secretary, in charge of the project. This turned out to be one of the best decisions I ever made.

As far as I was concerned, nothing would do for us except what Washington real-estate people call a "monumental site," a lot which faces the national Capitol. We found such a site at the corner of Indiana Avenue and First Street, Northwest. It consisted of just about seven thousand square feet and was available for around $79,000.

We then consulted architects Harvey Miller and, later, Arthur S. Anderson, both top-flight men. We soon learned that we could not afford a small building; we could afford only an eight-story building large enough not only to house us, but also to accommodate tenants whose rent would help pay our operating costs. Rough plans were drawn up for such a building, and the cost was estimated at $1,800,000.

Keating was able to report this progress to the membership at our convention in Detroit in 1946. The plans were approved, and it was agreed to allot one dollar of each member's *per capita* tax to the building fund.

Provision was also made, somewhat later, for individual contributions from active or retired members of the NALC, and this proved to be a valuable source of revenue to us. As a matter of fact, 75 per cent of our local branches and Ladies' Auxiliaries contributed to the fund over and above the regular *per capita* tax deduction. This idea of independent contributions was originated by Brother C. Lignon, and the first such gift came from his own Branch 1690, at West Palm Beach, Florida. The largest single independent contribution came in 1949, and was a complete surprise to us. Fred B. Hutchings, a devoted member of our Branch 134, Syracuse, New York, died, making the National Association of Letter Carriers the beneficiary under his will. The building fund received $37,000 from his estate. Hutchings Hall, the beautiful auditorium in the NALC building is named in his memory. Oddly enough, Fred Hutchings, who by all accounts was a quiet and kindly gentleman, was unknown to any of the national officers and had never been particularly prominent in NALC affairs. He was simply devoted to his fellow letter carriers.

By November 1950 we had progressed sufficiently to break the ground for our new headquarters. This was done on November 20, and Bill Green, president of the AFL, turned the first shovelful of earth to start us on our way.

Green was there also on August 20, 1952, when we formally dedicated the new building. So was my dear friend George Meany, who was then secretary-treasurer of the AFL and who is now president of the combined AFL–CIO.

The dedication speech was delivered by former Postmaster General James A. Farley. Understandably, Postmaster General Donaldson was not invited to participate in the ceremonies. We had a full complement of congressmen, letter carriers, and friends of the postal service. This was a proud day in the lives of all letter carriers and, as their president, a particularly proud day for me.

From a prestige point of view, the decision to build for ourselves was the wisest the leadership of the NALC ever made. As this is being written in the president's office on the eighth floor of our building I can look straight across the Taft Memorial at the Capitol and the office buildings of both the House and the Senate.

And, more important, those worthy ladies and gentlemen who labor on Capitol Hill can look straight at us. Whenever they see our tall, white building gleaming in the Washington sun they know we are here, they know we are in business to stay, and they know we are in the Big Leagues.

From a financial point of view, the decision was equally wise. As of today we have paid off all but about $600,000 of our debt, and the building itself is almost breaking even on its operating and maintenance costs. We occupy the equivalent of three floors of the building, renting out the other five floors. Of course, the over-all value of the building in these days of inflation is just about twice what we paid to have it built.

Our building is no pleasure dome. The emphasis is on functionalism rather than on grandeur; it is dignified and comfortable but not gaudy. Certainly it reflects accurately the prestige and the growth which the National Association of Letter Carriers has achieved, and in its own way it is a fitting symbol of the new importance of organized labor in the political and economic life of the nation.

Our national convention was held in New York City in 1952, and it was perhaps the biggest and most dramatic of all our conclaves.

It opened on Labor Day, right in the middle of the presidential campaigns. Organized labor, then as now, was strongly Democratic in its voting sympathies. The Democratic candidate, Adlai Stevenson, was inundated with invitations to speak before impressive Labor Day audiences. The Republican candidate, General Eisenhower, was almost ignored. His supporters told me he had literally nothing planned for this politically important occasion.

Democrat though I am, I felt this was both unjust and unwise. After all, Eisenhower was just a *soi-disant* Republican, untainted by the Taft-Hartley brush and uncontaminated by the most reactionary elements in his adopted party. He was surrounded by comparatively "liberal" Republicans and there seemed to be hope that, whether he won or lost, he would be able to impart to his Republican colleagues a healthy glow of modernism.

Then again it seemed quite possible that Ike would win the election. The polls were in great disrepute in 1952 after the debacle of 1948, but there had to be some truth behind the substantial majorities they were attributing to Eisenhower in almost every sector of the country. Some of my brethren in the labor movement were inclined to indulge in wishful thinking. They believed that the same sort of miracle which returned Harry Truman to office four years earlier would send Stevenson to the White House in 1952.

I had my doubts. As far as the personalities of the candidates were concerned, the position of the two parties had been somewhat reversed. In 1948 Harry Truman's controversial but undoubtedly warm personality had reached the heart of the average voter and elicited from him a response, while Dewey's public personality was undeniably frosty. In 1952 the Republican candidate was the warm and endearing public personality while Stevenson, great man though he is, had a somewhat specialized appeal. He never did excite the average working man in the same way Roosevelt or Truman did. I am being objective when I say this, because I voted for Stevenson in 1952 and again in 1956 and have never regretted that I did so.

It is a pity, but it is true that presidential elections usually boil down to a popularity contest and the successful candidate is chosen for attributes that have nothing to do with his fitness or lack of fitness for the job. Thus it is quite possible that Adlai Stevenson would have made a better President than Dwight D. Eisenhower. It is even possible that Tom Dewey would have made a better President than Harry Truman.[5] There can be no

---

[5] A very wise man who had considerable experience in these matters once said that, if elected, Tom Dewey would have been the most efficient and the most unpopular President in our history.

telling about such things. But, in any event, the decision of the electorate in each case was based on considerations far removed from those which would be decisive if we had a utopian republic.

So it was a combination of my innate sense of fair play and my suspicion that Dwight D. Eisenhower was going to be the next President of the United States that led me to invite him to address our national convention in New York City on Labor Day, 1952.

I went out to Denver to deliver the invitation in person. Acting as the essential intermediaries in this adventure were my good friends, and Eisenhower's good friends, Senator Frank Carlson, of Kansas, ranking Republican member of the Senate Post Office Committee, and Congressman Bob Corbett of the House Post Office Committee.

The invitation was swiftly, graciously, and even gleefully accepted. When I left the Brown Palace Hotel that day I was the golden-haired boy. I had, after all, eliminated the very real possibility that Eisenhower would be totally snubbed by organized labor on its great holiday.

The occasion of his appearance at our convention was a typical Eisenhower triumph. His infectious grin and obvious sincerity warmed up the entire convention hall. Just by waving his hand he made friends of letter carriers who had never believed they would be chanting, "I like Ike." But they did. Eisenhower has that kind of personality.

The speech he made proved to be a vital one. It was important not so much for its content as for its mood. He was not an expert in labor matters and made no pretense of being one. He convinced everyone in that convention hall, however, and, eventually, almost everyone in the labor movement, that he desired above all things to be fair. "I am reminded that yesterday morning I decided to write to the people who work in America a pledge," he said. "And in that pledge I said that, if I have assigned to me for the next four years the responsibility of filling the highest post in the land, I am going to have one ambition: that, at the end of these four years, every working man and woman in the United States would say: 'He was fair.' "

There were two sections of General Eisenhower's speech which were of major importance to me. He said: "I want to repeat to the full convention what I promised, and the request that I made to your president out in Denver only a couple of weeks ago. I said to him: 'Mr. Doherty, if I have this grave responsibility, I request that, if ever you find anything coming up that you believe is damaging the postal service, or is unfair to any member thereof, you bring that to me, and I promise in advance you won't sit on the doorstep any time to get to me.' " (Applause and cheers) [6]

The second vital passage was this: "I couldn't be a friend of yours if I didn't try my very best to understand your problems through your leaders and by mingling with you, and if I didn't try to carry out the definite pledge of the Republican platform: More efficient service with more frequent deliveries of the mail."

Of course, things did not work out that way. The same candidate Eisenhower who spoke so warmly and convincingly became the President Eisenhower who three times (up to the present writing) vetoed wage increases for postal employees.

The same candidate Eisenhower who promised "more efficient service with more frequent deliveries of mail" has done nothing up until the time of this writing to restore the all-important second delivery in residential areas.

And the same candidate Eisenhower who promised that I could always go to him with my troubles became almost completely inaccessible to me when I was badly in need of help.

And yet, I do not think there was an ounce of cynicism or hypocrisy in the man. I believe he was speaking with the utmost sincerity. He simply did not understand that the President of the

[6] Cf. Official Proceedings of the Thirty-eighth Biennial Convention of the NALC (1952), p. 9.

United States can be so insulated by his advisers from the realities of everyday life that he has only a vague idea of what is really going on among ordinary people. He must believe what his advisers tell him, and he is pretty well at their mercy as far as the things that reach him and the things that do not reach him are concerned. Unfortunately, his advisers were overly protective, and they hurt his popularity by withholding pertinent information from him.

Certainly, when I finally did get to see him during a wage dispute some years later, after getting a complete run around for several months, he was genuinely shocked when I told him how I had been systematically frustrated by his Palace Guard. I am utterly convinced that President Eisenhower did not even know I had been trying to see him.

But, in the final analysis, the real reasons that the glowing campaign promises to the letter carriers came to naught can be traced to the personality and the character of the man Eisenhower chose to be his Postmaster General, Arthur E. Summerfield.

CHAPTER 24

THE TRAGEDY
OF KING ARTHUR

WHEN January 1953 rolled around, the optimism among postal employees was endemic and contagious. We of the National Association of Letter Carriers were especially enthusiastic and happily expectant.

We had just moved into our own building and we were experiencing the euphoria which usually accompanies an advantageous change of surroundings. We had been freed, by virtue of the November elections of a postmaster general who had been for too long a thorn in our sides. And the newly elected President Eisenhower and his newly selected Postmaster General were making statements right and left which sounded to our eager ears like the most wonderful kind of music.

President Eisenhower, in an interview with Jerry Kluttz, the federal reporter of the *Washington Post,* promised "quick and sympathetic attention" to the postal employees' pay problems. "I am aware, despite wage increases, that the ordinary civilian federal employee is economically worse off than in 1939, due to inflation and high taxes," he said. "I do not believe we can enlist or keep employees competent to conduct the business of the United States with the kind of economic prospect confronting them. We can, and will, do better than that."

Arthur E. Summerfield, as chairman of the Republican National Committee, had managed General Eisenhower's successful campaign for the presidency. When he was appointed Postmaster General he severed his official political ties and announced that he was going to devote his time exclusively to running and improving the postal service. In his first official statement after his selection was announced he stressed "improvement of all branches of the Department and the increase of its morale" as the paramount objectives of his administration. "We will operate the postal system as it should be operated—in the service of the people and as their most vital means of all-important communications. I too, like you, am interested in two-a-day deliveries," he said, while the letter carriers' huzzahs rang through the land.

One would think that by this time in my life I would have accumulated a sufficient number of scars to look with suspicion upon the promises of politicians. But, alas! I was just as badly fooled as everyone else by these fair words and encouraging smiles. It looked like the beginning of a new and wonderful epoch in postal history. It is hardly remarkable that optimism was running rampant among letter carriers in that January of 1953.

It is a shame it had such a short run.

Future historians will find the Summerfield administration of the Postal Establishment an enigma. Certainly Arthur Summerfield has been the most controversial Postmaster General in our history, and were it not for some fatal flaws in his personal and political philosophy, he might well have become the best.

There has been no middle course with him. The things that

have been commendable in his administration have been almost incredibly good, and the things that have been reprehensible have been horrible.

In the field of business management and mechanical development he has shown great vision and courage. In the field of human engineering he has shown a persistent purblindness that will result in his leaving behind him, when he quits, an employee force that is, for the most part, sullen and embittered.

I write these words sadly. I have a real, though highly controllable, liking for the man. I have admired his "golden viscera" in times of travail. I have admired the way he has given the postal service his entire attention and energy, even to the point of seriously impairing his health. But I fear he has been sadly betrayed by his own weaknesses. Like so many men who have risen to great wealth from impoverished beginnings, he has shown little real sympathy for the working classes that gave him birth.[1] Too, like many others who have made their own way in life, he has, in my opinion, been dogged by a personal vanity which has made him on some occasions unwisely aggressive and on others unwisely cautious. During the past eight years, despite many violent disagreements with him, I have consistently tried to be Arthur Summerfield's friend. I have tried to be helpful by offering advice based on many years of practical experience. I have tried to convince him that postmasters general are remembered for their attitudes toward their employees and not for their financial acumen. I cannot claim any success. I have always found Mr. Summerfield interested, not in advice, but in consent.

During his earliest days in office he showed a unique courage in doing battle with the Congress. His fearlessness, at first, caught the public imagination. The postal service, which had always been considered pretty dull stuff by the people and the press of the nation, suddenly became exciting and controversial. But admira-

---

[1] His father was a rural letter carrier in Pinconning, Michigan. This has apparently had little effect on his attitude toward postal employees.

tion, even among his friends and supporters, turned to misgiving as it became more and more apparent that his only answer to even mild opposition was wild and indiscriminate slugging, with a touch of gouging thrown in for good measure. By nature Summerfield is a club fighter, not a main-event tactician.

In many ways it might have been better if Summerfield had taken all telephones out of his office. A choleric man at times, he has been much given to picking up the phone and ferociously bawling out senators and congressmen who, he felt, were not co-operating with his program of the moment. This is *not* the way to win friends or influence people. Since the Congress can cut off the Department's water at a moment's notice, and since congressional co-operation is necessary if any progress is to be made, this kind of approach is foolish indeed. Many of Summerfield's proposed reforms have been hamstrung because of the active dislike he has incurred on the Hill. Few cabinet officers in history have aroused as much congressional indignation as he has and this widespread disapproval has been ruinous to his hopes. His knee-in-the-groin approach to diplomacy has been a complete failure in the Congress and, according to informed sources, has caused concern even in the White House.[2]

When he took office he had the Congress, the employee force, the press, and the people solidly behind him. As his administration nears its end he has lost almost all of them. It is ironic that, despite his many real and permanent achievements, he will probably be remembered principally as the Postmaster General who made *Lady Chatterley's Lover* a best seller.

"But yet," as Othello says, "the pity of it, Iago . . . The pity of it!" How much in the way of reputation he could have achieved had he but tried only half as hard to achieve it. How much more

---

[2] I once tried to soften the anger of a congressman by remarking that in many ways Summerfield was his own worst enemy. The congressman growled: "Not while I'm still alive, he isn't!" This was a Republican member who, under normal circumstances, should have been Summerfield's friend.

he would have been remembered had he only stopped more often to remember others. How much more he would have accomplished had he not persisted in disregarding others in his quest for accomplishment.

Certainly he started out well. The postal service had drifted into decrepitude through constant lack of managerial attention. Summerfield began by selecting a team of executives from the top echelons of private industry rather than from the ranks of prominent politicians: Charles R. Hook, Jr., from the Chesapeake & Ohio; Norman R. Abrams, from Congoleum-Nairn; Ormonde A. Kieb, one of the best-known industrial real-estate men in New Jersey; John Allen, from Sears-Roebuck; Albert J. Robertson, a prominent midwestern banker; Eugene J. Lyons, from Merck & Co.; Ben H. Guill, a former Texas Republican congressman who turned out to be a most effective postal lobbyist; Gerald Cullinan, a top-flight public relations man and writer from San Francisco by way of Texas; and others. These men brought a new vigor and an entirely new tempo into the Postal Establishment and there was, in those early and formative days, a spirit of crusading which was like a living thing.

And the good Lord knows, the old postal system needed a crusading spirit. I have been told that most of the newcomers, accustomed as they were to the more orderly and progressive business *mores* of the outside world suffered a kind of traumatic shock when they discovered the business deficiencies that existed in the Post Office Department. For instance, at the very first staff meeting General Summerfield, so I am informed, asked for a financial statement as a starting point for their deliberations. He was told that no such thing existed. Financial statements, because of the antiquated accounting system in use, ran eighteen months behind events and were used as historical documents and not as management tools! (Summerfield engaged as consultant Maurice H. Stans, one of the nation's ablest certified public accountants. Stans mechanized and modernized the accounting system in one year so that financial data were up-to-the-minute, accurate, and more useful, and in doing so, he enabled the Department to save about $25,000,000 a year in man-hours. Stans later succeeded Charlie Hook as Deputy Postmaster General and then was made Director of the Budget.) In that first year the Summerfield team began the decentralization of postal operations, which, rightly or wrongly, has been called (by Summerfield) the greatest industrial reorganization ever attempted in or out of government. Also, when they found that there was no bureau responsible for the welfare of the half-million postal employees on the payroll, they got the Congress to create a Bureau of Personnel. When they found that, despite the fact that the mails were becoming more and more snarled by the mounting volume, there had been almost no attention whatsoever given to industrial research and development, they embarked on a massive program of modernization and mechanization. They boldly attacked the problem of plant obsolescence, inadequate transportation patterns, and other areas of inefficiency and waste.

All this was exciting and commendable. The year 1953 was probably the most revolutionary single year in postal history in every area except one: that of employee relations.

As much as we of the NALC admired the vision and energy of the new administration, we began to grow restive as each month passed without any positive suggestions regarding the economic welfare of the employees. Postmaster General Summerfield's speeches were very little like the statements he had been making before he became Postmaster General. He suddenly stopped referring to the post office as a service and began calling it a "business," or a "public utility." He also stopped emphasizing employee benefits and started emphasizing the necessity for balancing the budget. He refused to talk about a pay raise for employees, and went all out for a postage rate increase.

For a while the Postmaster General postponed any serious talk about a pay increase for postal employees by saying that he had to wait until the projected Bureau of Personnel was authorized by the Congress and set up in the Department. Although it was hard lines on the employee force to make them wait for a pay boost under such conditions, Summerfield's argument made sense, particularly when he drew for us a picture of the rosy future we could all look forward to when the Personnel Bureau would be a reality. We did not realize, of course, that the Bureau of Personnel would be used as a weapon *against* every effort to grant adequate compensation for postal employees.

The National Association of Letter Carriers participated in the postage rate hearings in 1953, strongly supporting Summerfield's request for an increase in postage. We insisted, as we always have insisted and always will insist, that rates and wages should be considered separately, and that they should in no way be dependent on one another. We are also eternally committed to the principle that the post office is a service and should not be expected to make a "profit." Nevertheless, we agreed that an increase in postage was long overdue. The Congress, however, refused to see things our way.

The lid blew off the relationship between the Department and the NALC in early 1954, and the explosion was sudden and loud.

We had been irritated by a series of minor incidents that pointed up, in our minds, a lack of cohesive leadership in the Department. We would go in to see Norman Abrams, the Assistant Postmaster General for Operations, and therefore the nominal boss of all postal employees, with our grievances. "Norm," as he was known throughout the postal service, is a warm person with an intuitive affection and respect for the human family. He would work with us, and more often than not, he would decide cases in our favor. But we found that in many of the most important cases these happy interviews did not result in corrective action. We were convinced that this was not Norm Abrams's fault. We believed then and believe now that he was simply being overruled by the Postmaster General. We could usually win our cases involving *individuals,* if we had justice on our side, but we had practically no success in winning cases in the Department involving general principles.

One of these instances involved the study regarding the reorganization of the pay structure within the Postal Establishment. It is true, the pay structure was a mess. Half a million employees had job *titles,* but there were no job *descriptions* to back up those titles. This enabled some politically favored employees to be called supervisors and to receive a supervisor's pay without actually doing the work of a supervisor. It also made it possible for a politically minded postmaster to make a rank-and-file employee perform many of the duties of a supervisor while getting no increase in his salary. Differentials in pay had little to do with the duties of the employees. Reform was needed, and needed badly. Because of generations of inattention, the pay structure of the Postal Establishment had indeed become an unweeded garden that had grown to seed.

Almost immediately after the authorization of the new Bureau of Personnel but before an assistant postmaster general was selected to head it, Summerfield engaged a business consultant firm called Fry Associates to make a study and report on the postal pay structure. In November 1953 I was told that representatives of the National Association of Letter Carriers would be invited to participate in the formulation of recommendations for the reform of the wage scales. Naturally, we were delighted at the prospect. But that was the last we ever heard of the suggestion. The Fry people, who naturally enough knew nothing about postal matters, were forced to make a rather hurried report without the assistance of any representatives from the field service. It is not surprising that the report, when released, was so shot through with inequities and inconsistencies that it was laughed out of committee, and produced nothing substantial in the way of pay reform.

Similarly, the letter carriers were asked to participate in a study, conducted in Dallas, Minneapolis, and Indianapolis, concerning the advisability of restoring two-a-day mail service. We complied with this request, and did so with pleasure. The tests were run to our entire satisfaction. Reports presumably were written on the results. We cannot be sure of this, however, because we never were able to see the reports. Nothing whatsoever came of these tests, and we were never given the courtesy of an explanation as to what they showed.

A disturbing pattern was emerging. We found that in matters concerning postal employees one of two courses was generally followed: either satisfactory agreements were made and then completely forgotten; or sweeping decisions were made without any pretense of previous consultation with us. It often happened that we learned about the most serious decisions concerning our welfare only by reading the daily newspapers. As the basic anti-unionism of the Summerfield administration unveiled itself, Departmental employees in the lower echelons were virtually forbidden to communicate with us, and those in the top levels were diffident about talking to us because they were afraid of being knifed in the back by their associates for doing so.

In all this, of course, we felt the subtle, deadly hand of the Inspection Service was showing itself. The Inspection Service does a wonderful job of selling itself to every new Postmaster General, and since most of the top career men in the various Departmental bureaus are graduates of the service, the influence of the service is much greater than its capabilities should warrant. It almost always happens, when a Postmaster General is sworn in, that the chief inspector performs a convincing snow-job on him almost before he has completed the reading of his oath of office. The Postmaster General is told that the Inspection Service is his own private police force, answerable only to him and loyal only to him. They are to him what the Swiss Guard is to the Pope. They are his eyes and ears, the only segment of the employee force he can trust. This is a beautiful routine and it appeals irresistibly to the ego of the boss. When he first takes over, a post-master general feels strange and alone in his new position and he welcomes the consoling idea of having a police force within his Department which he can trust without question. And to a man of even normal vanity, the idea of having a force of a thousand dedicated, selfless, fearless servants prepared to shed their last collective drops of blood for him at the drop of a memorandum is a heady one. Postmasters general almost invariably swallow the story without question. It is a beautiful dream.

Unfortunately, that is all it is—a dream. In my opinion, the Inspection Service is loyal to itself, period. To keep up appearances it might shed an occasional drop of blood for the Postmaster General, but he would be a fool if he expected any hemorrhages. It is generally conceded that inspectors are brainwashed as systematically as are the members of the secret police of totalitarian nations. They savagely resist change or any attempts by the postal administration to delegate authority to anyone who is not an inspector, because every time this is done the stranglehold of the inspectors on the postal service is a little weakened.

One of the greatest tragedies of Arthur Summerfield's administration is the faith and reliance he has placed in his Inspection Service.

Those who have worked closely with Summerfield contend that he is most likely to be swayed by the last person who speaks to him. The inspectors evidently cottoned on to this early and made sure that they got the last word in. That word was almost always negative. Encouraged by their success they grew bolder than they had ever grown before. They found themselves able to circumvent the Bureau of Operations and to kill major reforms before they could be placed in action. They resented experienced businessmen taking over positions of authority in the Department, since this weakened their power. In previous administrations, when the political appointees did not care to trouble themselves too much with the operation of the post office, the inspectors were uninhibited in their domination of the service. When Summerfield imported men for the top jobs who had every intention of personally running the bureaus for which they were responsible, this threatened to reduce the power of the inspectors. They fought back by devising ways of short-circuiting the assistant postmasters general. They are experts at infighting, and they are tireless in furthering their own ends.

So, during these early days of the Summerfield administration, while others in the Department were trying to establish a modern system of management-labor relations with responsible employee organizations, the Inspection Service was pouring poison into the Summerfield ear and solidifying his natural prejudice against the postal unions.[3]

The antagonism which was developing between Summerfield and the employee groups did not break into the open until early 1954, however, when the hearings began on a projected pay raise. Since the Eighty-third Congress had a Republican majority, Representative Ed Rees of Kansas was chairman of the Post Office Committee. Rees has been very close to the Postmaster General and is a man of intensely anti-labor sympathies.

There was considerable sentiment in the Congress in favor of a bill which had been introduced by Representative Gardner Withrow of Wisconsin, and which would provide for a flat across-the-board salary increase of eight hundred dollars for every postal employee. We of the NALC testified enthusiastically in favor of this bill. The Postmaster General was almost fanatically opposed.

However, Chairman Rees introduced his own bill, which, of course, had been worked out by the Post Office Department officials. It was based on the Fry Report and called for the establishment of a system of classification that was so faulty and unjust that, if it had been accepted, it would have created unmitigated

[3] The Summerfield Chevrolet Company in Flint, Michigan, is reputed to be the largest General Motors dealership in the United States. It is strictly a non-union shop.

chaos in the entire Postal Establishment. It would have given letter carriers an average of one hundred dollars apiece, and would have boosted the salaries of some supervisors as much as five thousand dollars a year. As a matter of fact, it would have given some letter carriers an increase of only ten dollars a year. It would have given pennies to the poor and armloads of greenbacks to those who needed them least. Naturally we resisted this shocking bill with considerable fervor.

This resistance on our part created a weird situation. The worthy gentlemen who had been imported to run the Department had come to Washington burning with a crusading spirit. They had thrown themselves into their work with evangelical fervor. Summerfield, at that time, was the peerless leader who could do no wrong. And even the most reasoned criticism on our part brought forth from them violent and almost frenzied retorts.

I must admit that this shook me more than a little. In the first place, these were men who, for the most part, had been brought up in the atmosphere of give and take which always exists in normal labor-management relations. They were all presumably real grownup kids, and here they were acting like rather immature Cub Scouts. This was unsettling. Summerfield would evidently exhort them to go out and do battle, and out they would go, eyes glistening and voices ringing with the new evangelism, denouncing William C. Doherty and the National Association of Letter Carriers in terms that would seem impolite if used in a group of reasonably scurrilous fishwives. As an experienced labor leader I was accustomed to having my opinions ignored upon occasion by the representatives of management. I was also accustomed, upon occasion, to have my opinions countered by managerial objections. But this was the first time I had ever had my opinions induce managerial hysteria.

The second thing that disturbed me was that this was *articulate* hysteria. Some of the evangelistic brethren in the Department, even though they were unencumbered by factual data, had the ability to pour it on. They had a talent for publicity. Naturally this made it necessary for me to answer their charges, and in the eyes of some of the Departmental zealots this was something very close to sacrilege. (Their attitude reminded me of Voltaire's phrase: "This is a vicious beast; when attacked, he fights back!") And for several months the air was almost literally blue, as charges and countercharges were shot off with a wild abandon. The battle of 1954 made Donnybrook look by comparison like a meeting of the Ladies Sodality in a silk-stocking parish. Much of the bitterness sprang from lack of humor in the Department. Unfortunately, crusaders seldom have a sense of humor, and Republican crusaders are usually the most humorless of all. I do not pretend to know why this should be so but, by and large, Democrats are more extroverted than Republicans and seem to enjoy life a good deal more. There are many exceptions to this rule of thumb, on both sides of the aisle, but Democrats generally seem to be more interested in people, and Republicans seem to be more interested in issues. This may explain the consistent popularity of the Democrats in congressional elections. After all, people vote and issues do not.

Certainly at this juncture there was very little evidence of a sense of humor in the Summerfield administration. Everybody was too busy going about the grim job of "saving" the world. Gerry Cullinan, who was both confidential assistant to the Postmaster General and special assistant to the Deputy Postmaster General, and who was an exception to the rule, once said in some despair: "This is the only administration in history in which a man can rise by his own gravity and sink by his own levity." Certainly, Departmental officials were taking themselves with fearful seriousness during these first few years of the Summerfield administration.

All the vituperation was pretty meaningless, because the Rees Bill, from the day it was introduced, had absolutely no chance of acceptance by the committee.

When this became painfully apparent, after twenty-four days of hearings and seven days of fairly wild executive sessions on the part of the Committee, Congressman Bob Corbett, at the risk of his political future, came to the rescue once again by introducing a substitute bill that called for a 7 per cent increase, with certain elements of sensible classification included. The bill was reported out by the Committee over the chairman's objections.

This maneuver caught Summerfield by surprise and infuriated him. (The fact that Corbett is a Republican did not improve the Postmaster General's temper.) He exerted intolerable pressure on the Congress, and since he had been the Republican National Chairman in 1952 he had considerable leverage. He was able to get the legislation tightly bottled up in the Rules Committee.

Fortunately, however, there were some members of the G.O.P. majority in the Congress who were humanitarians first and Republicans second. Bob Corbett was and is one of these. The late Congressman Harold C. Hagen of Minnesota was another. Hagen, who was the second ranking member of the Post Office Committee, introduced a petition in the House to discharge the Corbett Bill out of the Rules Committee.

Capitol Hill became a battlefield. Summerfield enlisted the postmasters' and supervisors' associations in his struggle to prevent members from signing the petition. He kept the telephone busy around the clock trying to charm, browbeat, and otherwise persuade members into a state of submission. Jerry Keating and I mounted a counteroffensive to get the required number of members to sign. The battle rocked back and forth as the opposing parties stormed the corridors of the House Office Buildings tracking down prospects.

There were enough people engaged in lobbying for and against this discharge petition to man a respectable assault on Gibraltar. At times the elevators and corridors seemed so crowded that one wondered how the congressmen could get to and from their chambers.

This went on for twenty-one days. In the end, we won the fight. The necessary 218 names were signed to the petition and the bill was duly discharged from the Rules Committee.

Summerfield would not accept defeat. He tried a number of diversionary tactics. He adopted the usual gambit of postmasters general of offering compromises which were more palatable to him than the Corbett Bill. We refused to compromise. We went for broke.

He then infuriated congressmen by intimating that Eisenhower would veto any bill that did not carry the personal approval of the Postmaster General.

The Congress of the United States does not yield to this kind of threat.

Summerfield's bludgeoning tactics backfired on him. When the Corbett Bill, with amendments, came up for a vote in the House he could find only 29 members to support him, while 352 members voted in favor of the bill.

It was even more embarrassing in the Senate, where the Postmaster General could muster only four votes in opposition, while sixty-nine senators voted against him.

Remember, this was a Republican Congress, and Summerfield, just two years previously had been the man-of-the-hour who had led his party to victory and had managed the campaign which had put Eisenhower in the White House. Because of his wild swinging, his threats and denunciations, he had even alienated most of the members of his own party in the Congress.

In view of the landslide in both Houses of the Congress I did not think the President would veto the bill. Eisenhower had expressed, privately and publicly, his devotion to postal employees and had sympathized with their economic plight on many occasions.

But he did veto it. Just as Calvin Coolidge had done three decades previously, Eisenhower waited until the Congress had adjourned (and therefore could not override him) and then he released his veto.

We won by 352-29 in the House.

We won by 69-4 in the Senate.

We lost 1-0 in the White House.

I know Arthur Summerfield considered this a victory. He had predicted a veto. Indeed, he had threatened one in the President's name! And, as it turned out, he prevailed.

But if this was a victory, it was, at best, a Pyrrhic one. His prestige in the Congress had been shattered, and among postal employees his name became anathema. He has never been able to recover from the "victory" he won over the Congress and the postal employees in the summer of 1954.

CHAPTER 25

THE VANITY
OF HUMAN WISHES

THE NALC biennial convention in 1954 was held in Cleveland, and for the first time in four years departmental representatives were invited to attend. As a matter of fact, I personally invited General Summerfield, hoping that he would be able to give some reasonable explanation of the hard-headed, hardhearted policies of his administration to date. Summerfield refused, but assigned Assistant Postmaster General (Personnel) Eugene J. Lyons in his place. Although Lyons was treated with every courtesy, his speech, through no fault of his own, was *not* a success. For the first time in the history of the NALC, mention of the Postmaster General's name from the platform incited such a chorus of boos that I had to work hard, in the interest of fair play, to quell them. Even Burleson's name had not been booed at our conventions. Although this had been partly due to fear of reprisals (since the laws and the customs of the country were not so protective of our liberties in Burleson's day), nevertheless that swelling wave of boos was a certain indication of the anger which letter carriers felt toward their boss. And the great pity of it is that, with just a touch of common understanding and sensible compromise on Summerfield's part, those boos could so easily have been cheers. The letter carriers had wanted so much to love Summerfield, but their offers of affection had been spurned. It was not that he loved them less, but that he loved a balanced budget more.

In the lexicon of letter carriers ever since Summerfield has been known as "Winterfield."

At the American Federation of Labor's annual convention in Los Angeles later that year I was forced to do something that was both difficult for me and distasteful. When President Eisenhower addressed the convention, I felt I could not in all honesty occupy the seat on the stage to which my position as vice-president entitled me. Instead, I sat with my fellow letter carriers on the floor of the convention.

I cannot be a phony. I was still so indignant at the way Eisenhower had vetoed our pay bill that I could not in good conscience sit on the stage and beam approval as he told the workers of America how much he loved them.

And yet I still think the President's veto was the result of weakness, not of malice. Summerfield had committed himself so far on the pay question that, in the event that the President *had* signed the bill, he would have almost certainly been forced to resign. This is symptomatic of Summerfield's entire *modus operandi*. He almost always pushes belligerently ahead, somewhat in the manner of General Patton, leaving his supply lines far in the rear, blowing bridges sky high behind him, allowing himself no possible opportunity for strategic retreat. He has only one way of operating and that is "Damn the torpedoes! Full speed ahead."

I feel that Summerfield, in 1954, through his stubbornness put Eisenhower on the spot. The President was torn between his desire, so often stated, of helping the letter carriers achieve economic equality, and his loyalty to the cabinet member who had organized and managed the campaign which had put him in the White House. It was a tough decision, one of many such which the Postmaster General has forced on the President. Although I understood the reasons for President Eisenhower's decision against us, I felt my presence on the stage during his speech would indicate a tacit approval of that decision. This would have been impossible.

My refusal received nationwide publicity, and in some quarters I was roundly criticized for what I did. I could not have done otherwise, and if the same circumstances prevailed, I would do it again.

As it turned out, President Eisenhower showed he also could do it all over again. He was destined to veto still another pay bill before 1955 came to an end, and a third pay bill in 1957. No President in history had ever vetoed two postal pay bills. Eisenhower, at Summerfield's insistence, vetoed three. (As this is being written a fourth pay-bill veto is being threatened.)

Summerfield's combination of stubbornness and vanity caused him even more grief during this period. During his first three years in office he insisted on returning to the United States Treasury, publicly, and even triumphantly, huge sums of money in the form of unused obligations that had been appropriated to the Post Office Department for its operation.

The first time he did this, in 1953, there was some political excuse for his action, since the money had been requested and granted by a Democratic administration and a Democratic Congress, although Summerfield's grandstanding before the klieg lights could not help but cause some irritation among Democratic congressmen.

However, he did it again in 1954 and 1955. On these latter occasions the original appropriations requests had been his. The Republican Bureau of the Budget and the Appropriations Committees in the Congress in each case had in good faith approved the final appropriations. Thus, at the same time that cameras were grinding while King Arthur took his bows, so were many Republican teeth.[1]

This glory-grabbing on Summerfield's part has cost his administration dearly. Just because the Bureau of the Budget had trusted his original submission as being honest, they found themselves holding the publicity bag at the end of the fiscal year. Just because the Appropriations Committees had gone easy on his budget request, they also were made to look bad.

For a congressman, assignment to the Appropriations Committee is a somewhat thankless honor. It is an all-important Committee, and those who serve on it must have certain special skills which are not required on other committees. But, even though some congressmen fight hard to get onto the Committee, they usually find afterwards that it has very little sex appeal for the voters.

As a general rule, a member of the Appropriations Committee can campaign in his district on only two bases: (a) pointing with pride to the federal money he has diverted to his own district; and (b) pointing with pride to the millions of dollars he has saved the taxpayer.

While Summerfield was making personal political hay out of his "saving" money for the taxpayer, the Bureau of the Budget and the Appropriations Committees of the Congress were swearing in their hearts that this would never happen again. As a result, when Summerfield did want a lot of additional money to pay for his program of automation and mechanization, the Bu-

---

[1] In 1953 the sum returned was $51,700,000. In 1954 it was $104,400,000. In 1955 it was $42,500,000. What irritated the Congress and the Bureau of the Budget particularly was that a major part of the "savings" consisted merely of transferring some items like subsidies to the airlines from the Post Office budget to the budgets of other government agencies. Many people in the Congress felt that there was not enough emphasis on this fact in the Post Office Department releases on the subject. There were even some who thought that Summerfield was running for vice-president at their expense.

reau of the Budget and the Appropriations Committees took out, not paring knives, but meat cleavers. They really went to work on his budget proposals, and many of his most cherished plans have been indefinitely delayed because of lack of funds.

It was not as if the money Summerfield returned could not have been used elsewhere, and to good effect, in the Postal Establishment. It could have.

There were those in the Department who strongly advised against this action. But the Postmaster General insisted on his hour in the sun, and he has paid for this by being consigned ever since to the Congressional doghouse.

The most successful agencies of government, as far as appropriations are concerned, are those that include in their budget proposals some recognizable fat, so that the Appropriations Committee can remove it publicly, for the edification of the voters back home. I do not say this is morally ideal; I am merely citing the rules as they exist. Ever since Summerfield broke the rules by making the Committee look bad, the Committee has tried to set a national record for cutting his budget requests all the way to the bone.

Naturally enough, letter carriers looked on all these administrative gyrations with a jaundiced eye. Since almost 80 per cent of all postal costs consists of salaries, we felt with good reason that Summerfield was publicly peacocking at our expense. While he was boasting of all the money he had saved, the letter carriers and other postal employees were struggling to maintain their families at a decent level of subsistence.

We finally did get a pay raise in 1955, through Public Law 68 (Eighty-fourth Congress), but it was only after thirty months of constant struggle, and another Eisenhower veto. By actual count this pay raise was granted only after the completion of thirty-two different legislative actions on the part of the Congress! There was really no excuse for the second Eisenhower veto, which occurred on May 9, 1955, except that the bill as passed provided for a system of classification somewhat different from that which was currently being proposed by the Department.

In his veto message the President objected to the cost of the legislation and said, "The bill imposes a heavier burden upon the taxpayer than is necessary to establish salary rates throughout the Department which will compare favorably with rates for similar work elsewhere in Government and in private industry."

Since certain Departmental officials were heard boasting that they had written the President's veto message before it was released, it would be churlish on my part to deny them the "credit" of having given the President bad advice and a surplus of misinformation.

The only reason for the veto, apparently, was that the bill did not carry the Department's trade mark. Instead, it had been introduced (as S-1) by Senator Olin D. Johnston, of South Carolina, chairman of the Senate Committee on Post Office and Civil Service, a great friend of the letter carriers and, indeed, of all federal employees, but no friend of Arthur E. Summerfield.

It is no wonder that we viewed the final passage of the Administration pay bill, Public Law 68, as an anticlimax. Postmaster General "Winterfield," through his own obstinacy, had lost any chance of winning the gratitude of the rank and file postal employees.

Public Law 68 was not a generous pay bill. It gave letter carriers a six percent increase and it did eliminate many of the inequities which had grown up in the postal pay structure. However, it vividly reflected the orientation of the Summerfield administration toward management, rather than toward labor. The bill was far more favorable toward postmasters and supervisors than it was to the letter carriers, post office clerks, and other rank-and-file employees who make up ninety percent of the postal work force.

I do not say this grudgingly. Many postmasters and a goodly number of supervisors were underpaid and deserved a raise. However, Arthur Summerfield's Public Law 68 was so weighted in their favor that it is not surprising that letter carriers did not go dancing in the streets upon news of its enactment. After thirty months and thirty-two separate actions on the part of the Congress, we were not overjoyed by a salary increase of six percent. We felt, in the words of the Roman poet, Horace, that the mountains had been in labor and had brought forth a ridiculous mouse. While we were happy to get economic relief of any sort, we left the rejoicing and the victory celebrations to our bosses in the post offices of the land. They had a great deal more reason to rejoice.

There was one piece of legislation which did gladden the hearts of letter carriers, however. An allowance of one hundred dollars a year was granted us for the purchase and maintenance of our uniforms.

This had been a project of the NALC since time immemorial and one of my major ambitions ever since I became its president. Letter carriers, despite the fact that they were underpaid, were expected to buy their own uniforms and to keep them neat and clean at all times. They were the only uniformed personnel on the government payroll who were denied an allowance for their uniforms. Although the hundred-dollars-a-year allowance is not adequate, Congress, in granting it, established an important precedent which will be beneficial in the future.

However, after the passage of Public Law 68, the relations between the NALC and the Summerfield administration were, on the surface at least, considerably smoothed out. We still had our disagreements, plenty of them, but through a tacit mutual understanding we were able to conduct our debates without undue acrimony.

Postal officials stopped indulging in indiscriminate name calling, and some of them actually became friendly. It became apparent that the abusive approach was getting them nowhere with the Congress and was, indeed, losing the administration support in areas far removed from that of postal pay.

We, on the other hand, grew used to the twists and turns of the administration. The optimistic glow had faded long ago. We had, to our sorrow, learned that we could not expect cooperation from the Department in any important area of endeavor. However, as Summerfield became more and more unpopular in the Congress, we found we could generally rely on our friends in both Houses for relief when we needed it.

We also found, through sad experience, that there was almost no relationship, at times, between what the Summerfield administration *did* and what it *said*. This was infuriating, of course, but with the passage of time it became a way of life which we did not like, but could not change.

This peculiarity of the present postal administration has been puzzling, and it can be traced, I think, to both a diffusion and a confusion of leadership.

In the first place, the program of decentralization which had been instituted so bravely in 1953 had been allowed to get considerably out of hand. The Inspection Service, which had bitterly opposed it, ended up by taking it over. Most of the top jobs were given to inspectors, and this has prevented regionalization from being the success it should have been.

The ascendancy of the inspectors in the regional program was due entirely to politics. During twenty years of Democratic rule very few known Republicans had been elevated in post offices to top supervisory jobs, which would equip them for executive positions in the regions. On the other hand, since post-office patronage was being directed by Republican congressmen who had been denied the right of appointment over the years, there was no possibility of placing any experienced Democrats in key positions. Postal inspectors are almost unique in the federal career service in that they must, by law, reveal their political affiliations. So Republican inspectors were given jobs in the new setup. It was a compromise and it has proved to be a poor one.

Once the Department had created decentralization it did not know how to live with it. In a moment of minor madness someone in authority had referred to the regional directors as "little postmasters general," and most of the directors took this bit of hyperbole right to heart. As the regional directors began to flex their muscles, the officials in the Department began to grow irritated, and the friction between the two elements of management caused a considerable amount of confusion. To this day nobody has been able to draw a sensible line of demarcation as to where the Department's authority ends and where the regional authority begins. It is not unusual for regional decisions to be overruled in Washington, particularly upon the insistence of an offended member of the Congress. On the other hand, it is not unusual for departmental orders to be ignored in the regions.

Then, after the exciting years of 1953–54, when so much was done for and to the postal service, a period of relative inaction followed. The great crusade began to lose its glitter. It was far less glamorous to activate plans than it was to create them, and a kind of departmental ennui set in. Certain of the top people in the Department began an internecine war for power which proved disastrous to executive morale.[2]

---

[2] There is even more rank consciousness in the Post Office Department than there is in the Pentagon. A great deal of the trouble stems from the custom of calling the top officials "General." I have never known a department official to demur at this gaudy title, even when he does not rate it. Then again, there is evidently a time in the career of each of them when he looks in a mirror, perhaps while shaving, and says: "By gosh, I'm an Assistant Postmaster General! Wow!" From that moment on the value of that particular individual is diminished. In the hothouse of official Washington life the average man's sense of insecurity proliferates, and he compensates by becoming overly aggressive and extremely jealous of his prerogatives. There are exceptions, of course, but they seldom last long.

Except for the area of research and development, the Summerfield administration suddenly began to run out of gas. The areas of authority became so confused and blurred that no one knew at any given time just where he stood, and every promise or agreement was subject to instantaneous change. This has been disheartening, but we have sadly adopted the philosophy of saying to ourselves, "This, too, shall pass away."

Part of the decline must be attributed to the failure of Summerfield's health. He has not been at all a well man during the last years of his administration, and there is a definite feeling that his leadership has suffered as a result. This has left a heavy burden on his deputy. His first deputy, Charlie Hook, was eminently capable of taking over, but he resigned before the problem became critical. His two immediate successors, Maurice H. Stans and Edson O. Sessions, while both brilliant in their fields (accounting and engineering, respectively), apparently did not have the special quality of leadership necessary to give the operation of the Department direction.

In any case, although our next pay increase did not come until 1958, the politicking on both sides was carried on with far less public wrangling. The effectiveness of departmental lobbying had been reduced to a minimum. Sometimes it seemed to me that departmental officials were too busy fighting among themselves to take us on. Whatever the reason, the struggle, although intense, was not particularly vituperative.

In July and August of 1957 both Houses of the Congress passed a pay bill which would have given letter carriers an increase of $456 a year. Once again, despite the overwhelming congressional sentiment in favor of the legislation, President Eisenhower, still following the advice of his anti-labor Postmaster General, pocket vetoed it after the Congress had gone home.

This was not a popular move on Ike's part, and the reaction among the public and the press was highly unfavorable. Pocket vetoes are generally looked upon as a rather sneaky device. Also, it was pointed out editorially on many occasions and in many places that it was unfair and illogical for the President to urge the expenditure of public funds for programs such as foreign aid, and then to single out a postal pay bill for disapproval because it was "inflationary." It has been the favorite confidence game of this Administration to try to label postal employees as the *causes* of inflation, when of course they are the *victims* of inflation.

The President issued his "Memorandum of Disapproval" from his vacation headquarters in Denver. Ironically, he refused to discuss the legislation with us before he vetoed it. Press Secretary James Hagerty announced that he would not receive any petitioning groups while on his vacation. This was a far cry from his speech to us at our convention in 1952 when he said: "Mr. Doherty . . . if ever you find anything coming up that you believe is damaging the postal service, or is unfair to any member thereof, you bring that to me, and I promise you in advance you won't sit on the door-step any time to get to me."

The only time I did get to see the President on a pay raise was in 1954. This was after moving heaven and earth, and when I finally succeeded it was too late. The veto message had already been written in the Department and was on the President's desk awaiting his signature.

On that occasion Ike was his usual charming self, but his hands were tied. He was all sympathy, but of no help. After that interview I made up my mind that it would be of no use trying to get favorable action from the President as long as "Winterfield" was his Postmaster General.

We are inured to adversity in the postal unions and we somewhat forlornly accepted the inevitable. We went right to work, and as soon as the Congress convened in January 1958, a reasonably equitable pay bill was introduced. This bill, which gave us a flat 10 per cent increase in pay, was signed into law on May 27, 1958, and was made retroactive to January 11 of that year.

The battle was not won without a compromise, however. Both the Postmaster General and the President were dead set on a raise in postage rates. It was obvious that they could not get a rate increase without giving in on postal salaries.

On the other hand, I was keenly aware that our members were in dire need of a substantial raise in pay. I felt that strict adherence to the principle of keeping pay and postage rates separate would only result in intolerable delay. So, after consultation with the other national officers of the NALC and with the leaders of some of the other postal groups, I agreed to go along with a combined postage rate-postal salary bill.

Summerfield fought hard and openly to keep the wage provisions of the bill as low as possible. When he found that his lobbyist, Harry Brookshire, was almost totally ineffective on Capitol Hill, he stationed himself in his official Cadillac just outside one of the entrances to the Senate Office Building and kept the telephone in his car working constantly.

Just before the Senate vote on the pay bill, he summoned me to his upholstered mobile office and asked me to go along with an 8½ per cent pay increase. He said he "thought" he could get the President to sign such a bill if it were joined to a rate bill. He intimated that this was the absolute limit and that Ike would veto any bill calling for a higher increase.

I refused to go along. I knew that he wanted a rate bill so badly that he would eventually agree to the 10 per cent increase on which I was insisting. I left him with his jangling telephone in the big black Cadillac and returned to work.

Shortly afterward the Senate turned down Senator Frank Carlson's offer of an 8½ per cent compromise and voted for a 10 per cent increase.

I was right about my prediction as to Summerfield's reaction. He went along with the 10 per cent all right. He recommended that President Eisenhower sign the bill.

The President did.

CHAPTER 26

THE SUMMING UP

AS I write these words, we of the National Association of Letter Carriers are once again engaged in a battle to get a pay raise.

Although we are optimistic about the future of this wage campaign, we shall miss the help of two devoted friends in the Senate who have died since our last salary struggle.

One of these was Senator William Langer (R), of North Dakota, and the other was Senator Richard L. Neuberger (D), of Oregon.

Many observers considered Bill Langer a controversial character. As far as letter carriers were concerned there was nothing whatsoever controversial about him. Both as chairman of the Senate Committee on Post Office and Civil Service,[1] and as its

---

[1] The word "Post Office" was put in the title of the Committee originally at my insistence. I mentioned the fact that the Post Office aspects of the Committee's work should be stressed in the Committee's title. Bill Langer agreed and fought successfully for its insertion.

ranking minority member, he was always our comrade and friend. The only disagreements I ever had with Bill Langer were when he thought I was asking for less money for letter carriers than he believed they deserved. Bill always wanted to give postal employees a better break than the Congress was willing to stand for.

The death of young Dick Neuberger was a shock to every intelligent student of government. This was a thoughtful man, with a brilliant mind and a delightful personality. The United States Senate is infinitely poorer for his passing. Our sorrow is assuaged only by the knowledge that he is survived by his lovely wife, Maurine, and by the hope that she may someday soon succeed to the seat which her husband occupied with such distinction.

Once again this year Postmaster General Summerfield is opposing a decent wage increase for postal employees. Once again we are being told that, despite the fact that both Houses of Congress have passed the legislation by overwhelming majorities, President Eisenhower will veto it. Indeed, every conceivable strategy has been employed to delay Congressional action long enough to permit a "pocket veto," which cannot be overridden. And once again the Postmaster General is trying to put postage rates ahead of postal salaries.

The old familiar patterns are just as repetitious as they are in the cheaper varieties of wallpaper.

On December 28, 1959, I rang up General Summerfield and asked for an interview with him. I wanted to state our position. He told me he was going to fight us on any wage increase, but he also said he would call me back within a few days. Three months later he did call me. By that time both he and the NALC had publicly committed themselves. There was no longer an opportunity for compromise.

When I finally did see General Summerfield, he spent most of the time talking about postage rates. He told me he was determined to go down in history as the first Postmaster General to put the Postal Establishment on a businesslike basis. Although he spoke a lot about the national debt and the national welfare, I received the distinct and unshakable impression that he had determined to occupy a certain niche in history, and that he was going to achieve that objective even if he had to sacrifice the welfare of every single member of the 525,000 employee force under his control.

I am conscious that during the latter stages of this account I have dwelt quite a lot on our struggles for pay increases. I feel strongly that for me, as national president of the NALC, the principal job is to put more money in the pockets of my members. Although I have been successful in this struggle, the slowness of the congressional machinery has kept us from maintaining economic equality with others in private industry. The three Eisenhower vetoes slowed down our advancement to a point where recovery is difficult.

The average letter carrier today is getting $4,640 a year, or $370 a month, or $89.23 a week, or $2.23 an hour. This is not adequate for a man to support his family in dignity and with reasonable security. This is particularly true since letter carriers live, work, and must rear their children in the thickly populated and generally industrialized metropolitan areas of the country where living costs are highest. A survey taken recently among fifty thousand of our members shows that in 93 per cent of the cases either letter carriers' wives must work to supplement the family budget, or the letter carrier himself must work at a second job, or else the family must operate on borrowed money.

As recently as eleven years ago the salaries of policemen and firefighters were generally comparable with those of letter carriers. Today they have far outstripped us.

We took thirteen typical major industry groups and found that each one of them was paying its employees far better than Uncle Sam pays his letter carriers. The average for all thirteen of these industries is $104 a week. This is an average of $15 a week more than a letter carrier's pay. The average worker in the mining industries is getting $114.24 a week, or $25 more than a letter carrier. In the construction industry the average wage is $117.81, or $28.60 a week more than a letter carrier's pay.[2]

As a result of inflation over the years street sweepers, dog-catchers and garbage men in many communities today are getting more pay than are letter carriers.

And here is the reason: In the past eleven years letter carriers have received only four pay raises. The average number of pay raises in thirteen selected major industries has been ten. In private industry the raises come easier, bigger, and more often.

And yet, looking back over the almost twenty years I have been president of the National Association of Letter Carriers, there has been a great deal to be thankful for. When I took office in 1941, letter carriers were getting a minimum wage of $1,700 and a maximum wage of $2,100. There had not been a single wage increase in sixteen years.

In the past ninteen years there have been nine wage increases. None was as large as we desired, but each one made us all work that much harder for a further increase. As soon as one struggle was completed we had to embark almost immediately on another struggle.

Today a letter carrier begins at $4,035 a year and at the maximum rate he gets $5,175, after twenty-five years. The average pay of a letter carrier, as I have said, is $4,640 a year.

So, the wages of a regular letter carrier have been increased almost 250 per cent in nineteen years. But they had remained static for sixteen years previously and were so low when the program of improvement began that they had become a national

[2] See *The Labor Force* (U.S. Dept. of Labor), January 1960.

scandal. We have never quite been allowed to catch up with the economic parade.

A substitute letter carrier, when I took office, was getting a flat 65¢ an hour, when he could get work. Today he begins at $2.00 an hour, and at his maximum receives $2.42 an hour. Thus, his wages have been more than trebled.

There have been other improvements in personnel relationships which have been equally inspiriting: national life insurance, national health, retirement benefits, sick leave liberalization, most of the fringe benefits which pertain in enlightened industries.

The fringe benefits in government service are not as liberal as they are in private industry generally,[3] but they are not a source of major complaint.

Our membership has nearly doubled since 1941, and it is still climbing with each passing year.

Certainly we could not have done all these things if we did not have at all times a strong and loyal group of national officers who have imaginatively and loyally implemented our policies.

In addition to those whom I have mentioned earlier I would like to give a special vote of thanks to such stalwarts as John Sullivan, of Portland, Maine; Philip Lepper, of New York City; A. F. Baker, of Austin, Texas; J. Stanly Lewis, of Burbank, California; Dean E. Soverns, of Denver, Colorado; James H. Rademacher, Jr., of Detroit; John W. Schmidt, of Milwaukee; Charles N. "Nick" Coyle, of Portland, Oregon; James C. Stocker, of St. Louis; Thomas H. Gerraty, of East Orange, New Jersey; Louis F. Seeback, of Brooklyn; Martin F. Kalbow, of Chicago; Carl J. Saxsenmeier, of San Francisco; Edward F. Benning, of Springfield, Illinois; and Nelson E. Sundermeier, of Cleveland. There are many others equally deserving, all of whom have left a large footprint on the history of organized labor in government.

We have come a long way from those grim days of suppres-

[3] The Cordiner Report of 1957 made this abundantly clear.

sion and oppression which drove the nation's letter carriers to organize in Milwaukee in 1889.[4] We have advanced a long way from the days when postal employees had to convene in secret, like the ancient Christians in their catacombs, and voice their complaints in whispers. We have left far behind us the shameful days of the "gag rule" when the President of the United States deprived postal employees of their constitutional right of appealing to the Congress. We survived Burleson, Hitchcock, Cortelyou, and Donaldson. We shall survive Summerfield. We have seen Congresses come and go. We have watched postmasters general enjoy their brief hour of authority and then depart. And through it all, in evil times and good, the National Association of Letter Carriers has grown and prospered and has been forged in the fire of adversity into a labor union unique for its influence upon all segments of the national life.

We have had our confident yesterdays. We shall have our joyous tomorrows.[5]

[4] However, the more things change, the more postmasters general remain the same. As early as 1825 Postmaster General John McLean wrote that he had no intention of paying postal employees a sufficient compensation to provide a livelihood without other means of support. Today, one hundred and thirty-five years later, the philosophy of Postmaster General Summerfield has produced results identical with those produced by his predecessor.

[5] On June 30, 1960, President Eisenhower did the expected and vetoed the Federal pay bill mentioned at the beginning of this chapter. This was his fourth veto of such a bill. However, on the very next day the Congress overwhelmingly overrode the veto by a vote of 345-69 in the House and 74-24 in the Senate. This was only the second Eisenhower veto (out of a total of 169) to be overridden in eight years. The bill will give a pay increase of about 8.5 per cent, on the average, to letter carriers. There were many Congressional heroes in this historic and successful "Crusade for Economic Equality," but the leadership of Senator Lyndon B. Johnson, of Texas, was especially decisive. We were also helped by the intemperate tone of the veto message itself, which irritated many of the members. Incidentally, a solid majority of Republicans in both Houses repudiated Summerfield and voted to override. This was the final curtain of "The Tragedy of King Arthur."

CHAPTER 27

WHERE DO WE
GO FROM HERE?

TWO things are consistently true about the postal system:
Everyone takes it for granted, and everyone complains about
it. As a matter of fact, people become so accustomed to complaining about poor mail service that they take the attitude that
the situation is hopeless, and that inefficiency will be always
with us.

Of course, under existing conditions it is a kind of miracle
that the postal service is as good as it is. Postal employees work
under conditions, in many communities, which would be considered substandard in the jute mill of a maximum security federal prison. Postmaster General Summerfield, to his credit, has
been making a valorous attempt to improve the physical plant
of the post office, but the task is immense and he has never been
granted the funds to do the massive job that is needed. In his
later years he became so obsessed with balancing the postal
budget that it is doubtful if he would have wanted to do the job

even if he could have got the funds. There are so many areas in which improvements can be made. Over the years the postal system has been America's "fabulous invalid" and "experts" have analyzed it and reported on it more than on any other department of government. Many of these suggestions have been sensible, many have not. None of them can be of any permanent benefit as long as each succeeding postmaster general allows himself to be seduced into considering the post office as a money-making public utility, instead of a public service.

The proposed reforms I am listing here are all basic. They are aimed at the improvement of the Postal Establishment's service to the American people. They do not constitute a complete list, since this would involve the compilation of a technical manual of abuses and grievances which would have no general interest. However, the things I list below could be started tomorrow, and the dividends to the American people would be immediate and generous.

Budgetary Questions: The Postmaster General should be prohibited by Congressional action from playing any part whatsoever in the determination of postage rates or postal salaries.

These questions should be left to the Bureau of the Budget, the Treasury Department, and the Appropriations Committees and Post Office Committees of the Congress.

This makes sense. It could be the psychological key to the service problem. The Department today is not permitted to make use of revenues it collects. The money the public pays for postage stamps goes into the United States Treasury. The Post Office Department must live within Congressional appropriations.

There have been attempts to induce the Congress to allow the Post Office Department a "business-type" budget. This would permit the Department to make use of its revenues for the betterment of the service. It would undoubtedly result in greater efficiency all around, but the Congress has never shown the slightest inclination to go along with this suggestion.

In the absence of a business-type budget there is no reason for the Postmaster General to be burdened with the task of attempting to raise revenues which his Department can never use. Certainly, upon request, his accountants could perform the necessary scholarship and research for, let us say, the Bureau of the Budget, but the information developed would not involve any enunciation of policy and would not be a burden on the Postmaster General himself.

An arrangement such as this would free the Postmaster General and his top staff to devote their entire time to what should be their proper job: the improvement of the postal service. If Arthur Summerfield had done this, instead of dissipating his energies in trying to prevent salary raises for his employees and getting postage rates increased, he would, I really think, have been one of the better postmasters general in our history. Because he has diverted his energies into fields which logically should be none of his business, he has failed to improve the service demonstrably, and neither has he achieved the budgetary balance he so greatly desired.

The psychological effect would be most beneficial since the executive thinking would be service-centered rather than deficit-centered.

If a postmaster general knew that his performance would be judged by posterity, not by the money he had saved but by the improvements he had made in the service, we would have a far better postal system than we ever can have while postal executives spend most of their efforts on penny-pinching and dreaming up possible service curtailments.

As a matter of fact, this change in procedure would make the job of postmaster general one of the most sought-after jobs in Washington. It would relieve the top postal executive of the most unpleasant aspects of his job and would permit him to concentrate on those aspects that would win popular favor. It would also serve to improve the caliber of men in the top levels of the Department.

This shift of emphasis in the duties of the postmaster general would also have a sweeping effect on his approach to wage levels.

Historically each postmaster general has opposed almost every attempt by postal employees to get a raise in salary, almost as if the additional funds were coming out of his own personal pocket. However, if he were to concentrate solely on improving the efficiency of the service he would be aware that greater efficiency derives from better morale, and that better morale derives from higher pay.[1] Therefore, he would be an *ally* of postal groups when they seek wage increases instead of an enemy. This, needless to say, would be a delightful change.

A case in point is the question of two deliveries a day in residential areas. Mr. Summerfield, before he took office, was very much in favor of restoring this service. However, once he took over the reins, the accountants began talking incessantly of the postal "deficit" and the added expense that would be involved in restoring proper service to the homes of America. Summerfield decided to go back on his word, and he has never restored that second trip.

And yet, despite all the efforts that have been made, the mail service can never be measurably improved until the second delivery is restored wherever the need exists. It is true that the experiment of flying regular mail by plane between certain cities has resulted in some improvements, but as long as there is but a single delivery a day to residential areas, improvements must be made on the basis of *a full twenty-four hours* if they are to be

---

[1] Mr. Summerfield evidently understands this in private life. On several occasions he has told me that he pays his nonunion workers in his Chevrolet agency in Flint, Michigan, wages considerably above the union scale. However, he does not believe, for some reason, that this procedure would work equally well in government service. In Summerfield's opinion what is good for General Motors is not necessarily good for the country.

made at all. In other words, if there is but one delivery a day, the mail must be speeded up *by a full day* to catch that delivery or else there will be no real improvement. There is no comfort to the householder in knowing that a letter has arrived earlier at his local post office if he cannot get that letter until the next day. While we approve of most of the mechanical and electronic developments on which the Post Office Department has been working, we regret that monetary considerations, which have been exaggerated out of all proportion, have prevented the one simple improvement that could speed up the service overnight.

As it is now, every postmaster general is torn on the horns of a dilemma. He interprets, as part of his job, the duty of balancing the postal budget, but he has no authority to do anything about it, since the Congress sets the rates of postage and the levels of payment to employees. Since the costs of the postal service are constantly rising, each postmaster general ends up by frantically trying to balance his budget almost to the exclusion of every other duty. Service considerations are ignored; the economic needs of the employee force are disregarded as he seeks to keep the expenses of the Postal Establishment within hailing distance of postal revenues which the Department does not receive and which it cannot use.

No one is so foolish as to say that a postal "deficit" is in itself a commendable thing. It would be wonderful indeed if the post office could give maximum service and still operate within appropriations which are roughly the equivalent of its revenues. But it boils down to the question of which shall be master. Shall the desire for a balanced postal budget dominate the Postal Establishment, or should service considerations dominate it?

This is no plea for extravagance or waste; it is a plea for common sense. The so-called "postal deficit" is really an investment by the taxpayers in the economy of America. The postal service is the taproot which nourishes the oak tree of our economy. There is not a business in America whose income does not derive in some measure from the postal service. If this service costs the taxpayer a small amount of money each year, it is money well spent. Certainly it is money better spent than that which is appropriated through taxes for many other government projects which provide less demonstrable benefits.

Oddly enough, this is a fact which is grasped by almost everyone in America except those who work in the Post Office Department. There are hundreds of organizations in the United States which have business with the Post Office Department and with the Post Office Committees of the Congress. Among all these groups and organizations there has never been a single one that advocated the reduction of postal expenditures or the curtailment of postal service.

There is one other budgetary consideration which should be mentioned at this time: The Postmaster General should be persuaded to obey the law of the land when publishing his fiscal balance sheet.

The Congress, in 1930, passed the Kelly Law, which established certain services of the post office as being nonpostal in nature, or in the public welfare, and directed that the cost of these services should not be counted as part of the "postal deficit." Postmaster General Farley did follow the law and, as a result, showed a "profit" in his operation of the Postal Establishment. When Farley retired, the Kelly Law was all but forgotten. The post office accountants went right back to the old system of totting up a deficit just as if the Kelly Law were never passed. Then, in 1958, the Congress passed the combined postage rate and postal salary act known as Public Law 426. The first title of that law expands and spells out in greater detail the public welfare elements of the postal service. If the Postmaster General would obey the mandate of this law he would be able to present a balanced postal budget almost every year. However, this definite statement of Congressional policy has been ignored.[2]

Actually, the effect of this change would, for the most part, be psychological. Each year the Postmaster General's Report lists the annual receipts and the annual costs, the difference between them being the postal "deficit" or "surplus" as the case might be. This is just about the only part of a Postmaster General's record that is permanently preserved. It is a little like the listing of the batting averages of baseball players, and postmasters general invariably find themselves trying to do better fiscally than their predecessors. This makes postal administrators more dollar conscious than service conscious.

It is a false yardstick, just as a batting average, taken by itself, can be a false yardstick by which to measure the true value of a ball player. But as long as post office accountants neglect to follow the mandates of the Congress, and include, as part of the postal "deficit," all the public welfare elements in postal costs, postmasters general will continue to insist on foolish economies at the expense of service.

Public Relations and Politics. Years of inattention have bred in the American people and in their congressional representatives

[2] There is a vast difference of opinion as to how much these nonpostal or public welfare costs come to. At the request of Chairman Olin D. Johnston, of the Senate Committee on Post Office and Civil Service, I served on the Citizens' Advisory Council on the Post Office, which made an exhaustive study of this subject in 1956–57. Our conclusion was that the public welfare costs of the Department amounted to $392,400,000 a year. This estimate was made the basis of the congressional policy enunciated in Public Law 426 (Eighty-fifth Congress). The Department at that time claimed its public welfare costs amounted to only $29,400,000! The items in question include the cost of the many nonpostal activities of the post office as well as the calculated loss the Department sustains as a result of congressional policy regarding the maintenance of below-cost postage rates on certain types and classes of mail and the retention of certain nonprofitable services in the interest of the public welfare. (Ninety per cent of the post offices of the country "lose" money, for instance, but they are kept open as a public service, whereas in a private industrial operation they would be shut down.)

a kind of patronizing attitude toward the post office. To the average citizen the post office is an object of affection, somewhat like an elderly maiden aunt who is hopelessly old-fashioned and absent-minded, but rather a dear person despite her exasperating habits. To too many politicians the post office is a kind of patronage dispose-all, the place where, historically, you could flush down all the faithful party hangers-on whom you could not place anywhere else.

As a result, hardly anyone outside the Post Office Department is accustomed to taking the *business* of the post office seriously. And yet this is the essential system of communications that holds the social and economic life of the country together!

Too often congressmen are inclined to insist that their friends and supporters be given top jobs in post offices regardless of their experience or professional qualifications. Many of these top positions are the key to the successful operation of the post office. When an inadequate person fills such a position, the efficiency of the post office suffers, and then the very same congressman who insisted in the first place on the unwise appointment is more than likely to be the first person to complain about bad service. Postal work is skilled work. To be done correctly it requires brains, training, experience, and integrity. It is not work that just anybody can do, and the persistent fallacy that it is simple unskilled labor has done a great deal of harm to the efficiency of the service and the morale of those who work in it.

Postal administrations have fostered this harmful view by trying to minimize the importance of post-office jobs whenever a wage dispute has arisen.

By the same token, the Committees on Post Office and Civil Service in both the House and the Senate are considered minor. They are ranked in prestige along with such Committees as those on merchant marine and fisheries, interior and insular affairs, and the Committee for the District of Columbia. Certainly the Post Office Committees are ranked far below, and get far less attention than, those on foreign relations, agriculture, and armed services.

This is both unrealistic and harmful. It means that postal matters almost always get the lowest priority as far as Congressional attention is concerned. The Senate and the House almost always take up postal matters only when they have finished considering everything else under the sun. (This is one reason why so many of our pay raises have been granted on the last day of Congressional sessions.) It also means that most congressmen try to avoid service on the Committee and if they are forced to serve against their will, they spend most of their time trying to get assigned somewhere else. This causes a large and steady turnover in membership which proves exasperating both to the Committee leadership and to those who must do business with the Committee. With each new Congress a new job of education must be undertaken to acquaint freshmen members with the postal facts of life and, in most cases, the neophyte students have their minds elsewhere.

As a matter of fact, it is amazing that the real postal professionals on the Committee have been able to do as well as they have done on behalf of the postal service. There have been, over the years, a goodly number of Senators and Representatives who have taken an intense professional interest in the postal service. It would be invidious to mention names at this point, but these serious-minded and knowledgeable postal professionals have held the Committee together and, with the help of the occasional interested new member, they have forced through a considerable amount of postal progress against great odds. But it has been tougher on them than it should be, and the progress has been less than it should have been.

The post office needs a constructive public relations program on the broadest possible scale. The people of the United States should know more about their postal service, how it works and why it works. Certainly the Congress should know more about postal *business*. The usual debate in the Congress on postal matters is so crammed with misinformation and erroneous theory that, I am convinced, if such ignorance were paraded publicly on international affairs or on the farm program, it would result in a national scandal. I am not necessarily blaming the congressmen. They have never been instructed in post office matters, and as long as the postal service remains a political plaything they will never treat it with the seriousness it deserves.

The National Association of Letter Carriers has done its best to conduct a public relations campaign along these constructive lines, but we have few of the tools necessary to do the job adequately. The National Association of Postmasters has also had a try at it. But is is really the business of the Post Office Department to do the job. It is a job that must be done before the Congress and the people of the United States can be expected to cooperate in the achievement of *ultimate* progress.

The late Congressman Clyde Kelly, author of the Kelly Law, in his book *United States Postal Policy* wrote:

> There should be a real selling campaign through which the American people could better realize the magnitude and the unexcelled efficiency of the public service. There has never yet been a real and effective attempt to sell the postal service to the public. The official attitude has generally been that the public could use such facilities as were offered or leave them alone. It is not unknown but *known* good that benefits mankind.[3]

To this we say "Amen."

Unfortunately no one has ever undertaken this job.

Arthur Summerfield has tried to create a public relations office in the Department. It has been merely a *publicity* office. It has achieved a great deal of publicity for Arthur Summerfield, and it has done an excellent job in publicizing itself, but there has

[3] Clyde Kelly, *United States Postal Policy* (New York: D. Appleton and Company, 1932), p. 252.

been no attempt at carrying out a public relations program with a broad concept behind it.

The Inspection Service. As early as 1891 the National Association of Letter Carriers advocated the abolition of the Inspection Service of the Post Office Department, and urged that the work they were doing could be better and more objectively done by established federal police agencies outside the postal service.

I do not advocate anything quite so drastic as that. However, I do advocate very strongly that the postal inspectors be cut down to size and returned to their proper jobs in the postal service.

Postal inspectors are policemen. In some respects they are also equivalent to bank examiners. They are not postal administrators or postal executives. They should be restricted to performing the functions of policemen and bank examiners.

Before the decentralization of postal operations, the lack of managerial leadership in the field created a vacuum into which the Postal Inspection Service rushed. Inspectors were not equipped to assume these managerial functions, and they did the job poorly. However, when postal operations were decentralized, the Inspection Service continued to insist on the retention of their management prerogatives, and no one has had the courage or the strength to put them firmly in their place.

The Inspection Service keeps complaining of how its members are overworked. They claim their case load is many times heavier than that of the Federal Bureau of Investigation, for instance. This is nonsense. The case load would be normal and manageable if only they would keep their hands out of management, a field in which they have no business and for which they have no aptitude or training.

The police mentality is a very real thing. It is a natural development that derives from constant association with criminals, and its principal characteristics are almost universal distrust and a kind of occupational paranoia that leads the policeman so affected to believe that every man's hand is against him. This psychological approach has its uses in the field of police work, if it is kept under reasonable control, but it is disastrous when employed in the area of management.

The average inspector is poorly trained for his job. His training, and his qualifications, compared to those of an FBI agent, for instance, are almost childishly inadequate.[4] Even in the task of inspecting post offices, they are usually incompletely equipped. In most cases they are experienced in just one aspect of postal operations and abysmally ignorant of almost every other aspect. Thus, if an inspector has been trained, let us say, in the money order section of a post office he will, most likely, give a thorough and tough inspection of that section of every post office he visits, and hardly give the time of day to such important operations as, for example, outgoing mails and city delivery service.

One improvement that could be made overnight is to increase the maximum entrance age for inspectors. Today it is set at thirty-six years. This age limit was established back in the days when inspectors were jumping aboard trains and shooting it out with mail thieves. That part of the job is almost completely a thing of the past, now. An inspector's job today, like that of a bank examiner, requires very little in the way of physical stamina.

But the thirty-six-year-old age limit still exists. In today's postal service this means that very few postal inspectors have had any supervisory experience by the time they take the badge. This is a great weakness in the system. It is a rare individual who can appraise the performance of a supervisor adequately unless he has been there himself, and has actually held down a supervisory position.

[4] An FBI agent, to qualify, must be a lawyer. Before he is put to work he is given a rugged fourteen-week course at the FBI school in Quantico, Virginia. There is no educational requirement for a post-office inspector. Also, there is no school which he must attend. He is put to work immediately upon selection and given some "on the job training." I do not think further comment on the difference between the two police organizations is necessary.

If the maximum age limit were lifted to, let us say, forty-five or fifty, there would be a healthy leavening of older and more experienced recruits who would bring to the Inspection Service a better balance and a greater degree of wisdom than is possible today.

Whenever this suggestion has been brought up in any administration, the Inspection Service has resisted it furiously. Admission that improvement could be made in the Inspection Service would also be an admission that the Inspection Service is not already perfect as it is, and few inspectors would ever make such an admission. Besides, if novitiates in the service were older and more experienced they would not be so susceptible to brainwashing.

Right now the Inspection Service is exerting a dead hand of control on the postal service. There is a mounting resentment against the conduct of the Inspection Service at every level of the employee force. Unless the service reforms itself, or permits the postal administration to carry out certain badly needed reforms, there could well be, one of these days, a full-dress Congressional investigation of the inspectors, and this would be performed in a way not at all to their liking. Such an investigation could conceivably result in the abolition of the Service and the transference of its duties to another federal police agency, just as *The Postal Record* advocated seventy years ago.

Union Recognition. The relationship between management and labor in the Post Office Department and in the post offices of the land is on very much of a "catch-as-catch-can" basis. It varies from administration to administration and from post office to post office.

This relationship should be regularized and "homogenized." The Congress should pass legislation formally recognizing the postal unions as an integral part of the Postal Establishment, and setting forth instructions for both Departmental officials (at the national policy level) and postmasters (at the local policy level) to sit down and consult with representatives of the responsible postal unions before formulating policies that affect postal workers.[5] This is everyday procedure in most modern industry, and it should be so in government service as well.

There are some enlightened postmasters who follow this procedure. There are many others who go through the motions of doing this but, in reality, they meet with union representatives only to tell them what has already been decided.

It is the same thing with the Department. We have been called in for "conferences" from time to time but these gatherings have been held merely to instruct us as to what has already been decided about our welfare. We were not consulted in advance even on such sweeping policy decisions as the decentralization program, the reclassification of postal salaries under Public Law 68, the curtailment of services, the use of "mailsters" and other devices on letter carriers' routes, and many other matters of equally vital importance.

Naturally, the official recognition of the postal unions in this manner would help us protect our members in advance from harmful decisions. But this is not the only consideration. Union recognition would also protect the Department itself from disastrous mistakes.

There is a great deal of difference in how a program or plan looks on paper and how it works out in terms of flesh and blood and local conditions. Department officials, even when they try to do otherwise, are forced by rank and by the magnitude of their authority to live in an ivory tower. They seldom get the true feeling of the employee force. They seldom know (or, it seems at times, care) what irritates and demoralizes employees and what pleases and encourages them. Permitting the representatives of labor to participate in the formulation of policies would help the

---

[5] This system was instituted in the British postal service in 1919 and works excellently. It is called the "Whitley Councils."

Department to maintain high morale and would give the top leadership the benefit of our experience and our knowledge of the employee force.

Postmaster General Summerfield and his aides have often bemoaned the fact that communication between the Department and the employee force in the field is almost impossible. There is no efficient apparatus available for such communication, and there are no funds to create such an apparatus. However, the means of communication have been close at hand all along. If Summerfield had leaned more upon the employee unions for guidance and assistance, he would have been able to communicate freely and effectively with every employee in the service.

The bitter wage struggle of 1954–55, for example, with its extremely deleterious and permanent effect on employee morale, could have been avoided if there had been union recognition at that time. In 1954 the Department relied solely on a group of outside consultants to draw up a plan of salary and job classification for the postal establishment.

Summerfield scorned to consult any employee group whatsoever, and the results were completely impractical and unworkable. The money spent on this report was wasted.

The Department tried again the next year. This time they called in the representatives of the postal supervisors for guidance. The bill was much better, but it was, not surprisingly, very much of a *supervisors'* bill.

The representatives of the rank and file employees were not consulted, despite the fact that there are about 460,000 of them as opposed to only 20,000 postal supervisors.

This fact caused a wave of suspicion to rise up against the legislation long before it ever left the drafting board. Postal employees were prejudiced against it before it was ever written. The attitude of most of the employees was: "Even if it was good we wouldn't like it."

As leaders of the postal unions we could not allay the fears of our members, because we ourselves were not allowed to know what was happening in the Department. We were never consulted, or even informed.

This complicated the passage of the bill considerably. And, of course, if we had been consulted the bill would have been much sounder, much fairer, and much more acceptable to the vast majority of postal employees.

Although this is an extreme case where the stubborn and stuffy refusal of General Summerfield to take the postal unions into his confidence had a demonstrably bad effect, the same kind of intransigence costs the Department in money, efficiency, and loyalty every day of the year.

Postal employees willingly do without two of the intrinsic rights which labor possesses everywhere else: the right to strike and the right to bargain collectively. However, because these rights are denied them is no reason for almost every other right of organized labor to be denied them also, and union recognition is one of those rights.

Union recognition would pay off immense dividends in terms of improved morale and improved teamwork among all segments of the employee front. We would have a better mail service as a result.

This may be heresy, but I do not believe that the handful of officials who work in the Post Office Department hold a monopoly on the nation's postal brains. I think that if post office officials did place more reliance on the experience, intelligence, and dedication of the more than 400,000 rank and file postal employees, they would learn a great deal to the betterment of the service. The American people would benefit greatly from such recognition.

Appeals and Grievances. One of the persistent anachronisms in the Post Office Department is its administration of "justice." The

Department is its own arresting officer, prosecuting attorney, jury, and judge.

When a letter carrier, for instance, is disciplined severely by his supervisor, and appeals, the appeal is usually reviewed by the selfsame supervisor who imposed the disciplinary action in the first place. There is no way that an employee can get an impartial and objective review of his case except by going through the expensive and time-consuming machinery of the federal courts.

It is idiotic but true that a postal employee can appeal to the United States Civil Service Commission only if he is a war veteran. Nobody has ever successfully explained or sensibly defended this discriminatory provision of the law.

Surely it is not too much to ask that postal employees, when their careers are threatened by disciplinary action, should have the right to appeal to a final authority who has had no involvement in the imposition of the disciplinary action in the first place! It is hardly remarkable under the present juridical setup within the Department that the average employee, as soon as he learns the postal facts of life, gets the impression that in personnel matters the Postmaster General is playing against him with a thoroughly stacked deck.

The appeal and grievance procedures of the Department should be completely modernized. All existing "star chamber" elements should be eliminated, and the distribution of objective, even-handed justice should be assured every employee. This seems very little to ask.

As a matter of fact the almost autonomous administration of "justice" by the Post Office Department keeps the Postmaster General consistently in hot water with the courts, the public, and the press.

A case in point is the role of censor that the Postmaster General has thrust upon him. Under present circumstances he can declare obscene or subversive practically anything he chooses and can bar such material from the mails. It takes a ruling of the federal courts to over-ride the Postmaster General's decision in such cases and this can be a lengthy and expensive procedure.

Heaven knows I am as strong an enemy of obscenity as anyone on earth, and I think every letter carrier in the country feels, as I do, that it is degrading to the service and to the job to have to transport some of the products of the muck-merchants through the streets of America and deliver them to the homes of our citizens.

I do not think it is necessary to proclaim my antipathy toward political subversion. This is a matter of public record.

But in principle it is a very dangerous thing to put the powers of censorship into the hands of one individual. Such powers can be terribly abused and misused, as witness the situation in 1911 when the Postmaster General arbitrarily held up the mailing of *The Harpoon,* an employee magazine, just because it criticized his administration.

The determination of what is and what is not mailable should be left to the courts. It should not be left in the hands of anyone who is answerable to the Postmaster General and whose decision can be influenced by the caprice of his superior.

Of course the recent furore over *Lady Chatterley's Lover* has brought this situation to a boil, but the issues involved go far beyond the matter of obscenity—they extend into the area of our personal liberties.

The office of Postmaster General is not a judicial one. It was never intended to be such and should not be allowed to retain any of the judicial prerogatives with which it has become almost accidentally endowed over the years.

One Big Postal Union. All the most effective and largest postal unions are gathered together under the protective banner of the AFL–CIO. Nothing has benefited the postal employee more than has this wholesome affiliation which gives him kinship with organized working men throughout the free world. Now there remains one further step: affiliation of all postal unions in the AFL–CIO into one big, effective postal union.

This makes great sense. Our postal organizations sprang up along craft lines, because the similarity of interests and of work performed drew men together.

But there is no further advantage in preserving these craft lines. Most matters which concern postal unions concern the postal work force as a whole. All postal workers come under the same department of government and the Congress legislates for all postal workers en masse. Although there are some specialized problems which pertain to only one service branch, there is no earthly reason why these problems could not be handled by subordinate branches of one mighty union of postal workers.

Both the National Federation of Post Office Clerks and the National Association of Letter Carriers have explored the possibility of forming a single federation in the past. However, craft jealousies have interfered, and the attempts at unification have failed because they have been premature and have not been prosecuted with sufficient imagination and understanding.[6] In my opinion the time has now arrived for the completion of such a move, and we in the National Association of Letter Carriers are determined to make this dream a reality.

In almost every other nation in the free world postal workers are united in one single, powerful union. I see no reason why the postal workers in the United States should be backward in this matter of unification.

The Post Office Department *opposes* any such amalgamation for the very same reasons that we propose it. They know that unification would put an end to management's frequent and occa-

[6] The first sentence of Article II of the National Federation of Post Office Clerks' constitution reads: "The objects of the National Federation of Post Office Clerks shall be to unite the postal employees in one brotherhood." It has remained that way for fifty years.

sionally successful attempts to capitalize on and aggravate craft jealousies and to play one postal union against another. The Department also comprehends the massive power that one aggressive postal union would have in legislative matters.

Postal employees are forbidden by law to strike or to bargain collectively. We do not dispute the wisdom of this policy.[7] There has never been a strike in a post office, even though some postmasters general have behaved with such autocratic brutality that, in any other type of industry, work stoppages would have been inevitable.

While it is undeniable that a strike should be unthinkable in the federal service, it is also undeniable that the lack of this weapon has weakened the position of postal workers in their attempts to get decent and proper justice from postal management.

The only way to compensate for this inherent weakness is to build up strength in the only way we can: in the unification and concentration of our collective forces. At the moment there are six postal unions affiliated with the AFL–CIO, with a combined membership of approximately 250,000. Of these, the NALC,

[7] The closest thing to a post-office strike occurred in Fairmont, West Virginia, in 1915. Postal employees were generally infuriated by the policies of the Postmaster General, Burleson, so when the postmaster fired three employees out of hand, without cause, twenty-five postal employees handed in their resignations in a body. Although this was not a strike but a mass resignation, the federal government moved with swiftness and viciousness against the offenders. Since none of the accused could afford to pay the cost of defending himself against the United States Government they all were forced to plead *nolo contendere* and received heavy fines. One of the defendants, W. H. Fisher, a letter carrier, broke down under the harassment to which he was subjected and committed suicide on the eve of his trial. Public opinion was so much behind the employees in this case, particularly since the postmaster was a known tyrant and an incompetent, that the government permitted very liberal terms for the payment of the fines. If such a situation as this were to arise today the entire strength and resources of the postal unions and the AFL–CIO would have been thrown into the fray in behalf of the persecuted postal workers. The Congress would almost certainly prevent the perpetration of injustice. But in 1915 the postal unions were comparatively weak and deficient in the necessary courage and prestige.

with 125,000 members is by far the largest and has been able to exert the greatest leadership.

If all postal unions were to forget their craft jealousies and pool their interests, the benefit to every postal employee in the country would be enormous. The benefits are so apparent that I feel I would be remiss in my duties to every postal employee who looks to us for leadership if I did not move forward in the name of the National Association of Letter Carriers to amalgamate all employees into one giant union.

It is not only the postal employees who will benefit from unification. The public and the service both will benefit.

One of the major bonds which unite the thinking of all postal groups is a shared dedication and devotion to the *service*. Postal workers insist that they are part of a national *service* and not of a national business venture or a national public utility. Their very loyalty and devotion are based on this concept, and so is their enlightened self-interest. Amalgamation would increase the influence of postal workers so that no postmaster general, no matter how devoted to nickel-nursing he might be, would be able to pervert the will of the Congress and the people into tolerating any other concept of the post office except the service concept.

The postal unions are much more service-minded than are postal administrators. We insist in passionate unanimity that postal service is not essentially a commodity nor can its value be measured in dollars and cents.

Guglielmo Marconi, the inventor of the radio, once said there was a two-fold measure by which we can judge the progress of civilization, "the decrease in labor and the increase in communication which diminishes space and eliminates misunderstanding."

This is so patently true that it is puzzling that so few postal administrations have paid heed to it. Most of the impediments to improved service have been created by executive orders issued by the Postmasters General over the years. Most of them could be removed in the same way. We are in great need of postal administrators who are zealously committed to the philosophy that the postal system is, above all else, a service and who will devote their energies without stint to the task of making this service more efficient and more useful to the people of the United States.

There are scores of ways in which this could be accomplished overnight. One of the most obvious is the restoration of the second delivery of mail in residential areas wherever possible. Another would be the improvement of the collection of mail so as to speed our letters on their way as soon as possible after they have been dropped in the box. A third obvious way is to extend the window hours in post offices so the patrons can make optimum use of their postal facilities.

By the same token, the insistence of postal administrations on foolish economies has scuttled the special-delivery system to a point where it is relatively meaningless. Except on Sundays and holidays a special delivery letter rarely gets any more preferential treatment than does an ordinary first-class letter.

Postmaster General Summerfield has made a lot of eloquent statements about the improvements that have been made in the service during his administration, but by and large he is flying in the face of the facts when he does so. The postal service has deteriorated during his administration, and it is getting worse each day. The indignation of the public is mounting. I know what I am talking about when I say this because it is to the letter carriers that the patrons usually complain.

As I have said earlier, mechanization of the postal service in several important areas is necessary and inevitable. The Summerfield administration has tried to make significant strides toward this goal. But all the mechanical devices in the world are of no avail unless they result in getting your letters into the hands of the letter carrier on his route faster.

There has been a great deal of talk about "facsimile mail," the proposed system by which a letter can be photographed and transmitted across the nation almost instantaneously. This sounds wonderful, but what good does it do if the letter must gather dust in the post office after it arrives, waiting for the letter carrier to pick it up the next day? When the first mail was flown by jet airplane from Los Angeles to Idlewild International Airport this year, the transcontinental journey took only four hours and three minutes. But letters on that airplane that were addressed to personnel working at Idlewild had to make the long, slow journey to the post office where they were processed. Then they had to wait overnight for the single delivery the next day. It was found that these letters, which had crossed the nation in record time, were delivered to airport personnel *forty-eight hours after they had arrived at the airport!*

It used to be that a housewife could sit down in the evening and write a letter, after her day's work was done, and then drop it in the corner letter box secure in the knowledge that it would be delivered the next day. A businessman used to be able to take his work home with him and then mail it, knowing it would reach its destination on the morrow. This is no longer possible because the collections have been curtailed. Letters mailed in the evening in most residential areas in the country will not reach the post office until around three o'clock the next afternoon.

It once was possible to mail a letter in the morning and have it delivered to someone in the same community in the afternoon. This is still the rule in most European countries, but it has long been forgotten in the United States of America.

The key to the whole problem is the philosophy of the man who occupies the position of Postmaster General. It is he who sets the pace. It is he who must make the administrative decisions that can result in improved service or impaired service.

The best Postmaster General in the past hundred years was Will H. Hays, who served only twelve months. In that short time General Hays set the course of the postal establishment along the lines of service above all else, and his influence was so great that his philosophy remained in force for a decade after he had departed.

The Post Office Department is badly in need of another Will Hays at the helm. It is in need of a man who will be passionately interested in the improvement and refinement of the service rather than in cutting financial corners and installing penny-pinching economies that eat away at the efficiency and the *usability* of this great system of communications on which the prosperity and social progress of the entire nation depend. Also, we are in need of a Postmaster General who recognizes the importance of morale in the postal service, who has a deep and abiding respect for the human beings who operate the service and for the importance of the jobs they perform.

In his annual report for 1921 Postmaster General Hays made the following statement, and in my opinion it should be required reading for everyone who aspires to the position of Postmaster General:

> I have met and shall continue to meet the heads of the postal organizations just as often as it is convenient for them to see me. There is no business in the world so dependent upon the human factor as the postal service. To treat a postal employee as a mere commodity in the labor market is not only wicked from a humanitarian standpoint, but it is foolish and short-sighted even from the standpoint of business. A postal employee who is regarded as a human being whose welfare is important to his fellows, high and low, in the postal organization, is found to do his work with a courage, a zest and a thoroughness which no money can buy. The most important element in any service is the spirit of the man doing it. . . . We have had employees; today we have co-workers.

Because Postmasters General Donaldson and Summerfield strayed away from this concept, the postal service has gone steadily down hill. Because postal administrations have insisted on paying postal workers starveling wages, the average capability of applicants for post-office jobs has declined with each passing year.

In some communities, as this is being written, the Post Office Department is conducting door-to-door canvasses begging for applicants for postal jobs. In other communities the post offices are running desperate want ads in the hope of getting applicants. The once-proud postal service is unashamedly scraping the bottom of the employment barrel. The percentage of applicants who fail the comparatively simple civil-service examinations is higher than ever before. Equally alarming is the unprecedentedly high percentage of employees who, once they are in the service, cannot meet the standards necessary for permanent tenure. This used to be a rarity. Today it is a commonplace.

You cannot operate the postal service efficiently under these conditions. And how about the future? Where will tomorrow's supervisors come from if today's employment crop is so unpromising? The efficient operation of the postal service of the future is being seriously imperiled by mere accountants. This should be of deep concern to us all.

In a speech delivered in Texas several years ago, Gerald Cullinan said: "Our system of communications—our mail service—has kept free men sane and courageous in times of trial. It has kept free men prepared to face the steeled cunning and the fortune of a scowling time. We are workers in and for freedom, and freedom is an endless river. Communications are its tributaries which enrich the land through which they flow."

This is a lofty concept and a true one. We who operate the postal service hold in our hands and hearts the power to help determine the course of freedom's river.

We who work together in the postal establishment are the ones who truly make it the "Messenger of sympathy and love, servant of parted friends, consoler of the lonely, bond of the scattered family, enlarger of the common life, carrier of news and knowledge, instrument of trade and industry, promoter of mutual acquaintance, of peace and good will among men and nations."

Knowing this, we shall never stand mute while soulless accountants attempt to bookkeep the glory of this thing we do together.

INDEX